UNIVERSALS AND PARTICULARS

READINGS IN ONTOLOGY

Michael J. Loux is an assistant professor and member of
the graduate faculty in philosophy at the University of
Notre Dame. He received his Ph.D. from the University of
Chicago in 1968.

UNIVERSALS AND PARTICULARS:
READINGS IN ONTOLOGY

Edited by Michael J. Loux

ANCHOR BOOKS

DOUBLEDAY & COMPANY, INC.

GARDEN CITY, NEW YORK

1970

Library of Congress Catalog Card Number 72–103791

TO ANN AND THE CHILDREN

PREFACE

In recent years, numerous anthologies have appeared covering problems in epistemology, the philosophy of mind, ethics, and the philosophy of religion. Despite the healthy proliferation of anthologies in these areas, however, there is no satisfactory collection of papers addressing general ontological questions; my intention here had been to fill this gap. I have tried to assemble a broadly representative collection of papers addressing one cluster of central issues in ontology, problems surrounding the distinction between universals and particulars.

Somewhat arbitrarily, I have broken the anthology into two sections—one incorporating papers concerned primarily with the problem of universals, and the other, those dealing with the nature of particulars. Papers on the problem of universals have been arranged chronologically. This is due to the importance of the historical element in this debate. Each paper builds on and criticizes the views expressed in the earlier papers, so that it is difficult (almost impossible) to understand any one of these papers without understanding those that precede it. Papers from the section on particulars, however, have been arranged topically. Thus, papers dealing with the identity of indiscernibles are presented first; next, papers addressing the notion of a bare particular; and finally, papers concerned with characterized particulars and essentialism. David Wiggins' paper, "The Individuation of Things and Places," while intimately related to all of these topics, does not easily fit any of these divisions; therefore it stands at the end of the section.

Although my aim has been a broadly representative

collection of papers, I have nonetheless tried to include the "classics." In this connection, I regret the absence of Chapter I of P. F. Strawson's *Individuals* from the second section of the anthology. This selection was simply too long for an anthology of this size. Fortunately, this book is available in paperback form. I strongly recommend that anyone interested in the problems covered by this anthology examine, if not the whole book, at least Chapters I, V, and VI.

My own contributions to the anthology, "The Problem of Universals" and "Particulars and Their Individuation," tend to be introductory in nature. In these papers I try to tie together the major issues addressed by the selections that follow, but exposition frequently gives way to philosophical argumentation of my own. I have tried to indicate where the one leaves off and the other begins.

I wish to thank Professors W. D. Solomon, E. A. Ludman, and P. K. Machamer, all of whom read large sections of the introductory material and offered valuable suggestions. I wish also to thank Professor V. C. Chappell, who provided helpful advice and friendly encouragement at every stage of this project. Finally, I wish to thank Professor H. J. McCann, whose keen insight and fertile imagination have, for several years, influenced my thinking on metaphysical questions. That influence, I believe, is obvious in what follows.

Contents

UNIVERSALS

PARTICULARS

UNIVERSALS

THE PROBLEM OF UNIVERSALS

Michael J. Loux

Much of our talk about the world around us is concerned with the characteristics which material bodies and persons possess, with things like the color of a shirt and the shape of a statue.[1] If we are not philosophers, we find little that is puzzling in this sort of talk. Language, as it is concerned with characteristics, seems relatively straightforward. No special insight seems to underlie its use, nor does it involve us in any serious theoretical tangles.

Nonetheless, philosophers have perennially found our talk about characteristics perplexing. This stems, I think, from what appears to be an incompatibility between two ways of talking about characteristics. We are all familiar with the fact that things can agree in one or more of their characteristics. Two pieces of cloth from the same dye lot, for example, agree in color. Now, we can describe this sort of agreement in at least two ways. We can say either that the two pieces of cloth are the same color or that the color of the one piece of cloth is exactly like the color of the other. It might seem that these two descriptions come to the same thing. Many philosophers, however, would argue to the contrary; the two forms of description, they would claim, are not only different, they are actually incompatible.[2] Thus, in using the first description, we imply

[1] Other philosophers have spoken of qualities, attributes, properties, etc. I choose the word "characteristic" because of its very familiar uses in ordinary, non-philosophical discourse. The term is used very broadly to include things as diverse as sense qualities, relations, and kinds.
[2] Nicholas Wolterstorff appears to take exception to this view. In his paper "Qualities" (included in this anthology), he argues that

that numerically one characteristic, a certain color, is exhibited by the two pieces of cloth; whereas in using the second, we make reference to two numerically distinct, yet exactly similar, colors. Of course, the difficulty can be generalized; for the same incompatibility seems to arise no matter which characteristics we bring into the picture. The fact is that there seem to be two incompatible ways of talking about agreement in characteristics. Philosophical discussion of characteristics centers on the question of which, if either, is the correct way of talking.

Some philosophers (traditionally known as metaphysical realists or Platonists) have preferred to express agreement in characteristics along the lines of the first description. They have maintained that there are two very different kinds of things, universals and particulars. Particulars, on this account, are things like Lyndon Baines Johnson and the Statue of Liberty; whereas universals are the characteristics which particulars possess, things like the color blue and the property of being circular. While particulars can occupy just one region of space at any one time, universals exhibit a divided mode of existence: at any one time, a universal can wholly and completely occupy each of indefinitely many different regions of space. Universals have instances but particulars, while being instances of one or more universals, cannot. Realists have expressed this notion of instantiation in a variety of ways; they have said that particulars exhibit, exemplify, partake of, or participate in universals. Disregarding these terminological differences, realists would want to claim that three different entities enter into our example: two particulars, the two pieces of cloth, and one universal, the color that is common to both.[3]

Philosophers who would prefer the second form of description are called nominalists. They would reject the first description because they find the notion of a universal

these two ways of talking are both internally consistent and that there are no grounds for choosing one over the other.

[3] For an attempt to distinguish universals from particulars, see P. F. Strawson's "Particular and General," reprinted in this anthology.

unintelligible, contradictory, or, for some other reason, untenable. They would argue that four distinct entities, all of them particulars, are involved in our example. There are the two pieces of cloth and two numerically distinct, although exactly similar, colors, each characterizing just one of the two pieces of cloth.

Still other philosophers (I shall call them extreme nominalists) would claim that, taken literally, both forms of description are inadequate. These philosophers have simply denied that there are such things as characteristics; and consequently, they have viewed the dispute between the nominalist and the realist as pointless. On this view, our example reduces to just two entities, the two pieces of cloth; and while the extreme nominalist would agree that these two things are colored, he would deny that this commits him to the existence of any additional entities.

Possibly, I oversimplify matters by identifying the problem of universals with these sorts of technical questions about characteristics; for certainly other philosophical problems have gone by that name.[4] Nevertheless, when philosophers have asked "Do universals exist?" they have generally been asking, "Are characteristics, if 'things' at all, the sorts of things which can, while remaining just one thing, be simultaneously possessed by several different individuals?"

Traditionally, the burden of proof has been on the side of the realist; and the arguments which realists have provided are both numerous and varied. In recent debate, however, arguments for the existence of universals have generally found their origin in considerations about the structure of language. More specifically, contemporary realists have felt that the distinction between subjects and predicates is of particular importance in establishing the existence of universals. In what follows, I shall try to sketch out an argument which is typical of this sort of approach, and I shall try to indicate the major objections nominalists and extreme nominalists have raised in opposition to it. The

---

[4] The expression "universal" has been a catchall in recent metaphysics. Thus, things as different as classes, numbers, and meanings have been called universals.

argument falls into two stages. The first stage attempts to establish the existence of characteristics, while the second argues for the view that characteristics are universals.[5]

STAGE I

In asserting a proposition of the subject-predicate variety, we pick out one or more particulars and say something about it/them. Now, we can analyze a proposition of this sort into two distinct elements, each of which corresponds to one of the acts we perform in asserting the proposition. There is the subject-term, by which we pick out or identify the particular or particulars we wish to talk about; and there is the predicate-term, by which we say something about it/them. In the proposition "Socrates is wise," we identify a certain individual by the expression "Socrates," and we go on to describe him or characterize him by the expression "is wise."

However, if our use of the predicate-term is to have any foundation in reality, there must be some*thing*, some non-linguistic entity, which is related to Socrates in such a way as to justify us in describing him by the predicate-term "wise." But what sort of relation is necessary here? If our language is to fit the facts, the required entity must characterize Socrates in the way we speak of him as characterized. This point can be generalized as follows:

> For any predicate-term, "F," which can be correctly ascribed to an individual, *a*, there is some entity, *F-ness*, which characterizes *a*.

STAGE II

By definition, predicates have generality of application. They can be affirmed of many different individuals or

[5] As far as I know, the argument I present here has never been presented formally by any philosopher, although something very much like it seems to underlie much of what P. F. Strawson says in the second half of *Individuals*. In this argument and in what follows in this introduction, I concentrate on "predicable" universals. For an account of non-predicable universals, see Nicholas Wolterstorff's "On the Nature of Universals," published for the first time in this anthology.

groups of individuals. What we said about Socrates, we could have said about many other men. But to each of these, the argument presented in Stage I applies: Each possesses some characterizing entity (a characteristic) which serves as the ontological basis for the applicability of the predicate-term.

However, it is not possible that there be a distinct, even if similar, characteristic for each entity to which a given predicate-term applies. We say the same thing about each of these things; and if the generality of the predicate-term is to have any basis in fact, the things to which it applies must all really be the same in some sense or other. But in what could this sameness consist other than in the numerical identity of characterizing entities? The point can be made in another way. A predicate-term does not apply arbitrarily to this or that thing. It is a principle of collecting things which agree in some way or other. The most appropriate way of describing this agreement is to say that all of the things to which one predicate-term applies exhibit or exemplify some one characteristic or set of characteristics. We can summarize this point, henceforth referred to as the "Realist's Principle," in the following way:

> A predicate-term, "F," can be truly affirmed of each of the members of a class $(a \ldots n)$ only if each possesses, exhibits, or exemplifies some numerically identical characteristic, *F-ness*.

The first stage of this argument has frequently come under attack by extreme nominalists. William of Ockham, Nicholas of Autrecourt, and W. V. O. Quine, to name a few, have challenged the claim that the applicability of a predicate-term presupposes the existence of a characterizing entity.[6] Philosophers of this bent would argue that the predicate-term "wise," for example, applies to Socrates simply because it is the case that Socrates is wise. One can go on to explain what it is to be wise, but this does not

[6] See, for example, Quine's paper, "On What There Is," reprinted in part in this anthology.

require the introduction of any additional entities, such as the characteristic of wisdom.

More generally, extreme nominalists have argued that the characterizing entities postulated by nominalists and realists are not essential to the explanation of any sort of phenomena; and since they are superfluous from this point of view, the extreme nominalist suggests that we eliminate them from our ontology. To support this proposal, extreme nominalists have argued that it is possible to eliminate from language all references to characteristics. One can, they claim, translate all of our characteristic-laden language into a language equally as rich as ours, but completely free of terms that purport to signify characteristics.

Realists and nominalists alike have criticized this sort of approach. Sometimes their attack is directed against the extreme nominalist's claim of translation. They argue that translation yields synonymy, but if our language implies commitment to an ontology of characteristics and the language of the extreme nominalist does not, then the sentences of his language are simply not synonymous with their correlates in our language. In other contexts, the relevance of this sort of translation is called into question. The claim is that even the completion of the proposed translation (which, critics are quick to point out, has never been achieved) would not establish the view that characteristics do not exist. It would only show that we need not refer to them, and, according to many philosophers, these are two quite different things.[7]

The premise of the second stage of the argument—that predicate-terms are essentially general—has seldom, if ever, been challenged, although possibly F. P. Ramsey, a philosopher of the first half of this century, had something like this in mind when he claimed that it is impossible to draw any sort of satisfactory distinction between the notions of subject-term and predicate-term.[8] Points similar

---

[7] C. A. Baylis in his paper "Universals, Communicable Knowledge, and Metaphysics" (included in this anthology) counters Quine's reductionism in this way.

[8] See F. P. Ramsey, "Universals," *Foundations of Mathematics*, pp. 116–17.

to those made in the remainder of the second stage, however, have been criticized more frequently.

According to one recurrent line of criticism, the realist's appeal to universals commits him to a number of absurdities. As we have seen, the realist maintains that characteristics have a divided mode of existence—each can occupy several different regions of space at any one time. Critics, however, argue that if this were possible, it would make sense to say of a characteristic that it lies at such and such a distance from itself, that it is drawing closer to itself, and so on.

Now, some realists have simply denied that statements of this sort are absurdities. It would be absurd, they argue, to speak of a particular as lying at such and such a distance from itself or as drawing closer to itself; but since a universal can occupy several different places at any one time, it is perfectly intelligible (indeed, often true) to say such things about it. Other realists, while conceding the absurdity of these statements, deny that they are genuine consequences of a realistic metaphysics. This sort of response generally involves a slight deviation from the doctrine of realism as I have presented it. Thus, some realists distinguish between a universal characteristic and the numerically distinct particulars which are its instances, claiming that particular characteristics can have spatial location, but that the universal characteristic which these instantiate cannot.[9]

According to another recurrent criticism, the account of predication that is inherent in the Realist's Principle generates an infinite regress. According to that principle, a predicate-term applies to several different individuals only in virtue of their possessing or instantiating some one characteristic. For the sake of proving it wrong, critics have asked us to assume this principle and have argued as follows: There exists some predicate-term, "F," which is applicable to each of several entities, $a \ldots n$. The applica-

[9] Alan Donagan in "Universals and Metaphysical Realism" (included in this anthology) seems to take the first response; whereas Nicholas Wolterstorff in "On the Nature of Universals" seems to take the second.

bility of this expression presupposes that each of the things, $a \ldots n$, possesses some one entity, *F-ness*. However, if each possesses *F-ness*, we can truly affirm of each the predicate-term "possesses the characteristic of *F-ness*"; but given the Realist's Principle, this presupposes that $a \ldots n$ possess a further thing, the characteristic of possessing the characteristic of *F-ness*. Of course, the possession by $a \ldots n$ of this new characteristic allows us to affirm of $a \ldots n$ yet another predicate-term, and this predicate-term presupposes that each of the things, $a \ldots n$, possesses yet another characteristic; and so on. The analysis never ends; for each new characteristic introduces a new predicate-term; and this, in turn, requires the postulation of still another characteristic. Conclusion? The Realist's Principle must be wrong since it cannot be applied without landing us in an infinite regress.[10]

Some realists have argued that this regress, while real, is not vicious; and in this context, that means that the regress does not render the explication of the applicability of a predicate-term impossible. On this view, the regress would be vicious if it were impossible to explain the applicability of a predicate-term without dealing with every member of the series of intrusive characteristics; but realists contend that nothing of the sort happens here. They agree that a new predicate-term is introduced with the postulation of each new characteristic, but they deny that the explication of the original predicate-term is thereby rendered incomplete. We can, if we wish, go on to explain the applicability of this new predicate-term by referring to its supporting characteristic; but we are free to discontinue the analysis at any point without invalidating what has gone before.

Even if we grant the realist this point, the objection still carries some force; for it indicates a certain implausibility in the realist's account. We are to believe that behind each predicate-term in our language there lies a hidden infinity

---

[10] This objection cannot be raised against the argument of Stage I; for at that point, it is not yet clear that "possesses a certain characteristic" is a predicate-term. One could hold the tenets of Stage I and argue, nevertheless, that the relevant characterizing entity is a particular, necessarily possessed by just one thing.

of entities; and surely this militates against our desire for simplicity of theory. One way of meeting this objection is to deny that realism actually involves an infinite regress. At each successive stage of the explanation, we can formulate what appears to be a new predicate-term; but one might argue that these expressions are all really synonymous. Thus, one might claim that, although "F" and "possesses F-ness" are grammatically distinct forms, they are indistinguishable at the semantic level and, consequently, presuppose exactly the same supporting characteristic.[11]

The objections that I have so far discussed have enjoyed a notoriously long history. Of more recent origin is the claim made by D. F. Pears that the Realist's Principle is essentially circular. We have already seen how the realist attempts to ground the generality of language in the generality of fact. He argues that predicate-terms apply to different things because each exemplifies some numerically identical characteristic. Now, Pears claims that if his account is to be successful, the realist must at least be able to identify for us the characteristic underlying the use of a predicate-term; Pears argues, however, that this can be done only by a backward reference to the predicate-term with which the analysis began. The realist claims that things are called red because each exhibits the color red; but this is circular; for the term whose use was to be explained appears as an essential ingredient in the explanation.[12]

Pears' criticism of realism has recently come under attack by Alan Donagan, a defender of one version of realism. According to Donagan, Pears' objection is based on a confusion of use and mention; that is, Pears fails to distinguish between the normal (first order) use of a term, to signify things that are not words, and the less normal (second order) use of a term, to signify linguistic expressions. The grammatical signal of second-order dis-

---

[11] In "Universals and Metaphysical Realism," Donagan dismisses a version of the infinite regress argument; but the version he considers is different from the one I have examined.

[12] See D. F. Pears' paper, "Universals" (included in this anthology).

course is the use of quotes. Now, Donagan suggests that
if the grammatical signal of second-order discourse is
made explicit, the circularity in the realist's account disappears. The realist, then, is taken to claim that things are
called by the name "red" because they all possess the
color red. There is no circularity here, Donagan argues,
since in the first case we refer to a word and in the second, to a characteristic, a non-linguistic entity supporting
the use of that word.[13]

In the later writings of Wittgenstein, we find another
objection against the Realist's Principle. Wittgenstein chal-
lenges the truth of the claim that all of the things to which
some general term applies possess some one characteristic
or set of characteristics. Wittgenstein uses the example of
games. Many different things are called games; and while
an examination of these things reveals many complex patterns of resemblance or similarity, there is, Wittgenstein
argues, no one characteristic or set of characteristics which
are all-pervading. There are certain characteristics which
recur again and again, but Wittgenstein contends that no
matter which characteristic one chooses, there will always
be some things bearing the name "game" which lack it.[14]

Unfortunately, it is not clear how general Wittgenstein
means his analysis to be. Does he mean to suggest that there
never are characteristics common to all the things to which
a general term applies, or does he merely wish to make the
weaker claim that this need not necessarily be the case?
Regardless of which view we take Wittgenstein to be defending, it seems that his position is compatible with at
least one form of realism. Wittgenstein assures us that
where a general term is used, one does find characteristics
which occur again and again. This claim can certainly be
interpreted along realistic lines. One could say that a re-
curring characteristic, although not present (necessarily?)

[13] See Donagan's "Universals and Metaphysical Realism."
[14] An account and defense of Wittgenstein's view is provided by
Renford Bambrough in his paper "Universals and Family Resemblances" (included in this anthology). Even a quick reading of this
paper indicates that Bambrough and I interpret Wittgenstein in different ways. See Wittgenstein's *Philosophical Investigations*, para-
graphs 65 ff., for the relevant texts.

in all of the cases where a general term is used, is numerically identical in those cases where it is present. Doubtless, the explanatory power of realism is lost in this interpretation; nevertheless, the realist's basic contention (viz., that there are entities having a divided mode of existence) is preserved.

Still, in Wittgenstein's emphasis on the notion of resemblance or similarity, one finds a hint of a view that has been explicitly held by most nominalists and extreme nominalists—the view that the applicability of a general term or predicate-term is grounded in the similarity among the things signified by that term.[15] This view has its source in considerations similar to those found in our argument for realism. In that context, we noted that there is an agreement among those things to which some one predicate-term applies. The realist went on to describe that agreement in terms of the numerical identity of characterizing entities. Now, neither the nominalist nor the extreme nominalist would deny that a predicate-term collects things which agree in some way; but both would prefer to describe this agreement in terms of the similarities obtaining among the things to which a predicate-term applies. As our initial discussion of the two pieces of cloth indicates, however, the nominalist and extreme nominalist would tend to express this view in different ways. The nominalist would ground the similarity among things in the similarity of their characteristics, whereas the extreme nominalist would argue that the similarity among things

[15] Although some of Wittgenstein's remarks may seem to point in the direction of realism, and others in the direction of nominalism or extreme nominalism, it would be a mistake to associate him too closely with any of these traditions. His own view, I suspect, is that the whole controversy over universals is based on a series of confusions, resulting from the strange interpretations philosophers put on our talk about characteristics. He would probably argue that if, as the realist and nominalist suggest, there are no criteria for distinguishing their use, our two ways of talking about characteristics (in terms of similarity and identity) cannot be incompatible. Likewise, he would doubtless find something absurd in the extreme nominalist's contention that these two ways of talking are both incorrect. If the speakers of a language customarily talk in these ways (following, as they do, something like a set of rules), such ways of talking are, by that fact alone, correct ways of talking.

called by one name is a fact that cannot be explicated in terms of any further entities.

Strangely enough, many realists have felt that this appeal to similarities actually supports their own position. Sometimes they argue that the claim that two or more things are similar is incomplete. We need to indicate the respect in which they are similar and, according to the realist, this involves a reference to a universal. In their view there is always some one thing with respect to which similar things are similar. Thus, the two pieces of cloth in our original example are similar with respect to some one color; and this, realists contend, is a universal.[16] In other contexts, realists argue that since resemblance is repeatable, it is itself a universal. Realists, however, have seen no point in accepting one universal and rejecting all of the others. As Bertrand Russell says, "Having been forced to admit this universal, we find that it is no longer worthwhile to invent difficult and implausible theories to avoid the admission of such universals as whiteness and triangularity."[17]

One might answer the first objection by denying that attributions of similarity are essentially incomplete; however, most nominalists and extreme nominalists would probably grant this point. What they would deny is that this concession commits them to realism. The extreme nominalist would probably argue that in filling in a similarity-claim, we need not refer to any entities distinct from the things we speak of as similar. Thus, he would say that the two pieces of cloth are similar in that both are, for example, red. The nominalist's account ultimately comes to the same thing. He would claim that the two pieces of cloth are alike in possessing exactly similar, although numerically different, characteristics, but he would deny that in admitting a similarity between the two colors, he commits himself to any additional entities.

[16] An account of this argument is presented by Baylis in "Universals, Communicable Knowledge, and Metaphysics" and by Pears in "Universals."

[17] See Bertrand Russell's "The World of Universals" (included in this anthology).

In response to the second objection, the extreme nominalist would argue that the realist goes wrong in construing similarity as a thing. He would want to claim that one can translate all sentences in which the term "similarity" or "resemblance" is used into sentences that contain no terms purporting to signify entities distinct from the material bodies and persons which are similar. The nominalist, on the other hand, might agree that similarities are entities; but he would contend that they are essentially particular. He would deny, that is, that the similarity obtaining between the two pieces of cloth from our example is numerically the same similarity as that obtaining between two other pieces of cloth from the same dye lot.

Much more could be said about the problem of universals. My brief remarks hardly do justice to the issues involved in the perennial controversy; but I think that they do indicate the extreme complexity of these issues. The notion of a characteristic, I hope I have shown, presents philosophical problems to which no easy solutions are available.

THE WORLD OF UNIVERSALS

Bertrand Russell

We saw that such entities as relations appear to have a being which is in some way different from that of physical objects, and also different from that of minds and from that of sense-data. In the present chapter we have to consider what is the nature of this kind of being, and also what objects there are that have this kind of being. We will begin with the latter question.

The problem with which we are now concerned is a very old one, since it was brought into philosophy by Plato. Plato's "theory of ideas" is an attempt to solve this very problem, and in my opinion it is one of the most successful attempts hitherto made. The theory to be advocated in what follows is largely Plato's with merely such modifications as time has shown to be necessary.

The way the problem arose for Plato was more or less as follows. Let us consider, say, such a notion as *justice*. If we ask ourselves what justice is, it is natural to proceed by considering this, that, and the other just act, with a view to discovering what they have in common. They must all, in some sense, partake of a common nature, which will be found in whatever is just and in nothing else. This common nature, in virtue of which they are all just, will be justice itself, the pure essence the admixture of which with facts of ordinary life produces the multiplicity of just acts. Similarly with any other word which may be applicable to common facts, such as "whiteness" for example. The word will be applicable to a number of particular things because they all participate in a common nature or essence. This pure essence is what Plato calls an "idea" or "form." (It must not be supposed that "ideas," in his sense, exist in minds, though they may be apprehended by minds.) The "idea" *justice* is not identical with anything that is just: it is something other than particular things, which particular things partake of. Not being particular, it cannot itself exist in the world of sense. Moreover it is not fleeting or changeable like the things of sense: it is eternally itself, immutable and indestructible.

Thus Plato is led to a supra-sensible world, more real than the common world of sense, the unchangeable world of ideas, which alone gives to the world of sense whatever pale reflection of reality may belong to it. The truly real world, for Plato, is the world of ideas; for whatever we may attempt to say about things in the world of sense, we can only succeed in saying that they participate in such and such ideas, which, therefore, constitute all their character. Hence it is easy to pass on into a mysticism. We may hope, in a mystic illumination, to *see* the ideas as we see objects of sense; and we may imagine that the ideas exist in heaven. These mystical developments are very natural, but the basis of the theory is in logic, and it is as based in logic that we have to consider it.

The word "idea" has acquired, in the course of time, many associations which are quite misleading when applied to Plato's "ideas." We shall therefore use the word "universal" instead of the word "idea," to describe what Plato meant. The essence of the sort of entity that Plato meant is that it is opposed to the particular things that are given in sensation. We speak of whatever is given in sensation, or is of the same nature as things given in sensation, as a *particular;* by opposition to this, a *universal* will be anything which may be shared by many particulars, and has those characteristics which, as we saw, distinguish justice and whiteness from just acts and white things.

When we examine common words, we find that, broadly speaking, proper names stand for particulars, while other substantives, adjectives, prepositions, and verbs stand for universals. Pronouns stand for particulars, but are ambiguous: it is only by context or the circumstances that we know what particulars they stand for. The word "now" stands for a particular, namely the present moment; but like pronouns, it stands for an ambiguous particular, because the present is always changing.

It will be seen that no sentence can be made up without at least one word which denotes a universal. The nearest approach would be some such statement as "I like this." But even here the word "like" denotes a universal, for I may like other things and other people may like things. Thus all truths involve universals, and all knowledge of truths involves acquaintance with universals.

Seeing that nearly all the words to be found in the dictionary stand for universals, it is strange that hardly anybody except students of philosophy ever realizes that there are such entities as universals. We do not naturally dwell upon those words in a sentence which do not stand for particulars; and if we are forced to dwell upon a word which stands for a universal, we naturally think of it as standing for some one of the particulars that come under the universal. When, for example, we hear the sentence, "Charles I's head was cut off," we may naturally enough think of Charles I, of Charles I's head, and of the operation of cutting off *his* head, which are all particulars; but we do not naturally dwell upon what is meant by the word "head" or the word "cut," which is a universal. We feel such words to be incomplete and insubstantial; they seem to demand a context before anything can be done with them. Hence we succeed in avoiding all notice of universals as such, until the study of philosophy forces them upon our attention.

Even among philosophers, we may say broadly, that only those universals which are named by adjectives or substantives have been much or often recognized, while those named by verbs and prepositions have been usually overlooked. This omission has had a very great effect upon philosophy; it is hardly too much to say that most metaphysics, since Spinoza, has been largely determined by it.

The way this has occurred is, in outline, as follows: Speaking generally, adjectives and common nouns express qualities or properties of single things, whereas prepositions and verbs tend to express relations between two or more things. Thus the neglect of prepositions and verbs led to the belief that every proposition can be regarded as attributing a property to a single thing, rather than as expressing a relation between two or more things. Hence it was supposed that, ultimately, there can be only one thing in the universe, or if there are many things, they cannot possibly interact in any way, since any interaction would be a relation, and relations are impossible.

The first of these views, advocated by Spinoza and held in our own day by Bradley and many other philosophers, is called *monism;* the second, advocated by Leibniz but not very common nowadays, is called *monadism,* because each of the isolated things is called a *monad.* Both these opposing philosophies, interesting as they are, result, in my opinion, from an undue attention to one sort of universal, namely the sort represented by adjectives and substantives rather than by verbs and prepositions.

As a matter of fact, if anyone were anxious to deny altogether that there are such things as universals, we should find that we cannot strictly prove that there are such entities as *qualities,* i.e., the universals represented by adjectives and substantives, whereas we can prove that there must be *relations,* i.e., the sort of universals generally represented by verbs and prepositions. Let us take in illustration the universal *whiteness.* If we believe that there is such a universal, we shall say that things are white because they have the quality of whiteness. This view, however, was strenuously denied by Berkeley and Hume, who have been followed in this by later empiricists. The form which their denial took was to deny that there are such things as "abstract ideas." When we want to think of whiteness, they said, we form an image of some particular white thing, and reason concerning this particular, taking care not to deduce anything concerning it which we cannot see to be equally true of any other white thing.

As an account of our actual mental processes, this is

no doubt largely true. In geometry, for example, when we wish to prove something about all triangles, we draw a particular triangle and reason about it, taking care not to use any characteristic which it does not share with other triangles. The beginner, in order to avoid error, often finds it useful to draw several triangles, as unlike each other as possible, in order to make sure that his reasoning is equally applicable to all of them. But a difficulty emerges as soon as we ask ourselves how we know that a thing is white or a triangle. If we wish to avoid the universals *whiteness* and *triangularity,* we shall choose some particular patch of white or some particular triangle, and say that anything is white or a triangle if it has the right sort of resemblance to our chosen particular. But then the resemblance must hold between many pairs of particular white things; and this is the characteristic of a universal. It will be useless to say that there is a different resemblance for each pair, for then we shall have to say that these resemblances resemble each other, and thus at last we shall be forced to admit resemblance as a universal. The relation of resemblance, therefore, must be a true universal. And having been forced to admit this universal, we find that it is no longer worth while to invent difficult and unplausible theories to avoid the admission of such universals as whiteness and triangularity.

Berkeley and Hume failed to perceive this refutation of their rejection of "abstract ideas," because, like their adversaries, they only thought of *qualities,* and altogether ignored *relations* as universals. We have therefore here another respect in which the rationalists appear to have been in the right as against the empiricists, although, owing to the neglect or denial of relations, the deductions made by rationalists were, if anything, more apt to be mistaken than those made by empiricists.

Having now seen that there must be such entities as universals, the next point to be proved is that their being is not merely mental. By this is meant that whatever being belongs to them is independent of their being thought of or in any way apprehended by minds. We have already touched on this subject at the end of the preceding chapter, but we must now consider more fully what sort of being it is that belongs to universals.

Consider such a proposition as "Edinburgh is north of London." Here we have a relation between two places, and it seems plain that the relation subsists independently of our knowledge of it. When we come to know that Edinburgh is north of London, we come to know something which has to do only with Edinburgh and London: we do not cause the truth of the proposition by coming to know it; on the contrary, we merely apprehend a fact which was there before we knew it. The part of the earth's surface where Edinburgh stands would be north of the part where London stands, even if there were no human being to know about north and south, and even if there were no minds at all in the universe. This is, of course, denied by many philosophers, either for Berkeley's reasons or for Kant's. . . . We may therefore now assume it to be true that nothing mental is presupposed in the fact that Edinburgh is north of London. But this fact involves the relation "north of," which is a universal; and it would be impossible for the whole fact to involve nothing mental, if the relation "north of," which is a constituent part of the fact, did involve anything mental. Hence we must admit that the relation, like the terms it relates, is not dependent upon thought, but belongs to the independent world which thought apprehends but does not create.

This conclusion, however, is met by the difficulty that the relation "north of" does not seem to *exist* in the same sense in which Edinburgh and London exist. If we ask "Where and when does this relation exist?" the answer must be "Nowhere and nowhen." There is no place or time where we can find the relation "north of." It does not exist in Edinburgh any more than in London, for it relates the two and is neutral as between them. Nor can we say that it exists at any particular time. Now everything that can be apprehended by the senses or by introspection exists at some particular time. Hence the relation "north of" is radically different from such things. It is neither in space nor in time, neither material nor mental; yet it is something.

It is largely the very peculiar kind of being that belongs
to universals which has led many people to suppose that
they are really mental. We can think *of* a universal, and
our thinking then exists in a perfectly ordinary sense, like
any other mental act. Suppose, for example, that we are
thinking of whiteness. Then *in one sense* it may be said
that whiteness is "in our mind." We have here the same
ambiguity as we noted in discussing Berkeley in Chapter
IV. In the strict sense, it is not whiteness that is in our mind,
but the act of thinking of whiteness. The connected ambiguity in the word "idea," which we noted at the same
time, also causes confusion here. In one sense of this word,
namely the sense in which it denotes the *object* of an act
of thought, whiteness is an "idea." Hence, if the ambiguity
is not guarded against, we may come to think that whiteness is an "idea" in the other sense, i.e., an act of thought;
and thus we come to think that whiteness is mental. But
in so thinking, we rob it of its essential quality of universality. One man's act of thought is necessarily a different
thing from another man's; one man's act of thought at
one time is necessarily a different thing from the same
man's act of thought at another time. Hence, if whiteness
were the thought as opposed to its object, no two different
men could think of it, and no one man could think of it
twice. That which many different thoughts of whiteness
have in common is their *object,* and this object is different from all of them. Thus universals are not thoughts,
though when known they are the objects of thoughts.

We shall find it convenient only to speak of things *existing* when they are in time, that is to say, when we can
point to some time *at* which they exist (not excluding the
possibility of their existing at all times). Thus thoughts and
feelings, minds and physical objects *exist*. But universals do
not exist in this sense; we shall say that they *subsist* or
have being, where "being" is opposed to "existence" as
being timeless. The world of universals, therefore, may
also be described as the world of being. The world of being
is unchangeable, rigid, exact, delightful to the mathematician, the logician, the builder of metaphysical systems,
and all who love perfection more than life. The world of

existence is fleeting, vague, without sharp boundaries, without any clear plan or arrangement, but it contains all thoughts and feelings, all the data of sense, and all physical objects, everything that can do either good or harm, everything that makes any difference to the value of life and the world. According to our temperaments, we shall prefer the contemplation of the one or of the other. The one we do not prefer will probably seem to us a pale shadow of the one we prefer, and hardly worthy to be regarded as in any sense real. But the truth is that both have the same claim on our impartial attention, both are real, and both are important to the metaphysician.

ON WHAT THERE IS

Willard Van Orman Quine

Now let us turn to the ontological problem of universals:
the question whether there are such entities as attributes,
relations, classes, numbers, functions. McX, characteristically enough, thinks there are. Speaking of attributes, he
says: "There are red houses, red roses, red sunsets; this
much is prephilosophical common sense in which we must
all agree. These houses, roses, and sunsets, then, have something in common; and this which they have in common is
all I mean by the attribute of redness." For McX, thus,
there being attributes is even more obvious and trivial than
the obvious and trivial fact of there being red houses, roses,
and sunsets. This, I think, is characteristic of metaphysics,
or at least of that part of metaphysics called ontology: one
who regards a statement on this subject as true at all must
regard it as trivially true. One's ontology is basic to the
conceptual scheme by which he interprets all experiences,
even the most commonplace ones. Judged within some
particular conceptual scheme—and how else is judgment
possible?—an ontological statement goes without saying,
standing in need of no separate justification at all. Ontological statements follow immediately from all manner of
casual statements of commonplace fact, just as—from the
point of view, anyway, of McX's conceptual scheme—'There

is an attribute' follows from 'There are red houses, red roses, red sunsets'.

Judged in another conceptual scheme, an ontological statement which is axiomatic to McX's mind may, with equal immediacy and triviality, be adjudged false. One may admit that there are red houses, roses, and sunsets, but deny, except as a popular and misleading manner of speaking, that they have anything in common. The words 'houses', 'roses', and 'sunsets' are true of sundry individual entities which are houses and roses and sunsets, and the word 'red' or 'red object' is true of each of sundry individual entities which are red houses, red roses, red sunsets; but there is not, in addition, any entity whatever, individual or otherwise, which is named by the word 'redness', nor, for that matter, by the word 'househood', 'rosehood', 'sunsethood'. That the houses and roses and sunsets are all of them red may be taken as ultimate and irreducible, and it may be held that McX is no better off, in point of real explanatory power, for all the occult entities which he posits under such names as 'redness'.

One means by which McX might naturally have tried to impose his ontology of universals on us was already removed before we turned to the problem of universals. McX cannot argue that predicates such as 'red' or 'is-red', which we all concur in using, must be regarded as names each of a single universal entity in order that they be meaningful at all. For we have seen that being a name of something is a much more special feature than being meaningful. He cannot even charge us—at least not by *that* argument—with having posited an attribute of pegasizing by our adoption of the predicate 'pegasizes'.

However, McX hits upon a different strategem. "Let us grant," he says, "this distinction between meaning and naming of which you make so much. Let us even grant that 'is red', 'pegasizes', etc., are not names of attributes. Still, you admit they have meanings. But these *meanings,* whether they are *named* or not, are still universals, and I venture to say that some of them might even be the very things that I call attributes, or something to much the same purpose in the end."

For McX, this is an unusually penetrating speech; and the only way I know to counter it is by refusing to admit meanings. However, I feel no reluctance toward refusing to admit meanings, for I do not thereby deny that words and statements are meaningful. McX and I may agree to the letter in our classification of linguistic forms into the meaningful and the meaningless, even though McX construes meaningfulness as the *having* (in some sense of 'having') of some abstract entity which he calls a meaning, whereas I do not. I remain free to maintain that the fact that a given linguistic utterance is meaningful (or *significant*, as I prefer to say so as not to invite hypostasis of meanings as entities) is an ultimate and irreducible matter of fact; or, I may undertake to analyze it in terms directly of what people do in the presence of the linguistic utterance in question and other utterances similar to it.

The useful ways in which people ordinarily talk or seem to talk about meanings boil down to two: the *having* of meanings, which is significance, and *sameness* of meaning, or synonymy. What is called *giving* the meaning of an utterance is simply the uttering of a synonym, couched, ordinarily, in clearer language than the original. If we are allergic to meanings as such, we can speak directly of utterances as significant or insignificant, and as synonymous or heteronymous one with another. The problem of explaining these adjectives 'significant' and 'synonymous' with some degree of clarity and rigor—preferably, as I see it, in terms of behavior—is as difficult as it is important. But the explanatory value of special and irreducible intermediary entities called meanings is surely illusory.

Up to now I have argued that we can use singular terms significantly in sentences without presupposing that there are the entities which those terms purport to name. I have argued further that we can use general terms, for example, predicates, without conceding them to be names of abstract entities. I have argued further that we can view utterances as significant, and as synonymous or heteronymous with one another, without countenancing a realm of entities called meanings. At this point McX begins to wonder whether there is any limit at all to our ontological immunity. Does *nothing* we may say commit us to the assumption of universals or other entities which we may find unwelcome?

I have already suggested a negative answer to this question, in speaking of bound variables, or variables of quantification, in connection with Russell's theory of descriptions. We can very easily involve ourselves in ontological commitments by saying, for example, that *there is something* (bound variable) which red houses and sunsets have in common; or that *there is something* which is a prime number larger than a million. But this is, essentially, the *only* way we can involve ourselves in ontological commitments: by our use of bound variables. The use of alleged names is no criterion, for we can repudiate their namehood at the drop of a hat unless the assumption of a corresponding entity can be spotted in the things we affirm in terms of bound variables. Names are, in fact, altogether immaterial to the ontological issue, for I have shown, in connection with 'Pegasus' and 'pegasize', that names can be converted to descriptions, and Russell has shown that descriptions can be eliminated. Whatever we say with the help of names can be said in a language which shuns names altogether. To be assumed as an entity is, purely and simply, to be reckoned as the value of a variable. In terms of the categories of traditional grammar, this amounts roughly to saying that to be is to be in the range of reference of a pronoun. Pronouns are the basic media of reference; nouns might better have been named propronouns. The variables of quantification, 'something', 'nothing', 'everything', range over our whole ontology, whatever it may be; and we are convicted of a particular ontological presupposition if, and only if, the alleged presuppositum has to be reckoned among the entities over which our variables range in order to render one of our affirmations true.

We may say, for example, that some dogs are white and not thereby commit ourselves to recognizing either doghood or whiteness as entities. 'Some dogs are white' says that some things that are dogs are white; and, in order that this statement be true, the things over which the bound variable 'something' ranges must include some white dogs, but need not include doghood or whiteness. On the other hand, when we say that some zoölogical species are cross-fertile we are committing ourselves to recognizing as entities the several species themselves, abstract though they are. We remain so committed at least until we devise some way of so paraphrasing the statement as to show that the seeming reference to species on the part of our bound variable was an avoidable manner of speaking.

Classical mathematics, as the example of primes larger than a million clearly illustrates, is up to its neck in commitments to an ontology of abstract entities. Thus it is that the great mediaeval controversy over universals has flared up anew in the modern philosophy of mathematics. The issue is clearer now than of old, because we now have a more explicit standard whereby to decide what ontology a given theory or form of discourse is committed to: a theory is committed to those and only those entities to which the bound variables of the theory must be capable of referring in order that the affirmations made in the theory be true.

Because this standard of ontological presupposition did not emerge clearly in the philosophical tradition, the modern philosophical mathematicians have not on the whole recognized that they were debating the same old problem of universals in a newly clarified form. But the fundamental cleavages among modern points of view on foundations of mathematics do come down pretty explicitly to disagreements as to the range of entities to which the bound variables should be permitted to refer.

The three main mediaeval points of view regarding universals are designated by historians as *realism, conceptualism,* and *nominalism.* Essentially these same three doctrines reappear in twentieth-century surveys of the philosophy of mathematics under the new names *logicism, intuitionism,* and *formalism.*

Realism, as the word is used in connection with the mediaeval controversy over universals, is the Platonic doctrine that universals or abstract entities have being independently of the mind; the mind may discover them but cannot create them. *Logicism,* represented by Frege, Rus-

sell, Whitehead, Church, and Carnap, condones the use of
bound variables to refer to abstract entities known and
unknown, specifiable and unspecifiable, indiscriminately.

Conceptualism holds that there are universals but they
are mind-made. *Intuitionism,* espoused in modern times in
one form or another by Poincaré, Brouwer, Weyl, and
others, countenances the use of bound variables to refer
to abstract entities only when those entities are capable of
being cooked up individually from ingredients specified in
advance. As Fraenkel has put it, logicism holds that classes
are discovered while intuitionism holds that they are invented—a fair statement indeed of the old opposition between realism and conceptualism. This opposition is no
mere quibble; it makes an essential difference in the amount
of classical mathematics to which one is willing to sub-
scribe. Logicists, or realists, are able on their assumptions
to get Cantor's ascending orders of infinity; intuitionists
are compelled to stop with the lowest order of infinity, and,
as an indirect consequence, to abandon even some of the
classical laws of real numbers. The modern controversy
between logicism and intuitionism arose, in fact, from disagreements over infinity.

Formalism, associated with the name of Hilbert, echoes
intuitionism in deploring the logicist's unbridled recourse to
universals. But formalism also finds intuitionism unsatisfactory. This could happen for either of two opposite reasons. The formalist might, like the logicist, object to the
crippling of classical mathematics; or he might, like the
nominalists of old, object to admitting abstract entities at
all, even in the restrained sense of mind-made entities. The
upshot is the same: the formalist keeps classical mathematics as a play of insignificant notations. This play of
notations can still be of utility—whatever utility it has already shown itself to have as a crutch for physicists and
technologists. But utility need not imply significance, in any
literal linguistic sense. Nor need the marked success of
mathematicians in spinning out theorems, and in finding
objective bases for agreement with one another's results,
imply significance. For an adequate basis for agreement
among mathematicians can be found simply in the rules

which govern the manipulation of the notations—these syntactical rules being, unlike the notations themselves, quite significant and intelligible.

I have argued that the sort of ontology we adopt can be consequential—notably in connection with mathematics, although this is only an example. Now how are we to adjudicate among rival ontologies? Certainly the answer is not provided by the semantical formula "To be is to be the value of a variable"; this formula serves rather, conversely, in testing the conformity of a given remark or doctrine to a prior ontological standard. We look to bound variables in connection with ontology not in order to know what there is, but in order to know what a given remark or doctrine, ours or someone else's, *says* there is; and this much is quite properly a problem involving language. But what there is is another question.

In debating over what there is, there are still reasons for operating on a semantical plane. One reason is to escape from the predicament noted at the beginning of this essay: the predicament of my not being able to admit that there are things which McX countenances and I do not. So long as I adhere to my ontology, as opposed to McX's, I cannot allow my bound variables to refer to entities which belong to McX's ontology and not to mine. I can, however, consistently describe our disagreement by characterizing the statements which McX affirms. Provided merely that my ontology countenances linguistic forms, or at least concrete inscriptions and utterances, I can talk about McX's sentences.

Another reason for withdrawing to a semantical plane is to find common ground on which to argue. Disagreement in ontology involves basic disagreement in conceptual schemes; yet McX and I, despite these basic disagreements, find that our conceptual schemes converge sufficiently in their intermediate and upper ramifications to enable us to communicate successfully on such topics as politics, weather, and, in particular, language. Insofar as our basic controversy over ontology can be translated upward into a semantical controversy about words and what to do with them, the collapse of the controversy into question-begging may be delayed.

It is no wonder, then, that ontological controversy should tend into controversy over language. But we must not jump to the conclusion that what there is depends on words. Translatability of a question into semantical terms is no indication that the question is linguistic. To see Naples is to bear a name which, when prefixed to the words 'sees Naples', yields a true sentence; still there is nothing linguistic about seeing Naples.

Our acceptance of an ontology is, I think, similar in principle to our acceptance of a scientific theory, say a system of physics: we adopt, at least insofar as we are reasonable, the simplest conceptual scheme into which the disordered fragments of raw experience can be fitted and arranged. Our ontology is determined once we have fixed upon the over-all conceptual scheme which is to accommodate science in the broadest sense; and the considerations which determine a reasonable construction of any part of that conceptual scheme, for example, the biological or the physical part, are not different in kind from the considerations which determine a reasonable construction of the whole. To whatever extent the adoption of any system of scientific theory may be said to be a matter of language, the same—but no more—may be said of the adoption of an ontology.

But simplicity, as a guiding principle in constructing conceptual schemes, is not a clear and unambiguous idea; and it is quite capable of presenting a double or multiple standard. Imagine, for example, that we have devised the most economical set of concepts adequate to the play-by-play reporting of immediate experience. The entities under this scheme—the values of bound variables—are, let us suppose, individual subjective events of sensation or reflection. We should still find, no doubt, that a physicalistic conceptual scheme, purporting to talk about external objects, offers great advantages in simplifying our over-all reports. By bringing together scattered sense events and treating them as perceptions of one object, we reduce the complexity of our stream of experience to a manageable conceptual simplicity. The rule of simplicity is indeed our guiding maxim in assigning sense data to objects: we associate an earlier and a later round sensum with the same so-called penny, or with two different so-called pennies, in obedience to the demands of maximum simplicity in our total world-picture.

Here we have two competing conceptual schemes, a phenomenalistic one and a physicalistic one. Which should prevail? Each has its advantages; each has its special simplicity in its own way. Each, I suggest, deserves to be developed. Each may be said, indeed, to be the more fundamental, though in different senses: the one is epistemologically, the other physically, fundamental.

The physical conceptual scheme simplifies our account of experience because of the way myriad scattered sense events come to be associated with single so-called objects; still there is no likelihood that each sentence about physical objects can actually be translated, however deviously and complexly, into the phenomenalistic language. Physical objects are postulated entities which round out and simplify our account of the flux of experience, just as the introduction of irrational numbers simplifies laws of arithmetic. From the point of view of the conceptual scheme of the elementary arithmetic of rational numbers alone, the broader arithmetic of rational and irrational numbers would have the status of a convenient myth, simpler than the literal truth (namely, the arithmetic of rationals) and yet containing that literal truth as a scattered part. Similarly, from a phenomenalistic point of view, the conceptual scheme of physical objects is a convenient myth, simpler than the literal truth and yet containing that literal truth as a scattered part.

Now what of classes or attributes of physical objects, in turn? A platonistic ontology of this sort is, from the point of view of a strictly physicalistic conceptual scheme, as much a myth as that physicalistic conceptual scheme itself is for phenomenalism. This higher myth is a good and useful one, in turn, insofar as it simplifies our account of physics. Since mathematics is an integral part of this higher myth, the utility of this myth for physical science is evident enough. In speaking of it nevertheless as a myth, I echo that philosophy of mathematics to which I alluded earlier under the name of formalism. But an attitude of formalism may with equal justice be adopted toward the physical conceptual scheme, in turn, by the pure aesthete or phenomenalist.

The analogy between the myth of mathematics and the myth of physics is, in some additional and perhaps fortuitous ways, strikingly close. Consider, for example, the crisis which was precipitated in the foundations of mathematics, at the turn of the century, by the discovery of Russell's paradox and other antinomies of set theory. These contradictions had to be obviated by unintuitive, *ad hoc* devices; our mathematical myth-making became deliberate and evident to all. But what of physics? An antinomy arose between the undular and the corpuscular accounts of light; and if this was not as out-and-out a contradiction as Russell's paradox, I suspect that the reason is that physics is not as out-and-out as mathematics. Again, the second great modern crisis in the foundations of mathematics—precipitated in 1931 by Gödel's proof [2] that there are bound to be undecidable statements in arithmetic—has its companion piece in physics in Heisenberg's indeterminacy principle.

In earlier pages I undertook to show that some common arguments in favor of certain ontologies are fallacious. Further, I advanced an explicit standard whereby to decide what the ontological commitments of a theory are. But the question what ontology actually to adopt still stands open, and the obvious counsel is tolerance and an experimental spirit. Let us by all means see how much of the physicalistic conceptual scheme can be reduced to a phenomenalistic one; still, physics also naturally demands pursuing, irreducible *in toto* though it be. Let us see how, or to what degree, natural science may be rendered independent of platonistic mathematics; but let us also pursue mathematics and delve into its platonistic foundations.

From among the various conceptual schemes best suited to these various pursuits, one—the phenomenalistic—claims epistemological priority. Viewed from within the phenomenalistic conceptual scheme, the ontologies of physical objects and mathematical objects are myths. The quality of myth, however, is relative; relative, in this case, to the epistemological point of view. This point of view is one among various, corresponding to one among our various interests and purposes.

UNIVERSALS

D. F. Pears

'Do universals exist?' This question was debated so long
and vehemently because it was mistaken for a factual
question about some airy realm of being. But why was this
mistake made? One diagnosis is that general words were
tacitly assimilated to proper names,[1] and that, when this
practice is exposed, it becomes harmless but pointless.[2]
But this is a description of what happened rather than an
explanation; it gives something more like a symptom than
a cause. Could so many philosophers have been so silly in
such a simple way? Even moderate scepticism on this point
would lead to an attempt to supplement this suggestion.
This article is such an attempt.

'Universals exist' has a deceptive logic. Realists offer it
as the conclusion of many arguments: but unlike the
premises of these arguments, it cannot be understood as
a verifiable statement of fact. On the other hand, if it is
taken merely as an esoteric way of stating those premises
over again, the vehemence of the controversy becomes
inexplicable. Faced with this difficulty of interpretation,
some modern philosophers suggest that it is no good puzzling about its literal meaning, just as it is no good puzzling
about the literal meaning of dreams. For traditional phi-

From *Philosophical Quarterly*, Vol. I (1951). Reprinted by permission of the author and the editor of *Philosophical Quarterly*.
[1] Cf. J. S. Mill, *Examination of Sir William Hamilton's Philosophy*
(5th edn., London, 1878) chap. XVII, p. 381, and Berkeley, *Principles
of Human Knowledge,* Introduction § 18.
[2] Cf. M. Lazerowitz, 'The Existence of Universals' (*Mind*, 1946,
pp. 1 ff.).

losophy provided a small set of possible conclusions to
arguments about the generality of thought and language,
and tradition was strong. If a tribe educated its children to
dream according to a tradition which restricted their manifest dream contents within narrow limits, it would be
difficult to discover their much more varied latent dream
contents.[3] Similarly, although realists are argumentative,
it is difficult to answer the question why they maintain that
universals exist. Any answer must be based on a selection
from among the many reasons which they themselves
proffer: and a good selection will be diagnostic; it will
successfully explain the doctrine. There is no sharp bound-
ary here between descriptions of the premises of philosophical arguments and diagnoses of their conclusions:
because success in explaining, which is the criterion of a
diagnosis, is a matter of degree, and because the reasons
which philosophers themselves give for their doctrines
sometimes completely explain why they held them. Quine's
remark, that realists find a universal for every property
which can be existentially generalized,[4] is an extremely
brief description. The thesis of Berkeley and Mill was more
than this: it was a diagnosis, but an inadequate one. I shall
try to provide a less inadequate diagnosis.

'Because universals exist' is the answer to at least two
general questions: 'Why are things what they are'?[5] and
'Why are we able to name things as we do'? Though Plato
and Aristotle sometimes distinguished these two questions,
it was characteristic of Greek thought to confuse them.
Yet they can be clearly distinguished, the first requiring a
dynamic answer from scientists, and the second a static
answer from logicians. Now philosophy has often staked
premature claims in the territory of science by giving quick
comprehensive answers to questions which really required
laborious detailed answers. And clearly this is what happened to the first of the two questions. When detailed

[3] Cf. Freud, *The Interpretation of Dreams,* tr. A. A. Brill (London, 1913), p. 166.
[4] Cf. 'Designation and Existence' in Feigl and Sellars, *Readings in
Philosophical Analysis* (New York, 1949), p. 48.
[5] Aristotle criticized Plato's theory largely as an inadequate answer to this question.

causal answers were provided to it, the comprehensive answer 'Because universals exist' was no longer acceptable or necessary.[6] But what would detailed answers to the second question be like? Presumably they would be explanations of the meanings of words. But philosophers are easily led to neglect such detailed progressive answers to the second question, and to seek instead a comprehensive and ultimate explanation of naming. For, though comprehensive answers to the first question are clearly futile, there are no obvious penalties attached to answering the second question in a comprehensive way. Yet, I shall argue —and this will be my first thesis—that any comprehensive explanation of naming is necessarily circular: and that philosophers think that, in spite of this disadvantage, such explanations have some point largely because they wrongly assimilate naming to natural processes. Yet surely naming cannot be utterly artificial? My second thesis will be that the desire to understand naming leads to a hunt for a completely satisfactory analogy: but that all other processes either already contain the very feature of naming which was puzzling, or else are too natural or too artificial to be really analogous; and that it was the inevitable oscillation between these three points which prolonged the controversy about universals.

It is unnecessary to produce evidence that philosophers who proposed the existence of universals thought that they were explaining the unity of classes and hence the possibility of naming. What is debatable is whether this was an important motive, and this can be decided only in the sequel. My first thesis, which I must now try to establish, is that realism is necessarily a circular explanation of naming. Now the answer to the question 'Why are we able to name things as we do?' is 'The reason varies'. For it is always possible with more or less ingenuity, depending on the degree of atomicity of the name, to give a detailed in-

---

[6] Socrates in the *Phaedo* (100d) says that it is the only acceptable answer to the first question. But the advance of science has undermined this thesis more thoroughly than the advance of logic has undermined the thesis that it is an acceptable answer to the second question.

formative reason; and this reason will vary with the name. But ultimately there must be some exit from the maze of words, and, wherever this exit is made, it will be impossible to give an informative reason except by pointing. For the only other way of giving an informative reason is to give a new word, and this would prevent the exit from the maze of words from being made at this place.[7] Still at the place where the exit is made it is always possible to give a detailed reason like 'We are able to call things red because they are red', which is too obviously circular even to look informative. Or alternatively it is possible to say 'We are able to call things ϕ because they are ϕ', and this is a general reason which is almost as obviously circular and uninformative. What philosophers who propose the existence of universals do is to propose a general reason which looks informative because it shifts to another level, but unfortunately is not. It merely marks time: but marking time can look very like marching if only the movements of the performers are watched, and not the ground which they profess to be covering. Yet this ground could not be covered. For the reason could not be informative even if it were detailed; since there could be a non-circular answer to the question 'What universal?' only if the exit from the maze of words were made at some different point, which would merely put off the moment of embarrassment from which in the end neither speech nor thought can be saved. Thus realism fails to escape the limitations of all explanations of naming; that they can be informative only if they are not general but detailed, and then only if they are not given at the point where an exit is made from the maze of words.

Uninformative answers have their point. They are silencing. What is wrong with realism is not this, but that it masquerades as an answer which advances knowledge one step further. The analytic machine acquires a momen-

---

[7] Cf. the view sketched by Socrates in the *Theaetetus* 201e–202c, and Antisthenes' view given by Aristotle in *Met.* H, 1043 b 23–32; also L. Wittgenstein, *Tractatus* 5; M. Schlick, *Grundzüge der Naturphilosophie* (Vienna, 1948), p. 21; and A. J. Ayer, *Thinking and Meaning* (London, 1947), p. 28.

tum which carries it beyond the point where it ought to stop. And there is an inveterate philosophical habit which strengthens the tendency to go beyond this point, or rather to think that one has gone beyond it. 'A thing is called by a certain name because it instantiates a certain universal' is obviously circular when particularized, but it looks imposing when it is left in this general form. And it looks imposing in this general form largely because of the inveterate philosophical habit of treating the shadows cast by words and sentences as if they were separately identifiable. Universals, like facts and propositions, are such shadows; and too often philosophers by appealing to them in general terms have produced in their readers a feeling of satisfaction which ought to have been produced only by specifying them.[8] But universals are specifiable only by reference to words. Similarly facts may be brute and propositions may be definite, but what exactly it is about them which is brute or definite can be specified only by reference to the sentences which were the unacknowledged starting-points. In all these cases it is tacit re-duplication which makes philosophers think that they can enjoy the benefits of specifying without actually specifying. Yet the explanation of naming is incomplete until a particular universal is specified, and, when it is specified, the explanation immediately fails through circularity. Naming is hazardous,[9] and any attempt to make it foolproof by basing it on an independent foundation must fail in this way. It is impossible to cross the gap between language and things without really crossing it.[10]

Since the failure of realism to perform this feat is inevi-

[8] The same trick is played by those who say that laws of nature exhibit connections between universals. This gives the impression that we could independently know the eternal framework in which temporal things move and change, rather as we independently know how a piston must move by looking at a cylinder: cf. what Köhler says about Aristotle's astronomy and Descartes' neurology (*Gestalt Psychology*, London, 1930, pp. 82–86).

[9] Cf. Bradley, *Appearance and Reality*, p. 22 and p. 533; and C. S. Peirce, *Collected Papers* (vol. I, para. 145): 'Direct experience is neither certain nor uncertain, because it affirms nothing—it just is.'

[10] Cf. Stuart Hampshire, 'Scepticism and Meaning' (*Philosophy*, July 1950, p. 245).

table, its rivals fail too. Nominalism, conceptualism and imagism,[11] in so far as they are rivals of realism, are attempts to provide a unity which will explain naming. Nominalism says that a name is merely connected with a multitude of things, sometimes adding that these things are similar. Conceptualism says that the name is not directly connected with the things but only via a concept, thus changing the nodal point. Imagism says that the nodal point is an image. And realism says that there is really no nodal point, since a name, though it appears to be connected with a multitude of things is all the time connected with only one thing, a universal. This is an over-simplification of what these theories say about the One and the Many; but it is enough for my next purpose, which is to show that these rivals of realism cannot produce a non-circular explanation of naming at those points where an exit is made from the maze of words.

The two psychological theories say that one word can apply to many things only because of the mediation of a concept or of an image. Locke's abstract general idea is 'the workmanship of the understanding, but has its foundation in the similitudes of things'.[12] And Berkeley replaces it by an idea which 'considered in itself is particular but becomes general by being made to represent or stand for all other particular ideas of the same sort'.[13] But what similitudes, and what representation? In the end both Locke's concept and Berkeley's image are completely identifiable only by their use.[14] Of course we can partly identify images by describing their features: and in this way we may even almost completely identify them, since certain images most naturally stand for certain things. And the same could be said of concepts, if they were not merely philosophers' reifications of mental processes. But this

---

[11] Cf. H. H. Price, *Thinking and Representation* (British Academy Lecture, 1946).
[12] Locke, *Essay concerning Human Understanding*, Bk. III, Chap. III, § xiii.
[13] Berkeley, *Principles of Human Knowledge*, Introduction, § 12.
[14] This is due to Wittgenstein: cf. e.g. *Tractatus*, 3.326, 'In order to recognize the symbol in the sign we must consider the significant use'.

will not completely identify either of them, since thought
may not follow the most natural course; nor is it always
clear which is the most natural course. It is not so much
that thinking is speaking as that thinking is like speaking in
the only way that matters: it uses one thing as a symbol
to stand for many things. And the only tool which could
not be used differently is the use. Even something which
had its use written on it could be used differently.[15] And,
if the psychological tool, whether concept or image, can
be completely identified only by the things on which it is
used, it cannot explain naming without circularity. For,
unless we point, the use can be specified only by backward
reference to the name. Nor is this circularity surprising.
For psychological tools have no advantage over words:
they are like them in being symbols, and unlike them
only in being shadowy symbols.

The type of nominalism which says that a name is applied to a number of things which are similar immediately falls into the same circularity. For 'similar' is an incomplete predicate, anything being similar to anything in
some way, perhaps a negative way.[16] And in the end the

[15] W. T. Stace in 'Russell's Neutral Monism' in *The Philosophy of
Bertrand Russell*, pp. 381–83, complains that neither Berkeley's precise image nor Russell's vague image (in *An Inquiry into Meaning
and Truth*) succeeds in explaining the generality of thought. But
no description of any item of mental furniture which included only
its momentary properties and not its habitual use could possibly
explain the generality of thought.

[16] Hence the point of many riddles. Cf. Stuart Hampshire, 'Scepticism and Meaning' (*Philosophy*, July 1950, p. 238). Also Plato,
Protagoras 331 d. The Platonic theory avoids the 'similarity' difficulty, but not of course the general difficulty of which this is only
one form. Speusippus, who abandoned the Platonic theory, seems
to have held that, since every species is like every other species in
some way, it is impossible to define one species without defining
every other species. Cf. Aristotle, *Post. An.* 97 a 6–11. Cf. H. Cher-
niss, *Aristotle's criticism of Plato and the Academy* (I. 60), quoted
by W. D. Ross in his note on this passage. J. Stenzel, in Pauly-
Wissowa Real-Encyclopädie, *s.v.* Speusippus, pp. 1650 and 1655,
brings out the affinity between Speusippus' view and Post-Kantian
Idealism. Cf. Brand Blanshard on individuals (not species). 'One
never gets what is fully particular until one has specified its relations
of every kind with everything else in the universe', *The Nature of
Thought* (London, 1939), vol. I, p. 639. Curiously enough N. R.
Campbell arrives independently at a similar conclusion about species,
when he is discussing the definition of such substances as silver,

kind of similarity which is meant can be specified only by
a backward reference to the name. Equally the type of
nominalism which merely says that a name is applied to a
class of things cannot say which class without a backward
reference to the name. Here the circularity is so obvious and
there is so little to cushion the shock of the realization
that naming is naming that this type of nominalism seems
hardly tenable. For, however strongly nominalists react
against realism, they can never quite escape its influence:
once somebody had said that universals exist it could never
be quite the same again. Surely, one wants to protest, there
must be some way of giving the class besides reference
to the name? Well there is, of course, enumeration. But
this answer seems to fail to allow for the possibility of
ever using the name correctly in any synthetic sentence.
For, if the class is given by enumeration, surely every use
of the name must be either incorrect or analytic? Since, if
to call a thing 'ϕ' is to include it in the class of things called
'ϕ', then surely either it is incorrect to call it 'ϕ' or else the
class cannot be given without reference to it? It is the example of realism which encourages these protests. But it
is a bad example. Such neatness is not to be had. For, first
of all, these classes cannot be given by enumeration of
all their members, since, except for words belonging to
dead languages, they are never complete. Nor is it true even
that each member must either contribute or not contribute
towards giving a class; since a name may be applied to the
same thing twice, once analytically and once synthetically,
and even a single use of a name may be synthetic for the
speaker and analytic for the hearer. In fact the disjunction
'Analytic or Synthetic' cannot be applied simply to the
addition of a member to a class without further caveats.
But this in itself is not enough to remove the difficulty; it
only makes it reappear in a new form. For if the addition
of a member to a class can be synthetic for the speaker and

mercury or lead (*Physics. The Elements,* Cambridge, 1920, p. 50).
All attempts to explain the unity of a species by similarity—whether
by similarity of the individuals to one another, or by similarities and
differences between the species and other species—suffer from the
same incompleteness.

analytic for a subsequent lexicographer, then to what class was the member added? Surely we now have two classes on our hands instead of one? An analogy will help us to deal with this new form of the difficulty. Naming is like electing the sort of member who makes a difference to a club. Strictly we cannot say without qualification to what club he was elected, since it was one club before he was elected and another club after he was elected. The club building might be pointed out, and of course there is no parallel move in the case of naming, although realism pretends that there is. But, even if there were no building or anything else of that kind, the puzzle about the two clubs would not be very perplexing. Similarly, when we reject the simple application of the dichotomy 'Analytic or Synthetic' the resulting puzzle about two classes is not very perplexing. All that is necessary is to point out that a class is incompletely given by a changing quorum. This may be untidy, but why not? There is something radically wrong with a request to be given a class which is not satisfied either with a reference to the name or with progressive enumeration. It is a request to be given something without being given it; as if somewhere, if only philosophers searched long enough, there could be found something which possessed all the advantages of a word and none of its disadvantages, an epistemological vehicle which carried all its destinations.

I now turn to my second thesis, that nothing is sufficiently like naming without being too like naming. Defenders of realism, like defenders of the other theories of naming, might object that the criticism contained in my first thesis is obvious, superficial and directed against a man of straw. For realism does not offer a non-circular detailed explanation of naming—how could it?—but simply gives a general characterization of the sort of unity which makes naming possible. But notice how very like a dream realism is. Taken literally it seems to be of little importance. But, if it is taken as the expression of a doctrine which, if *per impossibile* it were true, would give it great importance, the suggestion is immediately repudiated. Yet it does express such a doctrine, even if its exponents intermittently

deny that it does; and it is to the devious expression of this
doctrine that it owes most of its attractiveness. Its manifest content is little more than a harmless caprice, but its
latent content is a serious error.

But has realism no point when it is taken simply as a
general characterization of the sort of unity which makes
naming impossible? One might answer that it has no point,
and that it succeeds in appearing to have some point only
by the device of inventing a new comprehensive term:
and that this device is considered effective only in philosophy, since outside philosophy it is too obviously like making an impressive gesture in the direction of the interesting
object, opening one's mouth and saying absolutely nothing. But such a denial would be tantamount to a denial that
any general characterization of the sort of unity which
makes naming possible could have a point. And surely
such a denial would be wrong, since something can be
done towards explaining the general possibility of naming
by finding analogous processes? For instance, what makes
naming possible is one thing which is in many things as an
ingredient.[17] But does this analogy throw much light on
naming? Any feature of logical mixing which is at all
interesting seems to distinguish it from all other sorts of
mixing. The values of an unrestricted variable are strange
receptacles. What prevents contrary ingredients from being
put in together, or an implicant from appearing without its
implicate, is never the causal consequences. And anyway
the whole notion of mixing ingredients which were not
there before the mixing is peculiar. Could there be a logical
conjuring trick?

Here defenders of realism might object that a new misunderstanding had replaced the old one. For, if realism is
to be understood, not only must a general characterization
of naming be allowed, but also the verification principle
must not be applied too crudely. And anyway, if mixing is
not a good analogy, this only means that some better
analogy must be sought. This objection might lead to a toler-

[17] Cf. A. N. Whitehead, *Science and the Modern World* (Cambridge, 1928), pp. 197 ff. For a criticism of this analogy, cf. Ben-
tham, *Works*, vol. VIII, p. 335.

ant examination of other analogies.[18] But fortunately it also opens up a short cut to the heart of the matter, which I shall soon take. Now it would be taking too short a cut to repeat the platitude that naming is *sui generis*. For it is natural to seek an analogy even if the search can never be completely successful. And anyway Butler's truism applies to everything. What is needed in order to explain the peculiar persistence of the debate about universals is something slightly longer, a demonstration that no analogy can be sufficiently close to satisfy philosophers without being too close.

It is most natural to seek a visible process as an analogy to naming, particularly for the Greeks who began this controversy.[19] Now previously I insisted that it is impossible in the end to give a detailed non-circular description of what makes it possible to name anything. Here, however, it would be unfair to object that, if naming in general is compared to a visible process, still that process itself must be named. For this sort of circularity is the inevitable result of the philosopher's predicament. However, it is dangerous to begin speaking at all where so little can be said. For it is fatally easy to think that one has separate access to what makes a name applicable just because one has separate access to whatever stands for this in the analogy. But, waiving this, let us now take the short cut and ask what sort of visible process could be analogous to naming. Let us try a rough analogy and say that one word is connected with many objects in the same way that the estuary of a river is connected with its many sources. But this analogy fails because this connection just happens naturally. We might then try to mend the analogy by saying that water follows the easiest course. But this could be called choice only anthropomorphically, in an extended and weak sense of 'choice'. In order to introduce choice in a restricted, strong sense, it is necessary to alter the analogy and say that people by directing the streams

[18] Metaphors must not be dismissed just because they are metaphors, as, e.g. 'copying' and 'participation' are by Aristotle, *Met.* 991 a 20.

[19] Cf. J. Stenzel, *Plato's Method of Dialectic* (Oxford, 1940), p. 37.

choose which sources shall feed the river. But, if the first
process was too natural to be like naming, the second is too
artificial, since, for the analogy to work, the sources ought
to have something in common besides the fact that the
river is fed from them. And it is difficult to find an analogy
which is neither too natural nor too artificial. The characteristic of naming which is difficult to match is that the
objects have something in common besides being called by
one name, but nothing in common which counts except
that in virtue of which they are called by one name. And
this characteristic can be matched only by allowing that
something makes it convenient but not absolutely necessary for people to canalize streams into the river in the
way they do, and that whatever it is which makes this
choice convenient is the only thing common to the sources
which counts. But this compromise between the two ex-
tremes introduces into the analogy the very feature which
it was intended to explain. For just how something works
in influencing usage was what was to be explained. Nor is
there a fourth alternative. So after all even general analogical characterizations of naming do fall into a circularity
which is closely related to the type of circularity which my
first thesis exposed. Neither in detail nor in general is it
possible to step outside language.

This short way with analogies looks too superficial. For
suppose that it is granted that one of the things that metaphysicians do is to seek the unattainable: that they hunt
for definitions which would in no way involve their defi-
nienda,[20] and for analogies which would in no way involve
what they were intended to explain. Yet even so metaphysics is a natural and inevitable pursuit, since the easiest
way to discover how far one can go is to try to go one stage
farther. And anyway there is a difference between complete failure and partial success; since, so long as analogies
do not reach the point of self-frustration they get better
and better as they approach it. These two qualifications
are just but they only serve to strengthen my thesis that it
was oscillation between the three points which prolonged

[20] Cf. J. Wisdom, 'Metaphysics and Verification' (*Mind*, 1938,
pp. 465 ff.).

the controversy about universals. For unless the possible analogies are mapped out in this simple way, it seems always conceivable that some altogether better analogy might lurk in an unexplored corner.

And what more are the rival theories of naming doing than seeking a completely satisfactory analogy? It is only jargon which makes them appear to be doing something more. The type of nominalism which suggests that things which are called by one name have only their name in common represents the extreme of artificiality.[21] It suggests that there are never any ways of telling even approximately whether a word is used in one sense or two senses. At the other extreme stands the type of realism which suggests that there is always one method of getting a precise answer to this question. In between are all the other theories of naming, which allow that it is neither impossible for the lexicographer to succeed in answering this question nor impossible for him to fail. None of these middle theories is really wrong, since of course we do bestow common names on certain chosen groups of things which exhibit certain similarities (else why should we do it?) or instantiate certain universals (why else were they invented?). But on the other hand none of them goes deep enough to satisfy the true metaphysician who is in all of us; since though they take us to the bottom of naming, we were in a simpler way already there, and they do not succeed in showing us how naming is founded on something else which lies even deeper. Hence each of these middle theories (except imagism, which says something empirical which seems to be false) develops its own thesis with embarrassing success up to a point, and can discredit its rivals only by accusing them of not going beyond that point. But, since naming cannot be explained by anything which really goes beyond a reasoned choice of usage, this is an unfair accusation. And its unfairness is concealed from those who make it only because each tacitly and wrongly assumes that his own theory alone does go beyond this point. Thus moderate nominalists maintain that similarity is a better expla-

---

[21] There are traces of such an extreme form of nominalism in Hobbes. Cf. *Leviathan*, Pt. I, chap. IV, p. 13 (Everyman edition).

nation of the unity of a class than the presence of a universal. (But why should people not *just* recognize the presence of universals?) And moderate realists retort that this admits the existence of at least one universal, similarity. (But why should the presence of a universal explain the recognition of similarity if it cannot explain the recognition of anything else? Why should people not *just* recognize similarity?) Really these are not two arguments but two bare assertions of superiority. They are manœuvres which are carried out in a way which suggests that they are difficult and that they must be advances: but both these suggestions are false. Yet these theories do seem to be striving towards something. And they are. Their goal is the unattainable completely satisfactory explanation of naming. And, as so often happens in metaphysics, progress is measured by distance from the starting-point and not by proximity to the goal whose unattainability each uses against its rivals without allowing it to deter itself.

Thus theories of naming, which seem to flout the verification principle without therefore saying nothing, can be interpreted as disguised analogies. And, though there is a common limit beyond which they cannot go, the success with which they stealthily approach this limit, camouflaged in the technical terms of epistemology, varies. But if this almost mechanical oscillation is avoided what else can be said about naming? Certainly as the first part of this article showed, detailed answers to the question why we name things as we do will in the end be circular. Only the trick of giving a general answer as if it were a detailed one cloaks their failure. If a word is explained ostensively, then however difficult this process may be it really is explained ostensively. It is no good trying to combine the concreteness of ostensive definition with the clarity of verbal definition. Verbal definitions have such an easy task just because ostensive definitions have such a difficult task. Surveyors find it easier to fix the positions of points which they can visit than to fix the positions of points which they cannot visit. Similarly it is easy to fix the relative positions of words: but the points in things to which words are related are in the end inaccessible to logicians.

Then what else can be said about naming? How *does* the lexicographer tell when a word is used in two senses rather than in one sense? Surely there must be something in common to all well constructed series of things? Yes, just that they *are* well constructed. For this question already contains the equivalent of any possible comprehensive answer which could be given to it. And, though in one way it is hard to see what detailed answers could be given to it, in another way it is only too easy to see. For we never reach a point where an exit *must* be made from the maze of words. Admittedly, if a verbal explanation is given at one point, it is only successful if at some other point a connection with things is already understood; and at some points it is more natural not to offer more words. But at no point is an exit obligatory. So, if detailed reasons why we call a thing what we do are required, it is easy to give them; but never ultimately or in the end, since here *ex vi termini* it is impossible to give them. But philosophers tend to ignore this kind of detailed answer and press on. But where to? Perhaps to experimental psychology, in order to discover how changes in the sense organs, in training and in interests alter the ways in which people group things. But this sort of investigation only gives the varying tests of the good construction of a series, and not its essence. But what could its essence be? When general analogical characterizations of naming have been mentioned, and detailed reasons why we call particular things by particular names, and the psychological background of all this, what is left? The desire to go on explaining naming is to some extent the result of the way these three fields have been confused, and to some extent the result of a natural feeling that in such a vast territory there might be something which lies outside these three fields. But above all it is the result of the Protean metaphysical urge to transcend language.

UNIVERSALS, COMMUNICABLE KNOWLEDGE, AND METAPHYSICS

C. A. Baylis

Except for an extreme sceptic the "problem of universals" can, I think, be formulated as follows. The existence of communicable knowledge requires shared meanings. Such knowledge, in its simplest form, is knowledge of the common characters exhibited by various objects and events. In the more advanced form of scientific knowledge it is knowledge of the interrelations of these characters in all their possible instances. If we call such potentially exemplifiable and conceivable common characters "universals," our problem is to explain their nature and their function in knowledge in terms that are neither mystical nor false to the facts of conscious communication. The extreme nominalist who denies the existence of such common characters seems unable to account for the knowledge we appear to share. On the other hand the speculative metaphysician who hypostatizes them tends toward mystification and eulogy rather than knowledge-yielding explanation. How can we avoid these opposite errors and present a straightforward account of universals that will explain the facts and yet not go beyond the evidence?

Scientific knowledge, whether empirical, as in a natural science like biology, or *a priori*, as in a rational science like logic or mathematics, depends on knowledge of the interrelations of specifiable characters. Even classification

From the *Journal of Philosophy*, Vol. XLVIII (1953). Reprinted by permission of the author and the editor of the *Journal of Philosophy*.

requires grouping by means of some character or group of characters. Empirical scientific study often begins with the discovery and examination of the properties of objects or events, e.g., of magnetic fields or of electric currents. The discovery of empirical laws rests on knowledge of the interrelations of such characters. Neo-Humeans describe the crucial relationship as one of uniform concomitance. Others, in growing numbers, remain dissatisfied until their evidence reveals a "real" or "natural" connection between such conjoined characters. But in either case knowledge of sharable qualities, properties, or relations constitutes the basis of scientific generalization.

That such knowledge is fundamental also in logic and mathematics is readily indicated. We study the relations between implication and logical consistency and between implication and truth values. Our knowledge of the interrelations of logical properties enables us to organize whole fields into deductive systems, of arithmetic, of geometry, of logic itself. In these fields, instead of concentrating attention on the primary characteristics of particular objects and events we study secondary and high-order properties. And in many cases, of course, we study defined properties of these higher orders without regard—at least for the time being—as to whether or not there are first-order objects which have the characters which in turn these higher-order properties might characterize. In any case, however, in the rational as well as in the empirical sciences, our knowledge rests on discernment of specifiable characters or universals. What is the nature of such universal characters? What kind of being do they have? How is knowledge of them possible?

That we can discriminate common characteristics in objects and events is admitted by all save extreme nominalists. Some describe the process as abstraction, others as focusing our attention on certain features of our experience and neglecting others. Even those determined would-be nominalists, Berkeley and Hume, were led to admit that by a "distinction of reason" we could notice, for example, the respects in which they differ.

There are perhaps three main types of extreme nominalists. One group confuses concepts with images. Finding that all images are particular, they deny the possibility of "abstract ideas." Their error can be indicated by pointing out that in many cases we know with great clarity the connotative meaning of a term without being able to form an image of that meaning. Thus we know precisely that a chiliagon is a plane polygon with a thousand angles, though psychologists assure us that we cannot imagine anywhere near that many angles at once. Again, if we accept something like Russell's and Whitehead's analysis of the meaning of the expression "cardinal number three" we realize that our meaning is not identical with any image we can form. Even where a relevant image can be formed, it cannot correctly be identified with our meaning. Berkeley and Hume have shown quite adequately that no image of a triangle is limited to precisely those properties which define triangularity.

It is easy to explain why some behaviorists are nominalists, for of course, since they shun introspection, they are not likely to meet a concept directly. Much credit is due those behaviorists who recognize that universals, at least in the sense of common characteristics, turn up even in nature.

A third class of extreme nominalists is composed of those logical positivists who, from admirable motives of logical economy and metaphysical clarity, deny the existence of universals. But their denial is inconsistent with their practice as long as they make use of variable symbols. For variable symbols are precisely such as can be replaced by any member of a certain class of constant symbols, and whether this class be specified by a class property or by enumeration, all of its members will have certain characteristics in common—in the first case, the class property, and in the second, the characteristic of having just been enumerated.

The denial by extreme nominalists[1] that particulars have common characteristics leads them to affirm that no two things can be precisely alike in any respect. This has the

---

[1] E.g., E. B. McGilvery, "Relations in General and Universals in Particular," *Journal of Philosophy*, Vol. XXXVI (1939), pp. 5–15, 29–40.

prima facie absurd consequence that, for example, no two books can be precisely alike in containing exactly 232 pages. The extreme nominalist tries to avoid this absurdity by urging that there is no one property of having 232 pages which is shared or exemplified by two or more books, but rather that there are two or more unique particular properties which, though not alike in any respect, are nevertheless similar. As Russell and others have pointed out, such a nominalist, to be consistent, must then go on to insist that all relations of similarity are also particulars, not alike in any respect, but only similar in some still different sense of "similar." Such a nominalist has at his disposal only particulars and names of particulars. This appears to make it impossible for him, without inconsistency, to make any descriptive statements, for all such statements assert or deny that something has, i.e., exemplifies, some character.

It seems likely that nominalism in the extreme form in which I have been discussing it is one of those views which C. D. Broad has suggested we call "silly"; that is, it is a view which only an extremely able philosopher would even try to hold. Let us turn from it, then, to a less extreme nominalism such as is represented by the position which W. V. Quine seems to take.[2]

Quine appears to admit general terms, e.g., "square," which often apply correctly to a number of particulars. But he wants at least to try to construct a language in which such terms do not designate or name anything. This involves, he agrees, giving up terms as substituends, save as an eliminable notational abbreviation.

He believes he has shown how by a contextual definition he can treat statements and statement variables as a mere abridged manner of speaking, translatable at will back into an idiom which uses no statement variables and hence presupposes no propositions.[3] He has worked also in the direction of providing contextual definitions of this

[2] "Designation and Existence," *Journal of Philosophy*, Vol. XXXVI (1939), pp. 701–9, and "Identity, Ostension, and Hypostasis," ibid., Vol. XLVII (1950), pp. 621–33.
[3] "A Logistical Approach to the Ontological Problem," *The Journal of Unified Science*, Vol. 9.

kind for terms which would otherwise designate concepts,[4] but this task is incomplete. He adds that until the nominalist can supply the relevant contextual definitions his plea that his apparent abstract entities are merely convenient fictions "is no more than incantation."[5]

Should Quine be able to overcome the difficulties which now block completion of his linguistic attempt to avoid all variables whose values would be abstract entities, his success would show only that a nominalistic language is possible. It would furnish no evidence as to whether or not universals exist. For evidence as to that we must seek to determine whether or not our abstract terms have clear and specifiable intensional meanings. Let us, then, ask what manner of entity universals are or would be, and what is involved in affirming that there are some. Perhaps a theory can be constructed which at once does justice to the facts of common concepts and communicable knowledge and also respects our desires for clarity and economy of ontological hypothesis.

Let us start with the common characters of particular things which moderate nominalists seem to admit. Such characters, as embodied or exemplified, we can call *characteristics*. We notice the resemblances between things and events and classify on the basis of them. We then go further and observe some of the relations which hold between these abstract, though not abstracted, characteristics. On such knowledge the empirical sciences are based.

It is an easy next step to think of abstract characters which might characterize but which as a matter of fact do not. We can safely assume that zoologists know and can specify the set of characters that any animal must have to be an American bison or buffalo. This knowledge, combined with knowledge of botany and biochemistry, makes it possible to know that some types of prairie flora will in general prove nutritious for buffaloes and other types will prove poisonous. Now, suppose that buffaloes become quite extinct. It will still be possible to think of those char-

    [4] "A Theory of Classes Presupposing No Canons of Type," *Proceedings, National Academy of Science*, Vol. 22 (1936), pp. 320–26.
    [5] "Designation and Existence," p. 709.

acters which are definitive of buffaloes even though nothing exemplifies all of them. And experts in such matters will still know the relation between possession of these characters and the suitability for food of certain prairie vegetation. Such knowledge is not destroyed by the death of all the creatures whose existence gave rise to it and made it applicable. We can still think or conceive of the characters that once characterized buffaloes and we still know what any creature which possessed such characters should and should not eat. Let us call abstract characters which are conceived but are not exemplified *concepts*.

Another way of bringing out these points is through the traditional distinction between denotation and connotation. Some such distinction becomes imperative where a meaningful symbol has no denotation. The words "hundred-dollar bill now in my pocket" convey a clear meaning to me, though I know that no such bill is there. The expression has significance, connotation though no denotation. In this sense the connotation of a term consists precisely of those characters whose possession is necessary and sufficient for anything to be denoted by it. Again, in the case of many terms, there must be some sense in which we are acquainted with their connotation before we can determine whether or not there are things denoted by them. Thus, for example, we must know what is meant by the expression "white crow" before we can search intelligently to see if there are any. We must know in terms of income what we mean by the phrase "rich man" before a study of income tax returns would be rewarding in identifying some.

These are trivial and obvious examples. But something like them seems needed in the face of persistent denials that there are concepts. These examples indicate that we are often aware of the connotative meaning of terms that denote nothing. But to be aware of such connotative meanings is to conceive abstract characters that are unexemplified, namely, concepts. We can select as a concept any character we wish, and we can limit this concept by stipulation to just that character or set of characters we choose. This ability is essential to classification and to the discovery of empirical laws.

At a second stage of abstraction we notice that concepts themselves exemplify characters which can in turn be conceived. Thus relations, a species of concepts, can themselves be classified as symmetric, asymmetric, or non-symmetric, transitive, intransitive, non-transitive, and so on. It is knowledge of second and higher-level concepts which makes logic and mathematics possible.

One way in which we can combine concepts to obtain more complex concepts is by simple conjunction. Since we can conceive of the concept *old* and the concept *man*, we can think of the concept *old man*. By conjoining *creature having the body of a horse* and *creature having the chest and head of a man*, we can conceive the defining characteristics of a centaur. Walt Disney goes us one better and by a happy modification conceives that titillating conjunction of characters possessed by every centaurette.

Unless we limit the principle that the conjunct of any two concepts is itself a concept, it follows further that there are self-inconsistent concepts such as round-square-ness. Though startling at first, a little reflection convinces us that there is nothing alarming in this. The elements of the concept round-square-ness are mutually incompatible in the sense that nothing can at once exemplify both these concepts. But the concept round-square-ness does not violate the principle of contradiction. It is neither round nor square, let alone both. It is composed of, but does not have in the sense commonly symbolized by ϵ, two incompatible characters which nothing whatever can possess. Round-square-ness is an unfamiliar concept but a harmless one. We are guaranteed that it can have no instances. To avoid such concepts one would have to complicate logic unduly by limiting the principle of conjunction to mutually compatible concepts. This would have as one unfortunate consequence the fact that in dealing with complicated concepts, for example, some of those of mathematics, we may not know whether we can conjoin certain pairs or not. Such a limitation would be analogous to forbidding statement conjuncts of p and q unless they are mutually consistent. This can indeed be done but our pragmatic interests in simplicity, like those of Quine and Lewis, militate against it.

Thus far we have distinguished two sub-classes of universals: (1) *characteristics,* those universal characters which are exemplified whether thought of or not, and (2) *concepts,* those universal characters which are conceived whether exemplified or not. There is, I think, a third subclass, (3) *pure universals,* or those abstract characters which are neither exemplified nor conceived. Here it is, of course, impossible to give examples, save by indirection. As Russell has remarked, we know that the product of any two positive integers which have never been thought of is more than 100, although by hypothesis these numbers have not themselves been conceived. We have knowledge about them but no acquaintance with them. Again, it has always been true, and always will be, that were there to be a plane triangle in the sense prescribed by Euclid, the sum of its interior angles would be 180°. The geometrical characters which Euclid had studied had exactly the interrelations he noted before he remarked them. And they will continue to have those relations even when all knowledge of Euclidean geometry fades away. Or consider the empirical laws mentioned earlier about nutritional foods for buffaloes. When all buffaloes are dead and all buffalo experts also, these laws, though unknown and unexemplified, will still be true in the sense that if there were buffaloes certain plants would nourish them and others would not. To be sure, the relations between characters which these laws state would probably not have been known unless buffaloes had existed and their essential characters had been conceived, but neither such existence nor such conception is necessary for these relations to hold.

What are the criteria which distinguish universals, of whatever kind, from particulars? They can be stated in terms either of the relation of exemplification or embodiment, whose converse is characterization, or of logical implication. Universals are the sort of entity which, except for conjuncts of mutually incompatible characters,[6] can characterize, that is, can be embodied or exemplified. If they are thus embodied we call them characteristics of that which exemplifies them. Universals also have characteristics. Particulars, on the other hand, though they have many characteristics, do not and cannot characterize anything.

Strict implication between concepts, which is the intensional counterpart of the relation of logical inclusion between classes, also serves to distinguish universals from particulars. Any concept either implies or is implied by some other concept. When a concept, A, strictly implies a concept, B, nothing *could* be a member of the class determined by A and fail to be a member of the class determined by B. But no particular thus implies any other particular. Either characterization, then, or logical implication, will serve to distinguish particulars from universals. Particulars can neither characterize nor imply, universals can do both.

Are universals as thus described independent of being thought of and independent of being exemplified? That exemplification is extrinsic to the nature of universals is shown by the fact that often we first conceive of a set of characters and then look around to see if that set is exemplified. Thus mathematicians have conceived of Riemannian geometry and also of Euclidean geometry. Though we do not know with certainty whether our world is Euclidean, Riemannian, or neither, the nature of each of these geometries, since it has been completely specified, is independent of exemplification.

That universal characters can exist as embodied in things though they have not yet been thought of, is indicated by every new discovery of a scientific law. Presumably the law of gravitation held before it was first thought of, let alone confirmed. Or again, suppose a time in the course of evolution when paramecia existed, but no human or other species capable of mathematical thought. Even then, when two paramecia swam over to two other paramecia there were four paramecia gathered together. Universals may be

_____

[6] The constituent characters of such conjuncts can characterize.

embodied without being thought of and in this sense, at least, they are independent of being conceived.

But further, pure universals are independent simultaneously of both conception and embodiment. To take one more example, let us suppose that Leonardo da Vinci was the first man who ever thought of airplaneness, that set of characteristics which anything must have to be an airplane and which, if anything has it, makes that thing an airplane. Yet airplaneness had at least this minimal sort of being before Leonardo thought of it, that many propositions were true about it. Though no one then knew it, we now know that it was true just before Leonardo's birth that airplaneness would be thought of within the next century. And if some mischance had killed Leonardo before he thought of it then it might well have been true that airplaneness would not have been thought of until some time later. In this minimal sense, then, that some propositions are true and others are false about characters or sets of characters that are neither exemplified nor thought of, the nature of such pure universals is independent both of exemplification and of conception.

It seems not unnatural to say of universals that are embodied that they exist as characteristics, and of universals that are conceived that they exist as concepts. Whether we want to say of pure universals that they exist or not seems largely a matter of verbal usage. If we use the term "exist" as many mathematicians do, we would say that they do exist, just as we would say that the thousandth decimal of "pi" exists even though what number it is has not yet been discovered. But if we wish to restrict application of the word "exist" to entities which have spatial and temporal properties, then we shall need some other term such as "subsist" to describe the kind of being that pure universals have.

Perhaps one reason why pure universals have been discounted and even denied in some quarters is their relative uselessness. We cannot discover instances of universals which are not embodied. And we cannot use in our thinking universals which have not yet been thought of. But is

uselessness a sound reason for denying to pure universals
the minimal being specified?

If it be urged against universals that they "clutter up" the
universe in infinitely chaotic fashion, the answer is obvious.
It is those who raise this objection, not proponents of such
an ontologically modest theory as this, who hypostatize.
Universals occupy no space and because of their fixed relations they are more neatly and precisely ordered than
anything else in our experience. Furthermore, their number does not surpass the bounds of the characteristics which
are exemplified, the concepts which are conceived, and
the characters which could be conceived if we but turned
our attention to them.

Nor are the unchanging or, if you like, eternal characteristics of universals at all incompatible with our changing interests and our changing language. Characters which once
were usefully conceived are no longer so and are neglected.
But if we wished, they could be used again because their
relations with other characters are still what they have always been. Though the same character may be signified
now by one term, now by another, and though different
characters may be signified by the same term, these facts
about the way in which characters are described do not alter their defining characteristics and relations.

Beyond the account of the minimal characteristics described here which universals must possess if we are to
justify scientific knowledge, it is of course possible to construct elaborate metaphysical theories. Some may wish to
think of universals as being more "real" than particulars;
others prefer to judge them less "real." Some may wish to
distinguish between the types of "reality" possessed by
pure universals, by concepts, and by characteristics. But
such addenda are not necessary for purposes of explaining
common meanings and communicable knowledge. They
are, I suspect, purely speculative undertakings. Even if
their usually undefined terms, such as "real" and "reality,"
can be given explicit meaning, the result tends to be only
a number of unverifiable though mutually incompatible
metaphysical theories. From their rivalries we can safely remain detached.

The discussion of this paper justifies, I think, the following conclusion: There are unchanging characters or universals at least in the sense that the same characters can be thought of again and again, that they can be exemplified repeatedly, and that certain relations obtain among these characters whether they are exemplified or not and whether they are thought of or not.

PARTICULAR AND GENERAL

P. F. Strawson

1. There is a certain philosophical question which, if antiquity confers respectability, is as respectable as any.[1] It was not long ago discussed by Ramsey in the form "What is the difference between a particular and a universal?",[2] and more recently by Ayer in the form "What is the difference between properties and individuals?"[3] Ramsey decided that there was no ultimate difference; but perhaps he set the standard for an ultimate difference higher than we should wish to, or drew it from a theory we no longer wish to hold. Ayer, after some interesting suggestions, changed the subject, and discussed instead two other questions: viz., what is the difference in function between indicator words and predicates, and could we in principle say what we want to say without using the former?[4] It may be that the original question is made

From *Proceedings of the Aristotelian Society*, Vol. LIV (1953–54). Copyright 1954, the Aristotelian Society. Reprinted by permission of the author and the editor of the Aristotelian Society.

[1] I am much indebted to Mr. H. P. Grice for his criticisms of an earlier version of this paper; and I owe much to the stimulus of an unpublished paper by Mr. Michael Dummett. For the errors and obscurities which remain in the present paper I am alone responsible.

[2] Ramsey, *Foundations of Mathematics*, pp. 112–34.

[3] Ayer, *Individuals*, "Mind," 1952.

[4] To the second question Ayer's answer was affirmative; and, things being as they are, this is no doubt correct as a matter of what is theoretically practicable. Ayer also acknowledges (*a*) that in actual practice we could scarcely dispense with indicator words, and (*b*) that the attempt to do so would always involve a theoretical failure to individuate, since no elaboration of predicates rules out the theoretical possibility of reduplication. But I doubt if the original question can be answered unless we take these two facts more seriously than he does.

easier to start on, and more difficult to settle, by an initial failure to make even fairly clear what types or classes of things are to be included in the two general categories between which a satisfying difference is sought. The words of the questions I quoted are not very helpful. Universals are said to include qualities and relations. But if, for example, we take the words "quality," "relation" and "property" in their current uses, much that we should no doubt wish to include on the side of the general, as opposed to the particular, would be left out; and if we do not take them in their current uses, it is not clear how we are to take them. Thus snow, gold and clothing are not properties; nor is man, nor any other species; nor is chess nor furniture; nor is the Union Jack—by which I mean, not the tattered specimen the porter keeps in a drawer, but the flag designed in the 19th century, examples of which are taken from drawers by porters and hung from windows. But all these are things which we might well wish to classify with properties correctly so-called, like inflammability, or with qualities correctly so-called, like prudence, when we contrast these latter with individuals or particulars. For there are individual flakes or drifts or falls of snow, pieces of gold, articles of clothing or furniture, games of chess,[5] members of species; and there are hundreds of Union Jacks. These are all (are they not?) particular instances of the general things named in *their* names. Sometimes the unlikeness of these general things to properties or qualities correctly so-called is masked by the introduction of expressions like "being (a piece of) gold," "being snow," "being a man," "being a Union Jack," "being a chair," "being a game of chess"—phrases like these being said to name properties. Now such expressions no doubt have a participial use; and some (*e.g.,* "being a man") may have a use as noun-phrases, as singular terms. But it is dubious whether many of them have a use as singular terms; and it is dubious whether any of them can be regarded as names of properties. And however we resolve these doubts in different cases, the following dilemma arises

[5] But a game of chess *may* be something which itself has instances.

in each. Either these verbal nouns (where they are nouns)
have the same use as the general names they incorporate—
and in that case they may as well be discarded in favour of
those general names, which are more familiar, and about the
use of which we are consequently less liable to be misled; or
they have a different use from those general names—and in
this case we still have on our hands, to be differentiated, like
properties correctly so-called, from particulars, the general
things designated by those familiar general names.

2. This initial unclarity about the limits of the two great
categories of general and particular shows itself also in that
arbitrary narrowing of the field which must be presumed
to occur whenever certain answers to our question seem
plausible. I shall consider again some of these answers,
which were dismissed by Ayer or Ramsey or both, not so
much on the ground that they thought them false as on the
ground that they did not think them fundamental. There is,
for example, the suggestion that general, unlike particular,
things cannot be perceived by means of the senses; and this
seems most plausible if one is thinking of the things designated by certain abstract nouns. It is not with the eyes that
one is said to see hope. But one can quite literally smell
blood or bacon, watch cricket, hear music or thunder; and
there are, on the other hand, certain particulars which it
makes dubious sense to say one perceives. Then there is
the suggestion that general, unlike particular, things, can
be in several places at once. There can be influenza in London as well as in Birmingham, and gold in Australia as
well as in Africa. But then so can many particulars be
scattered over the surface of the table or the globe. Moreover, it makes dubious sense to say of some general things
(e.g., solubility) that they are in any place, let alone in
many; and equally dubious sense to say of some particular
things (a sudden thought, a mental image, the constitution of France) that they have a particular spatial location. It may be said that I have missed the point of both
these theories; that, first, when we say we perceive general
things, what we really perceive is individual instances of
them, not the general things themselves; and, second, to

say that general things can be in several places at once is to
say that they may have different instances, differently
located; whereas it makes no sense to speak of different
instances of individuals. But so to explain these theories is
to give them up. It is to fall back on saying that general
things may have instances, and individual instances of
general things may not. This is, perhaps, an unexception-
able statement of the general distinction between the two
categories, but scarcely seems to count as an explanation of
it.

A third suggestion is that individual things, unlike general things, have dates or histories. But similar objections
apply to this. We may speak of the history of dress or en-
gineering, the origins of civilization, the invention of
golf and the evolution of man. This theory, like the others
(when taken at their face value), may draw a logically
interesting distinction; but, like them, does not draw one
that coincides with the categorial line between particular
and general.

A doctrine which might appear more promising,
because more general, than these, is that individuals can
function in propositions only as subjects, never as predicates; whereas general things can function as both. But it is
not clear what this doctrine amounts to. Suppose, first, it is
a grammatical point. Then if it says that the names of
individuals never have adjectival or verbal forms, whereas
names of general things do, it is false. If it says that individual names never form parts of grammatical predicates, or
alternatively, never stand by themselves after the word "is"
in a grammatical predicate, it is equally false. In any
case, a grammatical point could scarcely be fundamental,
since it is easy to imagine the elimination of those distinctions upon which such points must rely, in favour of the
device of merely coupling names of appropriate types, in
any order, in a singular sentence. We should not, by so
doing, eliminate the category-distinction. For we might
imagine changing the language once more, requiring that
our names should stand on one side or the other of the
phrase "is an instance of," and then simply distinguishing
the individual names as those that could never stand on the

right of this phrase.[6] So I think we must conclude that the point misleadingly made in the languages of grammar is simply once more the point that individuals, unlike general things, cannot have instances. To say that general things, unlike individuals, can be predicated of other things, is simply to paraphrase this; and neither expression seems more perspicuous than the other.

3. But will the word "instance" itself really bear the weight of this distinction? Of course, as a philosopher's word, understood in terms of that distinction, it cannot fail to bear it; but then it ceases to explain the distinction for us. If we ask what expressions we actually use to refer to or describe an individual thing as an instance of a general thing, we find that they are many; and that perhaps none of them is appropriate in every case. They include: "a case of," "an example of," "a specimen of," "a member of," "a piece of," "a quantity of," "a copy of," "a performance of," "a game of," "an article of," and so on. Though each can be followed by the name of a general thing, many can also be followed by expressions we should hesitate to regard as the names of general things. This is true of the phrase "an instance of" itself. We may speak of a signal instance of generosity; but we may also speak of a signal instance of Smith's generosity. Similarly we may speak not only of a piece of gold and an article of clothing, but of a piece of Smith's gold and an article of Smith's clothing. So if we seek to draw our distinction in terms of the words actually used to play the part of the philosopher's word "instance"—including the word "instance" itself—then it will not be enough to say that general things may have instances. For so may non-general things.

The point here may be put roughly as follows. We are tempted to explain the distinction between two types of things, T_1 and T_2, by means of a certain relation R; by saying, that is, that only things belonging to T_2 can appear

[6] Ramsey seems to suggest that this would simply be to manufacture an empty verbal distinction. (Cf. *Foundations of Mathematics*, pp. 132–33). But it would not. For it would not be an arbitrary matter to decide which names to put on which side of the coupling phrase.

as the second term of this relation, whereas both things belonging to T_2 and things belonging to T_1 can appear as its first term. R is something like, but more general than, *is characterized by* or *is a member of* or the converse of *is predicated of*. But then it appears that we really have no notion of R except one which is useless for explanatory purposes since it is itself to be explained in terms of the difference between T_1 and T_2; this is what I called the philosopher's notion of "an instance of." What we have instead is a lot of notions which are either too restricted to serve our purpose (*e.g.*, "has the property of"), or fail to be restricted in precisely the way in which we want them to be, or both. As a member of this set of notions, pre-eminent for its abstract character, we may take the logician's idea of class-membership. The difficulty is, roughly, that we can form closed classes on what principle we please; we could count almost any particular we are likely to mention as such a class, and hence as the second term of our relation. (These remarks are very rough and schematic; but they serve, I hope, to make the point in a general form.) Consequently, we shall have to give up the idea of explaining the difference between the particular and the general in terms of such a relation. This will not lead us, as it perhaps led Ramsey, to despise the philosopher's notion of an instance, and to think that there is nothing in it; for it is easy enough to teach anyone the application of it, without precise explanations. But it will lead us to look further for such explanations.

4. To begin with, I want to draw a rough distinction between three classes of nouns, all of which would traditionally be regarded either as themselves the names of universals (general things) or—in the case of the nouns of group (2)—as closely linked to such names. The distinctions are indicated only by examples; and the three classes are by no means exhaustive of the field. But this does not matter for my purpose.

(1) Examples of the first class are such partitive nouns

as "gold," "snow," "water," "jam," "music." These I shall call *material-names,* and what they name, *materials.*[7]

(2) Examples of the second are certain articulative nouns such as "(a) man," "(an) apple," "(a) cat." These I shall call *substance-names,* and what they apply to, *substances.*

(3) Examples of the third are such abstract nouns as "redness," (or "red"), "roundness," "anger," "wisdom." These I shall call *quality-* or *property-names,* and what they name, *qualities* or *properties.*[7] These three classes of nouns may be compared and contrasted with one another in a number of ways. But the contrast on which I wish to lay most emphasis is

(i) The contrast between the nouns of group (3) and those of groups (1) and (2). The nouns of group (3) are the most sophisticated and the most dispensable. They are derived from adjectives and the general things they name usually enter our talk by way of the adjectives from which their names are derived. When we consider the things which philosophers are prepared to count as individual instances of these general things, we find a considerable latitude in the categories of the things to which these instances may belong. Thus an instance of wisdom may be a man, a remark or an action. An instance of the colour red may be a material thing like a pillar-box, an event like a sunset, or a mental thing like an image. A word, a gesture, an expression, a man may all be instances of anger. In contrast, unsystematic ambiguities aside, there is no latitude at all about what category of thing can be an individual instance of a cat or an apple. There is some latitude, but one would often hesitate to call it a category-latitude, about what can be an individual instance of the general things named by the nouns of group (1). An instance of gold may be a vein, a piece or a quantity of gold; an instance of snow may be a drift, an expanse, a piece, and even a fall, of snow.

(ii) Next I want to emphasise a respect in which the nouns of group (2) differ from those of groups (1) and

[7] The terminology, evidently, is not to be taken too seriously. Anger is a state, not a property or quality.

(3). Philosophers may speak of "an individual (particular) instance (example, specimen) of ϕ," where "ϕ" is replaced by a noun from any of these three groups. Suppose the noun is drawn from group (2). Then we have such phrases as "an instance of a horse" or "an instance of an apple." It is to be noticed that what follows the expression "an instance of" is a phrase which can and does *by itself* function as an indefinite designation of an individual instance. (An instance of a horse is the same as a horse.) This is not the case if the nouns are drawn from groups (1) or (3). (Gold is not the same as a piece of gold.) It seems as if, when we say that x is an instance of y, then when y is such that there is no choice about the sort of thing we can count as an instance of it, we feel no need of a true general-thing name for y, *i.e.*, of a name differing from an indefinite designation of an individual instance of y. (It is true that we have the expressions "*the* horse," "*the* apple," etc., names of species or kinds, obvious collectors of homogeneous individuals; but these follow less naturally after the expression "an instance of" than does the phrase containing the indefinite article). Philosophers have felt this difference, and tried to blur it with the invention of such expressions as "horseness" (*cf.* "being a horse"). But it should rather be treated as a clue until proved an anomaly.

(iii) Finally, I want to note the existence of a special class of individual instances of general things whose names belong to group (3). The simplest, though not the only recipe, for forming the names of members of this class is as follows: in the formula "the . . . of . . . ," fill the first gap with the property-name in question and the second gap with the definite designation of a suitable individual. Thus we may speak of *the wisdom of Socrates* as an instance of wisdom; of *the redness of Smith's face* as an instance of redness; and we may also speak of *Jones' present mental state* as an instance of anger. This class of individual instances of properties, or property-like things, will include the "particular qualities" which Stout defended. And an analogy may be found between referring to a horse as "an instance of a horse" and referring to Jones' present stage of anger as "an instance of anger."

5. Next, I want to make some general, and still propaedeutic, remarks about the notion of an individual or particular.

(1) The idea of an individual is the idea of an individual instance *of* something general. There is no such thing as a pure particular. (This truth is too old to need the support of elaboration.)

(2) The idea of an individual instance of ϕ is the idea of something which we are able in principle

  (*a*) to distinguish from other instances of ϕ; and
  (*b*) to recognise as the same instance at different times (where this notion is applicable).

So, to have the idea of a particular instance of ϕ, we need (in general)

  (*a*) criteria of distinctness,
  (*b*) criteria of identity

for a particular instance of ϕ. On the need for these criteria the following comments must be made:

(i) It might be supposed that the distinction between the two kinds of criteria is a mistake; that there is no such distinction. For identity and difference are two sides of the same coin. It is possible, however, at least in some cases, to consider separately the criteria by which we distinguish and enumerate objects of the same sort, in a situation in which the question of identifying any one of them as, or distinguishing it from, the one which had such-and-such a history, does not arise or is not considered. It is to criteria of this kind that I give the name "criteria of distinctness". They might also be called "criteria of enumeration."[8]

(ii) What the criteria of distinctness and identity for instances of ϕ may be is obviously closely connected with what ϕ is, but is not wholly determined by it in every case. That it is not so determined is obvious in the case of properties, qualities, states, etc.; we have already seen how

---

[8] It might be true, if intelligible, that *if* we had so time-indifferent a perspective of things as to see them as four-dimensional objects in space-time, then there would be no point in giving separate consideration to criteria of distinctness. But we do not have such a perspective.

wide a range of categories their instances may be drawn
from (4 (i)). It is less obvious, but still true, in the case
of general things named by material-names. The *general*
question of the criteria of distinctness and identity of individual instances of snow or gold cannot be raised or, if
raised, be satisfactorily answered. We have to wait until we
know whether we are talking of *veins, pieces* or *quantities*
of gold, or of *falls, drifts* or *expanses* of snow. There are
cases, however, where this indeterminateness regarding the
criteria of identity and distinctness does not seem to exist,
where it seems that once ϕ is given, the criteria are given,
too. And among these cases are those where "ϕ" is a substance-name (4 (ii)). It should once more be noted that
these are the cases where we do not find a true name of a
general thing following the phrase "an instance of," but
instead an expression which can by itself function as an
indefinite designation of an individual instance (*e.g.*, "a
horse").

(3) When it has been said that a particular must be an
instance of something general, and that there must be
criteria of distinctness and (where applicable) of identity
for individual instances of a general thing, something of
central importance still remains unsaid. In giving the relevant criteria—or sets of criteria—for individual instances of
a certain general thing, we do not indicate how such particulars are brought into our discourse. Nor do we bring a
particular into our discourse by mentioning these criteria.
(To mention them is still to talk *in general*.) We bring a
particular into our discourse only when we determine,
select, *a point of application* for such criteria, only when
we mention, refer to, something to which these criteria
are to be applied; and no theory of particulars can be adequate which does not take account of the means by which
we determine such a point of application *as* a point
of application for these criteria.

6. In the rest of this paper I shall try to do two things.
First, I shall try to show how, in the case of *certain kinds*
of particulars (particular instances of *certain kinds* of
general things), the notion of a particular may be seen as

something logically complex in relation to other notions (a kind of compound of these notions). That is, I shall try to produce a partial explanation (analysis) of the notion of an individual instance, for certain cases; and then I shall try to show how this notion, as explained for these cases, may be used in the explanation of the notion of individual instances of *other* sorts of general things, and in the explanation of the notions of those other types of general things themselves. So in this part of the paper (sections 6–9), no general account is offered of the distinction we are concerned with. The procedure is essentially one of indicating, step by step, how certain types of notion can be seen as depending upon others; and it makes no claim at all to completeness. Second (section 12), this procedure is found to suggest a possible general account of the distinction we are concerned with; though the acceptability or otherwise of this general account seems to be independent of that of the step-by-step schema of explanation.

Now it might seem that the difficulty of finding an explanation of the notion of an individual instance arises from the fact that the category distinction between general and individual is so fundamental that there is nothing logically simpler, or more fundamental, in terms of which this notion could be explained. But I think this view can be challenged for a certain range of important cases, which can then perhaps serve as the basis for the explanation of others. To challenge it successfully, we have to envisage the possibility of making statements which (*a*) do not make use of the notion of individual instances, and (*b*) do not presuppose the existence of statements which do make use of this notion. The second condition may be held to rule out general statements; for though many general statements make no direct mention of individuals, they have often and plausibly been held in some sense to presuppose the existence of statements which do. So what we have to consider is the possibility of singular statements which make no mention of (*i.e.*, contain no names for, or other expressions definitely or indefinitely referring to) individual instances of general things. Now there certainly does exist, in ordinary use, a range of empirical singular statements answering to this description. I suggest, as examples, the following:—

> It is (has been) raining
> Music can be heard in the distance
> Snow is falling
> There is gold here
> There is water here.

All these sentences contain either the material-name of a general thing ("music," "snow") or a corresponding verb; but none contains any expression which can be construed as serving to make a definite or indefinite mention of individual instances of those general things (*i.e.*, falls or drops of rain, pieces of gold, pools of water and so on). Of course, when these sentences are used, the combination of the circumstances of their use with the tense of the verb and the demonstrative adverbs, if any, which they contain, provides an indication of the incidence of the general thing in question. Such an indication must be provided somehow, if empirical singular statements are to be made at all. But it is important that it can be provided by means of utterance-centred indications which do not include noun-expressions referring definitely or indefinitely to individual instances. *Such sentences as these do not bring particulars into our discourse.*

Languages imagined on the model of such sentences are sometimes called "property-location" languages. But I think the word "property" is objectionable here because (*a*) the general things which figure in my examples are not properties, and (*b*) the idea of a property belongs, with the idea of an individual instance itself, to a level of logical complexity we are trying to get below. So I propose to substitute the less philosophically committed word "feature"; and to speak of feature-placing sentences.

Though feature-placing sentences do not introduce particulars into our discourse, they provide the materials for this introduction. Suppose we compare a feature-placing *sentence* ("There is snow here") with a *phrase* ("This (patch of) snow") in the use of which an individual instance of the feature is mentioned. It seems possible, in this case, to regard the notion of the individual instance as something logically complex in relation to the two simpler notions of the feature and of placing. The logical complexity may be brought out in the following way. In making the feature-placing statement, we utter a completed sentence without mentioning individuals. If we *merely* mention the individual without going on to say anything about it, we fail to utter a completed sentence; yet what the feature-placing sentence does explicitly is, in a sense, implicit in this mere mention. So, as the basic step in an explanatory schema, we may regard the notion of a particular instance of *certain sorts* of general things as a kind of logical compound of the simpler notions of a feature and of placing.

But what about the criteria of distinctness and identity which were said in general to be necessary to the notion of an individual instance of a general thing? The *basis* for the criteria of distinctness can already be introduced at the feature-placing level, without yet introducing particulars. For where we can say "There is snow here" or "There is gold here," we can also, perhaps, more exactly, though not more correctly, say "There is snow (gold) *here*—and *here*—and *here*." And when we can say "It snowed to-day," we can also, perhaps, more exactly, but not more correctly, say "It snowed twice to-day." The considerations which determine multiplicity of placing become, when we introduce particulars, the criteria for distinguishing this *patch of* snow from that, or the first *fall of* snow from the second. Of criteria of identity I shall say more in general later.

It might be objected that it is absurd to speak of an imagined transition from feature-placing sentences to substantival expressions definitely designating particular instances of features as the *introduction* of particulars; that it is absurd to represent this imagined transition as part of a possible analysis of the notion of a particular instance, even for these simple cases of material-names which seem the most favourable; and that at most what is achieved is the indication of a possible way of looking at certain *designations* of certain particulars. For are not the particulars as much a relevant part of the situation in which a feature-placing sentence is employed as they are of a situation in which a substantival particular-designation is employed? To this I would reply by asking what philosophical question there would be about particulars if we did not designate them, could not make lists of them, did not predicate qualities of them and so on. What we have to explain is a certain mode of speech.

7. When we turn from material-names to substance-names, the attempt to provide an analogous explanation of the notion of an individual instance seems much harder. But though it is harder, it is perhaps worth making; for if it succeeds, we may find we have then an adequate basis for the explanation of the notion of an individual instance in other cases, and for the explanation of further kinds of general things. In order for the attempt to succeed, we must be able to envisage a situation in which, instead of operating with the notion of an individual instance of a cat or an apple, we operate with the notions of a corresponding feature and of placing. Ordinary language does not seem to provide us, in these cases, with feature-placing sentences. And it might be argued that the idea of such sentences was, in these cases, absurd. For (1) it might be pointed out that an all-important difference between such things as snow and such things as cats lay in the fact that different instances of snow are, in a sense, indefinitely additive, can be counted together as one instance of snow; while this is not true in the case of instances of cats; and it might be suggested that herein lay a reason for the possibility of feature-placing sentences in the case of snow and for their impossibility in the case of cats. And (2) it might be added that we have no name for a general thing which could count as the required feature in the case of cats. It is true that we speak of *the cat* in general; but "the cat" ranks as a species-name, and the notion of a species as surely presupposes the notion of individual members as the notion of a property involves that of individual things to which the property belongs or might belong. It is also true that we may speak of an instance (specimen) of *a* cat, as we may

speak of an instance of gold; but here what follows the phrase "an instance of" is not, as "gold" is, a general-thing name which could figure in a merely feature-placing sentence, but an expression which also serves as an indefinite designation of an individual. Does not all this strongly suggest that there *could* be no concept of the "cat-feature" such as would be required for the analysis to work, that any general idea of cat must be the idea of *a* cat, *i.e.*, must involve criteria of identity and distinctness for cats as individuals and hence the notion of an individual instance?

These objections have great force and importance; but I do not think them decisive. For they do not show that it is logically absurd to suppose that we might recognise the presence of cat or signs of the past or future presence of cat, without ever having occasion to distinguish one cat from another as the cat on the left, or identify a cat as ours or as Felix.[9] The second argument merely reminds us that the resources of our language are such that on any actual occasion of this kind we in fact use, not a partitive noun, but the indefinite forms ("cats" or "a cat") of the articulative noun. But this fact can be explained in a way consistent with the advocated analysis (see section 10). Nevertheless, these arguments show something. The point about the species-name, for example, is sound; the notion of a species, like that of a property, belongs to a level of logical complexity we are trying to get below. Second, and more immediately important, the first argument shows that if there is to be a general concept of the cat-feature, corresponding in the required way to the notion of an individual instance, it must already include in itself the *basis* for the criteria of *distinctness* which we apply to individual cats. (Roughly, the idea of cat, unlike that of snow, would include the idea of a characteristic shape). But to concede this is not to concede the impossibility of the analysis. It is worth adding that sometimes we do find verbal indications of our use of feature-concepts such as those we are trying to envisage; as, *e.g.*, when we speak of "smelling cat" or

[9] Cf. Price, *Thinking and Experience*, pp. 40–41, on identity of individuals and of characteristics.

"hunting lion," using the noun in the singular without the article.

There might seem to exist a more general objection to this whole procedure. For it seems that it would always be possible in practice to paraphrase a given feature-placing sentence in use, by means of a sentence incorporating *indefinite* designations of particular instances; *e.g.,* "There is gold here" by "There is *a quantity of* gold here"; "Snow has fallen twice" by "There have been *two falls of* snow"; "There is snow here—and here" by "There are *patches (expanses) of* snow here and here"; and so on. And if sentences incorporating definite *or* indefinite designations of particular instances bring particulars into our discourse; and if statements made by the use of feature-placing sentences are *equivalent* to statements made by the use of sentences incorporating indefinite designations of particular instances; then do not feature-placing sentences themselves bring particulars into our discourse? But this argument can be turned in favour of the explanation it is directed against. Suppose there is a statement S made by means of a feature-placing sentence; and an equivalent statement S′ made by means of a sentence incorporating an indefinite particular-designation; and a statement T made by means of a sentence incorporating a definite designation of the particular indefinitely designated in S′. *Now only if a language admits of statements like T can it admit of statements correctly described as I have described S′.* (There are no *indefinite* designations of particulars where there are no *definite* designations of particulars.) But a language might admit of statements like S without admitting of statements like T. So the existence of statements like S′, in a language which admits of both statements like S and statements like T, is not destructive of the analysis, but is a proof of its correctness.

8. If the argument so far is acceptable, then at least in the case of some materials and some substances, we can regard the notion of an individual instance as partially explained in terms of the logical composition of the two notions of a feature and of placing. When we turn to

properties and qualities, we may make use of a different
kind of explanation which is also, in a sense, the completion of the first kind. I shall not, that is to say, try to explain the notion of individual instances of anger or wisdom
or red in terms of the logical composition of a feature,
such as *anger* or *red,* and placing. But nor shall I maintain that it would be wrong or impossible to do so. We
might think of such general things as anger (or red) *not*
primarily as qualities, properties, states or conditions of
persons or things, but primarily as instantiated in, say, situations (or patches) which acquired their status as individuals from just such a logical composition. But though this
is how we might think, it is not, for the most part, how
we do think. It is natural, rather, to regard those general
things which are properly called qualities, conditions, etc.,
as belonging at least to the same level of logical complexity
as the idea of individual instances of the kinds we have so
far been concerned with; to regard them, that is, as feature-
like things, the incidence of which, however, is primarily
indicated, not by placing, but by their *ascription* to individual instances of material or substantial features the
incidence of which *is* primarily indicated by placing.[10] We
have seen that the notion of an individual instance of some
materials and substances can be regarded as a logical compound of the notions of a feature and of placing. We have
now to see the ascription of a quality (etc.) to such an
individual as an operation *analogous* to the placing of a
feature. Indeed, we may find in the possibility of this operation the point—or one important point—of that logical
composition which yields us the particular. The individual
instance of the simply placeable feature emerges as a possible location-point for general things other than the feature of which it is primarily an instance, and hence as also
an individual instance of *these* general things, its properties
or qualities or states. One might exaggeratedly say: the
point of having the idea of individual instances of material or substantial features is that they may be represented
as individual instances of property-like features. The in-

[10] These remarks, of course, apply only to some of the things correctly called properties, states, qualities, etc.

dividuals are distinguished as individuals in order to be contrasted and compared.

Other notions call for other treatment. I consider two more.

(a) I mentioned, at 4 (iii), a rather special class of individual instances of properties or property-like things. We form the notion of such an instance when, for example, we speak not of a man or an action as an instance of wisdom or anger, but of the wisdom of Socrates as an individual (a case of wisdom) or of Jones' present mental state as an individual instance of anger. Here the notion of the individual instance can be seen as a new kind of logical compound, namely, a compound which includes as elements both the notion of the general thing (property) in question and that of the material or substantial individual which is an instance of it; it may sometimes include a further element of temporal placing (cf. "his *present* state of anger").

(b) Instances of events, processes and changes I have so far scarcely mentioned. Most of our most familiar words for happenings strike us essentially as names for the actions and undergoings of individual instances of material or substantial features. But there is a difference between these happening words and quality or state-words. A wise man is an instance of wisdom, but a dead or dying man is not an instance of death. Only a death is that. As regards such happening-words as these, then, we have to see the idea of an individual instance as reached by a kind of logical composition analogous to that considered in the paragraph immediately above: an individual instance of a material or substantial feature is an element in the compound. But these, though perhaps the most important, are not the only kinds of happening-words.

9. The general form of these explanations may be roughly indicated as follows. The notion of placing a feature is taken as basic, as consisting of the logically simplest elements with which we are to operate. It is pointed out that neither of these elements involves the notion of an individual instance, nor therefore the notions of certain

types of general things, such as properties and species; and it is shown that the idea of operating solely with these simplest elements can be made intelligible for certain cases. (Features in fact of course belong to the class of general things; but so long as we remain at the feature-placing level, they cannot be assigned to it; for there is nothing to contrast the general with.) From this basis we proceed by composition and analogy. The designations of individual instances of (some) material and substantial features are first introduced, as expressions, not themselves complete sentences, which include placing-indications; and, complementarily, certain types of general things (*e.g.*, properties and types of happening) are introduced as items the designations of which do not include placing-indications and which are ascribed to material or substantial individuals. The ascription of such a thing as a property to a substantial individual is represented simply as an operation analogous to the placing of a feature; so no circularity attends the word "ascription." Individuals of certain other types (*e.g.*, events happening to substances, states of substances and "particularised" qualities) are then introduced as the designata of expressions which include the designations of individuals of earlier types, and hence indirectly include the notion of placing.

There are many types of individual and of general things besides these here considered. Some may admit of analogous treatment; and it might be possible to introduce others, on the basis already provided, by other methods of construction and explanation. But every introduction of a particular, in terms of such a schema, will either directly contain the notion of placing or will preserve, by way of individuals already introduced, the original link with this notion. Of course the value of this suggestion, as it stands, is small. For the notion of an individual instance extends itself indefinitely, by way of far more complicated connexions than I have so far indicated; and the limits of plausibility for the kinds of construction-procedure I have used would, no doubt, soon be reached, if they are not already over-passed. Nevertheless, I think this sketch of a procedure has certain merits:

(1) Some of the difficulties which attend any attempt to elucidate the category-distinction between the particular and the general arise from the fact that these two classes include so many different category-distinctions within themselves. This fact creates a dilemma for the theorist of the distinction. On the one hand, he is tempted, in a way illustrated at the beginning of this paper, into drawing distinctions which indeed separate one or more sub-categories of one class from one or more sub-categories of the other, but which fail to yield the desired result if applied over the whole field. Or, on the other hand, in the effort to escape from this domination by irrelevant category differences, he is tempted by the prospect of a purely formal distinction, drawing for this purpose on the terms and concepts of grammar or of formal logic. But distinctions so drawn can only seem to succeed by forfeiting their formal character and silently incorporating the problematic category-distinction. The present procedure offers at least a hope of escape from this difficulty. For it fully allows for the differences between types of general thing and of individual; and instead of producing one single explanation, the same for every case, it offers a serial method of explaining later types of general or particular things on the basis of earlier ones, while preserving a continuous general differentiation between the two major categories in the course of the explanation. Too much must not be claimed for the suggested procedure, however; in particular, it must not be thought that it has been so described as to provide a *criterion* for the distinction we are concerned with.

(2) Another characteristic of the schema of explanation is that it accords a central place to the notion of an individual instance of certain kinds of general things, viz., of material and substantial features. This (see section 8) is not an essential characteristic; it could be modified. But there is reason to think that it corresponds to our actual way of thinking; that these individuals *are* the "basic particulars." Why this should be so, and whether it might not be otherwise, are questions which I shall not now consider.

(3) Finally, while not itself providing a criterion of general and particular, the schema points the way to a possible

general distinction which might be defensible even if the procedure which suggests it should prove unsatisfactory. This general distinction I shall outline in section 12. Before I do so, some further points remain to be considered.

10. Something further must first be said on the subject of criteria of identity for individual instances of a general thing. We saw (5 (2)) how in many cases the question of the criteria of distinctness and identity of an individual instance of a general thing was incompletely determined when the general thing was named. This was particularly evident in the case of some properties and was evident also in the case of materials. Where substance-names were concerned, however, this indeterminateness seemed not to exist; when the name was given, the criteria were fixed. And this was connected with the fact that in these cases there seemed to exist no true general-thing name, apart from expressions which ranked as species-names and obviously presupposed certain definite criteria of identity for individual members. As far as criteria of distinctness are concerned, this raises no particular difficulty. We saw, for example, how the idea of a simply placeable feature might include—might indeed *be*—the idea of a characteristic shape, and in this way provide a basis for criteria of distinctness for individual instances of the feature. But it is not so easy to account for the apparent determinateness of criteria of identity. The explanatory schema advanced required that we should theoretically be able to form concepts of some substance-features which were logically prior to, and independent of, the corresponding concepts of an individual instance of such features; and this requirement seems to clash with the apparent determinateness of the criteria of identity for such individuals. A parallel answer to that given in the case of criteria of distinctness is theoretically available, but is unattractively unplausible. If we reject this answer, and cannot find an alternative, then we must at least radically revise, though in a not unfamiliar direction, the basis of the explanatory schema. (The difficulty is essentially a more specific form of that encountered already in section 7).

I think, however, that an acceptable alternative can be found. For in all cases where a feature-concept can be assumed to be possible, the criteria of identity (and of distinctness) for an instance of the general thing in question —or the sets of such criteria, where there is more than one set—can be seen as determined by a *combination* of factors, viz., the nature of the feature itself, the ways in which the feature empirically manifests itself in the world, and—to adopt a possibly misleading mode of expression—the kind of incentives[11] that exist for having a notion of an individual instance of the feature in question. The relevance of this third factor even, perhaps, gives us the right to say that there is something arbitrary about the criteria we adopt, something which, given the other two factors, is—in at any rate a stretched sense—a matter of choice. In extreme cases this is obvious. Even those who had witnessed the whole of the affair under discussion might, for example, give varying answers to such a question as: Is this the same quarrel going on now as was going on when I left? The answer we choose may depend on just what distinctions we are interested in; and one can imagine many situations for this example, and many different things which might influence us. There may, on the other hand, be very many cases of features where the adoption of a certain particular set of criteria of identity (and distinctness) for their instances is so utterly natural that it would seem to be stretching the phrase "matter of choice" intolerably to apply it to them. But, even in these cases, the naturalness may still be seen as depending on the combination of factors I mentioned; and, if we bear this in mind, we can sometimes imagine the possibility of alternatives. (Here is a question which might with advantage be explored for many different types of case.)

It seems reasonable to view substantial features as cases of this kind. If this view is acceptable, we can find in it an

---

[11] What I mean by "incentives" here may be illustrated from the convenience of the institution of property. Suppose there is a general feature, ϕ, which human beings wish to make use of. Even if there is enough ϕ for all, friction may be avoided if criteria are used for distinguishing my ϕ from yours. ("Mine" is indeed one of the earliest individuating words used by children.)

explanation of that difference between substance-names and certain other true general-thing names to which I have several times referred. Given a true general-thing name, like "gold" or "wisdom," the question of the criteria of identity of its instances cannot be answered until the kind of instance is specified, by such a phrase as "a *piece* of gold" or "a wise *action*". But where one set of criteria of identity is peculiarly dominant, its adoption peculiarly compelling, we find no such non-committal general name in current, adult, unsophisticated use. All that we might wish to do with it, we can equally well do without it, by the use of the indefinite singular or plural forms of the ordinary substance-name (*e.g.,* "a horse" or "horses").

11. It is, perhaps, necessary to guard briefly against a misunderstanding. Of course, I am not denying that we can very well use individual-designations as such without being, or ever having been, in a position to make a relevant placing of some feature which, in terms of the explanatory schema I have defended, is immediately or ultimately relevant to the explanation of the type of instance concerned. To deny this would be absurd. It would be to deny, for example, that when we talk about remote historical characters, we are really talking about individuals. But the view I am defending does not require such a denial. For this view seeks merely to explain the notion of an individual instance of a general thing in terms, ultimately, of feature-placing. It does not at all imply that we cannot make use of this notion in situations other than those in terms of which it is explained. In fact, of course, the expansiveness of our talk about individuals is in marked contrast with the restrictedness of our contacts with them. Both the possibility of, and the incentives to, this expansiveness have an empirical ground; in the variousness of individuals, the non-repetitiveness of situations. But this fact may nevertheless mislead us, may make the theoretical problem of individuation look more difficult than it is by distracting our attention from an essential element in the notion of an individual instance. The problem would scarcely seem difficult for the case of an imagined universe

in which all that happened was the repetition of a single note, varying, perhaps, in volume. Individual instances could then be described only as, say, "the third before now" or "the next one to come". But in such a universe the incentives to forming the notion of an individual instance would be small. We might say that, in general, what is essential to the notion of an individual instance is not what is interesting about individuals.

12. To conclude. I remarked earlier that the explanatory schema I have sketched points the way to a possible general distinction between the two major categories we are concerned with. To recall, first, some vague, figurative and unsatisfactory terms I have already used: the schema suggests that the notion of a particular individual always includes, directly or indirectly, that of placing, whereas the notion of a general thing does not. Now placing is characteristically effected by the use of expressions the *reference* of which is in part determined by the context of their use and not by their *meaning*, if any, alone. And this suggests the possibility of formulating a general distinction in a more satisfactory way. We may say: *it is a necessary condition for a thing's being a general thing that it can be referred to by a singular substantival expression, a unique reference for which is determined solely by the meaning of the words making up that expression; and it is a necessary condition of a thing's being a particular thing that it cannot be referred to by a singular substantival expression, a unique reference for which is determined solely by the meaning of the words making up that expression.* This specification of mutually exclusive necessary conditions could be made to yield definitions by stipulating that the conditions were not only necessary, but also sufficient. But there is point in refraining from doing so. For as we consider substantival expressions increasingly remote from the simplest cases, there may be increasing reluctance to apply the distinction at all. Nor is this reluctance quite irrational; for the simplest cases are those which form the basis of the general distinction. (Hence, roughly, the association of particularity with concreteness). We may admit that the

traditional distinction was vague as well as unclear, and respect its well-founded vagueness in this way.

To elucidate this quasi-definition of particular and general, I add some miscellaneous comments of varying degrees of importance.

(1) It might be objected to the conditions given that expressions like "The third tallest man who ever lived or lives or will live" answer to the specifications for a general-thing designation. If they did, it would perhaps not be difficult to legislate them out, by suitable amendments of those specifications. But in fact they do not. For their meaning does not suffice to determine for them a unique object of reference. It is, if true, contingently true that there is a single thing answering to such a description. This case, however, does raise a problem about how the words "expression a unique reference for which is determined solely by the meaning" are to be construed. If we construe them as "expression the *existence* of just one object of reference for which is *guaranteed* by the meaning," we may find ourselves in (possibly circumventable) trouble over, *e.g.,* "phlogiston" and "the unicorn." Yet this is the construction at first suggested by the present case.[12] It will be better, therefore, to construe them as follows: "expression the (or a) meaning of which is such that it is both logically impossible for it to refer to more than one thing (in that meaning)[13] and logically impossible for the expression to fail to have reference because of the existence of competing candidates for the title". And the sense of "competing candidates" can be explained as follows: *x, y* and *z* are competing candidates (and the only competing candidates) for the title D if, if any two of them had not existed, D would apply to the third.

(2) It may seem, perhaps, a more troublesome fact that the names we commonly employ for certain *types,* like Beethoven's Fifth Symphony, do not answer to the specifi-

---

[12] This difficulty was pointed out to me by Mr. H. P. Grice.

[13] This qualification allows for the possible case where there is no convenient unambiguous designation of the general thing in question; but is not strictly necessary since an unambiguous designation could always be framed.

cations given for a general-thing designation, although we may be more than half inclined to count such types as general things; for these names include, as a part of themselves or of their explanation, proper names like "Beethoven." We have, however, an easy remedy here. We can regard the pattern of sounds in question as a general thing for which there might (perhaps does) exist a general description the meaning of which uniquely determines its reference; and then it will appear as the contingent truth it is that Beethoven stands to the general thing so designated in a certain special relation. This does not commit us to saying that it is a contingent truth that Beethoven's Fifth Symphony was composed by Beethoven; but the necessity here is simply a consequence of the fact that we ordinarily and naturally refer to the general thing in question by means of an expression which incorporates a reference to a particular individual who stands in a special relation to it. Analogous considerations apply to many other types. Of course, the alternative is always open to us of declining to apply the criterion in such cases.

(3) It is clear that numbers, if we apply our criterion to them, will emerge as general things. But this is a result which will disturb few, and will certainly disturb no one who continues to feel the charm of the class-of-classes analysis.

(4) If we choose to apply the test to facts, we get the not wholly unappealing result that, *e.g.*, the facts that $2 + 2 = 4$, that all crows are black and that crows exist (in one use of "exist") are general things, while the facts that Brutus killed Caesar and that all the people in this room are philosophers are particular things. For propositions, of course, the result is similar. The distinction will correspond roughly to the old distinction between those propositions (or facts) which are "truly universal" and those which are not. In the case of facts and propositions, however, we may well feel a *very* strong reluctance to classify in this way at all; and, if we do, there is no reason why we should struggle to overcome it.[14]

---

[14] What I have said here of facts and propositions must not lead

Some points of more general significance remain.

(5) As historical evidence for the general correctness of this doctrine, we may note that Russell who, for so large a part of his philosophical life, showed an anxiety to equate meaning and reference in the case of *names,* finally inclined to the conclusion that the only true names are those of universals.[15] We do not, of course, need to adopt his idiosyncratic use of the word "name," in acknowledging the correctness of his implied view of universals.

(6) It will be clear that the quasi-definition I am suggesting has points of contact with some of those more familiar ways of marking the distinction which turn out to be more or less unsatisfactory. For instance, it will not do to say that general things do not have spatio-temporal positions and limits, whereas particular things do. Some general things, those of appropriate categories, like gold, do have spatial distribution; and some may have temporal limits. It is rather that when we refer to general things, we abstract from their actual distribution and limits, if they have any, as we cannot do when we refer to particulars. Hence, with general things, meaning suffices to determine reference. And with this is connected the tendency, on the whole dominant, to ascribe superior reality to particular things. Meaning is not enough, in their case, to determine the reference of their designations; the extra, contextual element is essential. They are, in a quite precise sense, less abstract; and we are, on the whole, so constituted as to count the less abstract as the more real.

(7) Finally, we may, if we choose, revert to the original philosophical way of marking the distinction in terms of the concept of an instance, and give it a sense in terms of the final definition. Instantiability, in the philosophers' sense, ends precisely at the point at which contextual dependence of referring expressions begins, or where refer-

---

us to suppose that we should obtain a similar result for *sentences.* These, and expression-*types* generally, will emerge as general things (*e.g.,* in virtue of the conventions for the use of inverted commas, the expression "the word 'and' " may be said to determine, by meaning alone, a unique object of reference).

[15] See *Enquiry into Meaning and Truth* and *Human Knowledge: Its Scope and Limits.*

ring expressions, as being proper names of individuals, have meaning only in a sense in which it is altogether divorced from reference. So general things may have instances, while particular things may not.

QUALITIES

Nicholas Wolterstorff

1. Pointing is a kind of drawing attention to. Suppose, then, I point at the tail of a dog. How does this differ from pointing at a dog? That it does differ is clear. For if someone asks me, "Are you pointing at a dog?" I can say, "No, I am pointing at the tail of a dog." And if, pointing, I say, "This would not be so short, but it became gangrenous and we had to cut it off," I cannot be viewed as pointing at a dog. But then, how do these pointings differ? Someone might venture that, since pointing usually involves an aiming of the finger, perhaps one aims one's finger differently in the two cases. This will not do at all, however, for it takes only a moment's reflection to see that the same aiming may be used either to point at a dog or to point at the tail of a dog. So knowing what someone is pointing at involves knowing more than the rule: when someone points, follow the aim of his finger in order to know what he is pointing at.

But what else does it involve? Well, suppose you point at a dog, and as the direct result of your pointing my attention is drawn to the dog's tail and not to the dog. In this case something has gone wrong; I failed to know what you were pointing at. And, it would seem, the cause of the failure was that my attention was not drawn to what you intended it to be drawn to. You intended to draw my attention to the dog, and instead it was drawn to the dog's tail. So pointing seems to be an intentional action, an inten-

From *Philosophical Review*, Vol. LXIX (1960). Reprinted by permission of the author and the editor of *Philosophical Review*.

tional drawing attention to something; and knowing what
you are pointing at involves knowing your intention. Hy-
dras can and do aim their limbs in certain directions, and
their aiming of limbs may well draw our attention to things,
but they cannot point.

Yet this seems clearly wrong, for we do say that the
weather vane is pointing to the west, and that the spinner is
pointing to the 7. But how does the weather vane's pointing
to the west differ from its pointing to the large oak? And
how does the spinner's pointing to the 7 differ from its
pointing to the red background? It seems to me it does
not. We can say, indifferently, that the spinner points to the
7 or to the background, though gamblers seem by and
large to be interested in the numbers and not in the colored
backgrounds. But when a man points at a number he is
not pointing at a colored background. So what we should
have said above is that *one kind* of pointing involves a
reference to intention, and that this is the kind which is
relevant when we say that a man is pointing at the tail of
the dog and not at the dog.

But how can *you* know what I intend to call your attention to? The simplest method is, of course, for me to accompany my pointing with the words "this dog" or "the
tail of this dog." But such verbalization is not essential;
indeed, it is clearly subsidiary. For we call attention to
things not only *by means* of words, but *in order to teach*
words; the words "dog" and "tail," for example, are customarily taught children by pointing. So imagine that these
words are not available; how then can I let you know that
I am pointing at the dog and not at his tail? The most
straightforward way is probably to point again, this time
aiming my finger at the dog's head and not at his tail. But
just this is certainly not enough. For how are you to know
that I am pointing twice at the same dog and not once at
his tail and once at his head? The answer to this is simple
enough: I accompany my second pointing with the words
"This is the same as that," or words to this effect. Of
course, I do not first point at the dog's tail and then at his
head, and say "This is the same as that"; for a dog's tail is
not the same as a dog's head. Rather I aim my finger first

at the dog's tail, then at his head, and, by then affirming
the identity of the object pointed at, I show it to be something bigger than and different from either the dog's tail or
his head.[1] It is, in short, a dog. And to make my intention
more and more unambiguous, I point more and more times
at the dog, each time affirming the identity of the object
pointed at.

So for you to know what I am pointing at, you must
know the circumstances under which I would be willing to
say that I am pointing at the same thing as that at which I
pointed previously. I shall call this *knowing the identity
criteria* for the thing pointed at. The utility of using terms
like "dog" and "tail of a dog" to accompany our pointings
may then be viewed as due to the fact that singular terms
like these are, in a sense, ossified identity criteria. Telling
you that I am pointing at a dog is a way of informing you
of the circumstances under which I would be willing to say
that I am pointing at the same thing as that at which I
pointed previously.

Now I wish to suggest, as preliminary to what I shall
argue in this paper, that the difference between qualities
and particulars is to be explicated in essentially the same
way in which I have explicated the difference between a
dog and a tail of a dog. Suppose, for instance, that I point
and say, "This is green." What then am I pointing at; that
is, does "this" refer to a particular or to a quality? I suggest that it may be either, and that the way to find out is to
determine the identity criteria of the entity referred to. Suppose I say, "This is green and that is green, only this is a
tree and that is a carpet, so this is not identical with that";
here it is clear that I am pointing at two distinct particulars
and not at one identical quality. But if I say "This is green"
while pointing in the direction of a tree, and then, pointing
in the direction of my carpet, say "And this is green, and
this is identical with that," then I would be pointing at a
quality. And so would a father who in teaching his child
says, "Here's green, and here's green, and here's green
again." (And incidentally, if we *do* say these things, it dis-

[1] Cf. W. V. Quine, "Identity, Ostension, and Hypostasis," in *From
a Logical Point of View* (Cambridge, Mass., 1953), pp. 65–79.

poses of the traditional prejudice that qualities and universals cannot be pointed at.) But what I have shown does not quite prove what I have concluded; for how do I know that, when you are apparently pointing at a quality, you are not rather pointing at a larger and scattered particular? The difference lies, I suggest, in the *reason* that you give for asserting the identity. Though every case of pointing at a certain quality *might* also be viewed as pointing at a scattered particular, the difference lies in the *criteria* used for asserting identity.

Now what I wish to discuss in this paper are the identity criteria for qualities. And my fundamental thesis will be that there are two distinct interpretations of these criteria, each being perfectly intelligible and consistent in itself, but that our ordinary language about qualities gives us no ground for saying that either is the correct, or even preferable, interpretation. In the tradition one of these interpretations has been preferred by nominalists and the other by realists—meaning by "nominalist" one who holds that qualities are to be interpreted in terms of particulars and classes of particulars, or *quality-classes* as I shall call them; and meaning by "realist" one who holds that qualities are *universals*. Hence I can also put my thesis thus: the dispute between nominalists and realists is a pointless dispute, incapable of solution except by arbitrary fiat. But in spite of this it is not a meaningless dispute, for the position of each disputant can be given an intelligible and consistent, yet distinct, formulation.

2. For the issue which I wish to discuss a consideration of predicates is irrelevant. Indeed, if the case for the existence of qualities or universals rested on an analysis of such terms, I should regard it as a very shaky case. For to hold that, in "Socrates is wise," "Socrates" refers to a particular and "wise" to a universal, is certainly to confuse names with predicates.[2] And to hold that the repeated applicability of predicates like "red" can be explained only by saying that each of the entities to which it is applicable

[2] Cf. M. Lazerowitz, "The Existence of Universals," *Mind,* LV (1946), 1–24.

possesses redness, is to utter something uninformative at
best and tautologous at worst.[3] But then I do *not* think that
the case for the existence of qualities and universals rests
on an analysis of such terms.

Rather the issue first joins, I think, when we consider
expressions like "the color of his hat," "the wisdom of
Socrates," and "the pitch of St. Mary's bell." Each of these
is a description in which the word preceding the "of" ordinarily names or refers to a quality, and the word succeeding the "of" ordinarily names or refers to a particular.
I shall henceforth call these *quality-descriptions,* without
implying anything as to their analysis. Now the offhand
inclination of the nominalist is to take these expressions as
referring to aspects of particulars, to "abstract particulars"
if you will, whereas the offhand inclination of the realist is
to take them as referring to qualities. I shall eventually
show that neither the realist nor the nominalist need stake
his case on his ability or inability to follow out this original
inclination; but it will be important first to consider who is
right on this issue.

The realist would hold that, if the color of my coat is in
fact green, then "the color of my coat" refers to the same
entity as does "greenness." Is there anything in our use of
quality-descriptions to show that this view is mistaken? One
fact which seems to show its incorrectness is that we say
such things as, "What *was* the color of your coat?" (when
the coat is destroyed) and "What *was* the pitch of St.
Mary's bell?" (when the bell is broken). The use of the
past tense here would seem to indicate that we are referring
to something which was destroyed when the coat or the bell
was destroyed; and what could this be but a certain aspect
of the coat or the bell? For colors are not destroyed by
burning coats, nor pitches by breaking bells. But this argument is inconclusive. For one might also say, while
pointing in the direction of a color sample, "This *is* the
color that my coat *was*," and while playing a note on the
piano, "This *is* the pitch that St. Mary's bell *had*." And
this seems to indicate that tenses here are determined by the

[3] Cf. D. F. Pears, "Universals" in *Logic and Language,* II, ed. by
A. Flew (Oxford, 1955), pp. 51–64 [included in this anthology].

fact that the coat which formerly possessed the indicated color no longer exists, rather than by the fact that the color of the coat is an aspect of the coat which is destroyed along with the destruction of the coat. And second, we sometimes even tense the verb in statements which refer unambiguously to qualities. We would not say, of course, that "green *was* a color"; but we might say, "What *was* the pitch you just gave?" and "The cloying sweetness you smelled *was* insect repellant."

But there is another class of cases which conclusively shows that the realist cannot be wholly right. For suppose a painter friend of mine comes to me one day and says, "I want you to see the wonderful green on my latest canvas." So I pull a color chart from my pocket and ask him to point to the color he has in mind. He *may* then point to one and say, "This is it." But he may also summarily wave the chart aside and say, "No, that won't do, you'll have to see my canvas in order to see what I'm referring to." In this latter case "the green on my canvas" is used to refer not to a certain color but to a particular qualitative aspect of my friend's canvas; for the friend might admit that the color of my sample was just like that on his canvas, but still deny that they are identical, since after all his canvas is not in the same place as my sample. Thus it is clear that quality-descriptions are not always used to refer to qualities.

So is the nominalist then right, or are there also cases in which quality-descriptions *must* be viewed as referring to qualities and not to aspects? The sort of case one naturally thinks of here is "The color of this hat is the same as the color of this blotter"; and "The pitch of this chorale is the same as the pitch of St. Mary's bell." In these cases it seems that we are asserting the existence of a quality shared by two different particulars. But these examples raise a new issue which is central to the whole debate over universals. For "the same" is an ambiguous expression, meaning either "identical" or "similar." Thus if two children have the same father, they have the identical father and not two similar ones; and if two college boys wear the same tuxedo so that they cannot go to dances together, they wear the identical tuxedo.[4] But on the other hand, though every soldier wears the same uniform, all soldiers can appear on parade clothed. The difference between these two senses of "the same" is also clear from our use of qualifying adverbs. One speaks of two things as being almost the same, or nearly the same, or not at all the same. And here we clearly mean "similar," for identity does not hold in degrees.

Now with this distinction in hand the nominalist can easily show that statements like "The color of his coat is the same as the color of this blotter" do not refute his position. For "is the same as" can here be construed to mean "is exactly or closely similar to"; hence the statement does not say that this quality is identical with that but that this aspect is similar to that. The realist obviously has a way of blocking this answer, however; for one might *also* say, "The color of this blotter is *identical* with the color of his coat." And though this is a rather stiff way of speaking, and though the nominalist may wish to hold that, in some sense, no information is conveyed by this sentence which is not conveyed by "The color of this blotter is exactly similar to the color of his coat," yet the two sentences are not synonymous.

There is also another class of statements which gives the nominalist trouble. Examples are, "This is the color of his coat," said while pointing in the direction of a blotter; "This is the pitch of *Nun ist das Heil*," said while playing a note on the piano; and "You too can have the wisdom of Socrates," proclaimed by an encyclopedia advertisement. Here we seem unambiguously to be asserting that one quality is shared by two distinct particulars; and the nominalist cannot now escape by distinguishing senses of "the same." Of course, on the analogy of "He has his father's hands," he might attempt to reformulate these and say that "This is the color of his coat" *really* means "This is exactly similar to the color of his coat." But I see no defense that could be given for such a reformulation.

In summary, then, quality-descriptions may be used to

---

[4] This example is from D. C. Williams, "On the Elements of Being," *The Review of Metaphysics*, VII (1953), 6.

refer either to aspects or to qualities; and in ordinary speech we usually do not make it clear how we are using them. The reference can, however, be made clear by asking for the circumstances under which the speaker would be willing to say that he was referring or pointing again to the same entity, with "the same" understood now as meaning "identical" and not "similar." Having done this, it turns out that neither the realist's inclination to regard these expressions as referring to qualities, nor the nominalist's inclination to regard them as referring to aspects, can be wholly correct. This, however, need give the realist no anxiety, since all he has to show is that, whatever else there be, there are universals. The nominalist, however, contends that there are *only* particulars and classes of particulars; so unless he can find a nominalistic interpretation of these references to qualities, an analysis of quality-descriptions will show already that nominalism is not a possible view.

But before considering the two alternative analyses of qualities, I think it worth remarking that a good many confusions in the history of philosophy have been caused by a failure to see that quality-descriptions may refer either to particulars or universals. For example, I think this failure is responsible for the extreme ambivalence in all classical modern philosophy on whether we *really* perceive only particulars or only universals. And it is clearly responsible for the views of G. F. Stout[5] and D. C. Williams,[6] and for G. E. Moore's total failure to understand Stout.[7] Stout says, for instance, that "of two billiard balls, each has its own particular roundness separate and distinct from that of the other, just as the billiard balls themselves are distinct and separate. As Jones is separate and distinct from Robinson, so the particular happiness of Jones is separate and distinct from that of Robinson." Of course, Stout is wrong in holding that "the roundness of this ball" can

[5] "The Nature of Universals and Propositions," Hertz Lecture, *Proceedings of the British Academy*, X (1921–23), 157–72.

[6] *Op. cit.*

[7] "Are the Characteristics of Particular Things Universal or Particular," symposium in *Proceedings of the Aristotelian Society*, Supp. vol. III (1923), 95–113.

refer *only* to a particular; but Moore is equally wrong in holding that it can refer *only* to a universal.

3. In addition to quality-descriptions referring to qualities, the terms we must now consider are ones like "greenness," "circularity," and "stickiness." I shall give these the traditional name of *abstract singular terms*. And what I wish to see is whether, at this stage, either realism or nominalism can be shown to be mistaken.

In analyzing abstract singular terms, the nominalist seems in general to have two courses open: he can say that all statements using such terms can be translated into synonymous statements whose singular terms refer only to concrete particulars; or, failing this, he can say that abstract singular terms refer not to universals but to certain classes of particulars, quality-classes.

According to the first suggestion, a statement like "Greenness is a color" is to be paraphrased as "For every entity, if it is green, then it is colored." Now is this paraphrase really synonymous with the original? It is not, I think. For the analysis assumes that "is a color" is synonymous with "is colored." But this is surely false, if for no other reason than that the ranges of meaningful application of these two terms are different. Green is a color but is not colored; and a blotter is colored but is not a color. There are also other flaws in the paraphrase; for certainly the connection between being green and being a color is in some sense a necessary connection, as well as being in some sense a relation of subsumption. But neither of these features is brought out by the proposed analysis. Thus the only plausible interpretation of nominalism seems to be that which regards hues, pitches, virtues, and so forth as classes of particulars.

Now the strongest objections to the class theory are based on the belief that the classes which nominalism proposes to identify with qualities cannot actually be defined. I think, however, that they can be; and so I shall take it as my main task to show that this objection is invalid.

Classes, according to the usual conception, are identical if and only if they have the same members. Hence the first thing we must do is decide when quality-classes do and when they do not have the same members; and for this we shall first have to know what criterion is used in determining the membership of such classes. Well, what criterion *do* we use? Suppose I come into a paint store with a sample of the color of my living room wall, and ask for some paint of the same (identical) color. How do I go about deciding whether the color of the paint handed to me is or is not identical with that on my wall? The answer seems clear: I bring a sample of the paint and a sample of the wall-color close together, and if they resemble each other I say they have the same (identical) color. Similarly, to find out whether St. Mary's bell has a pitch identical with that of St. Thomas' bell, I listen carefully to a peal from each and compare. In short, similarity is the criterion for membership in quality-classes; and our chief task is therefore this: given particulars and the relation of similarity holding among pairs of particulars, how can qualities be defined as certain kinds of classes?

But before describing what sort of class a quality actually is, we must deal with several complexities in the ordinary concept of similarity. In ordinary language things are not merely similar but are more or less similar, and, to make the situation worse, they are more or less similar in two quite different ways. For by saying that x is more similar to y than to z I may mean either that x is similar to y in more respects than it is to z, or that, whatever the respect in which they are similar, x is more closely similar to y in that respect than to z. For example, a nickel resembles a dime in both color and shape, while resembling a penny only in shape; and the color of a dime is more like that of a quarter than like that of a nickel. Now both the fact that things are similar in different respects, and the fact that things are similar in varying intensities, give trouble to the nominalist.

Consider first the difficulties arising from the varying intensities of similarity. The problem is just this: what degree of similarity is necessary for identity of qualities? That it is less than exact similarity seems to be implied by the fact that green things are by no means all exactly similar in color. Sage, lakes, blotters, grass, lamps, flower pots, bruises—all are green, but all are not exactly similar in color. On the other hand, if I ask for paint of the same color as that already on my wall, I would not be satisfied with just a green, or even an olive-green. And if a psychologist tells me to adjust a second light until it has the same brightness as the first, he clearly means *exactly* the same. Indeed, it always makes sense to say of qualities that they are almost the same but still not identical. So it is not clear what degree of similarity is necessary for identity of qualities. I am inclined to think, however, that it is exact similarity, and that the difference in shades of green can be given another explanation. But whether I am right or wrong on this point will make no difference. For I shall show later that precisely the same difficulties arise for the realist; and hence the difficulties arising from varying intensities of similarity cannot be used as a ground for preferring realism. I shall, in what I say further, mean by "similarity" always exact similarity; but this will in no way prejudge my central thesis.

The difficulties arising from the fact that things are similar in various respects are more troublesome. A quality-class would seem, quite clearly, to be a class of all and only those things which are similar in a certain respect. Or, to put it more precisely, a quality-class is a class which fulfills these two requirements: (i) of the members of the class, each is similar to every other; (ii) no thing outside the class is similar to every member of the class. But it would seem that, unless we introduce more conditions, this definition by no means yields only those classes which can plausibly be identified with qualities.

One of the difficulties which arises is called by Goodman the difficulty of imperfect community.[8] Suppose the universe included a class of things of the following description: one is green and hard, another is hard and square, and a third is square and green—symbolized as *gh, hs,* and *sg.* Now this class fulfills our requirements for a quality-class, since each member is similar to every other, and we are to sup-

[8] N. Goodman, *The Structure of Appearance* (Cambridge, Mass., 1951), pp. 124 ff.

pose that there is nothing outside the class which is similar
to every member of the class. Yet there is no quality common to the three members, and consequently the class cannot be identified with a quality. A second difficulty Goodman calls the companionship difficulty. Suppose that
everything green is sticky, and everything sticky is green.
In this case the class of green entities would be identical
with the class of sticky entities. But then the qualities greenness and stickiness cannot be identified with this class; for
greenness is not identical with stickiness.

Now it would seem that, to prevent these difficulties, we
must somehow get at the inside of particulars and distinguish the different respects in which they resemble each
other. Thus we might try taking similarity as a triadic
relation, saying always that x is similar to y in respect to z,
and then defining a quality-class as a class of particulars
similar to each other in only one respect, and that the same
respect throughout. But this would be to give up the game
immediately. For suppose we do regard similarity as a
triadic relation, always saying, for instance, that the blotter
is similar to the coat in respect to its color. What then does
"color" refer to? A class of particulars? If so, we have
precisely the same difficulty that we were trying to escape.
So apparently it refers to a universal, with the usage of
"the same respect" determined according to the criteria
recommended by the realist. But this was just what the
nominalist wanted to avoid. Thus, since respects in this
context are universals, the nominalist can make no use of
them.

But there *is* a way of avoiding the difficulties of companionship and imperfect community, and this is just to
keep in mind that the class of particulars includes not only
concrete physical objects and events but also what I have
called the aspects of these. The color of the Taj Mahal (on
one interpretation of this phrase), as well as the Taj Mahal,
is a particular; and a color patch as well as a tree is an
instance of greenness. Furthermore, there are aspects of
aspects, for instance, the hue of the color of the Taj Mahal.
We are, then, to remember that the relation of similarity
holds among aspects as well as among concrete particulars.

Now no doubt an apprehension will arise over using qualitative aspects of things in order to define qualities. I do not think, however, that such a procedure is circular. For I may very well recognize the shape of Eisenhower's face without having an independent recognition of that shape itself—without knowing what kind of shape it is, without being able to say in what way this shape differs from other shapes, without being able to sketch it, and so forth.

The inclusion of aspects in our quality-classes immediately eliminates the companionship difficulty. This arose, it will be remembered, whenever we had a class of things of this schematic form: gs, gs, gs. But now we also have the two particulars g and s. According to our rules then, gs, gs, gs, g will form one quality-class; and gs, gs, gs, s will form another. The two classes have different memberships, and are therefore not identical, because s and g do not resemble each other. The difficulty of imperfect community is likewise solved. Our example illustrating this was, schematically, gh, hs, sg. We are now directed to allow also the three aspects $g, h,$ and s. This gives us the three classes $gh, sg, g; gh, hs, h;$ and $hs, sg, s;$ and the difficulty is resolved.

In summary then, a quality, according to a nominalist, is a class of all and only those particulars which bear a certain resemblance to each other. Hence qualities A and B are identical if and only if they have the same instances (members); and we determine whether they do or do not have the same instances by observing the relations of similarity and dissimilarity among the instances.

4. Now the realist regards all this as wrong, and insists that qualities are not classes of particulars but are instead universals. Such classes may, in some way, be associated with qualities, but they are not to be identified with them.

What then does the realist propose as the identity criterion for qualities? Consider again the example of my coming into the paint store and asking for some paint of the same color as that on my wall. How *do* I decide whether the color of the paint is identical with the color of my wall?

Obviously what I do is compare the colors. And if I find that they resemble each other exactly, I say that this color is identical with that. Similarly, to find out whether the pitch of St. Mary's bell is identical with the pitch of St. Paul's, I listen carefully to see whether I can discern any difference in pitch. And to find out whether the flavor of this cheap Scotch is really identical with the flavor of this expensive Scotch, I taste each carefully and compare the flavors. Thus the relation of similarity constitutes the identity criterion for universals.

The contrast between nominalism and realism is often drawn by saying that the former makes use of the relation of similarity holding between particulars, whereas the latter makes use of the notion of universals shared by particulars.[9] But it can now be seen that this contrast between resemblance-theorists and universals-theorists is improperly drawn. Both theories make use of the relation of resemblance, the only difference being that they use it in different ways. The nominalist uses resemblance as the criterion for membership in quality-classes, whereas the realist uses resemblance as the criterion for identity of universals. And it is because both theories use the relation of resemblance that any vagueness which appears in the one theory as a result of vagueness in the notion of resemblance will make a parallel appearance in the other.

Now the usual objections to the realistic interpretation of qualities are made, not on the ground that it involves a program impossible of being carried out, but rather on the ground that it involves a commitment to queer and weird entities, things best shunned. This seems to me a baseless prejudice, and I shall concentrate my attention on showing why the objection is not applicable.

There is, for instance, a long and by no means dead tradition to the effect that only particulars can be perceived, that universals may be objects of reason but not of perception. But this is certainly mistaken. For we can play a pitch on a violin, relish a sweetness on our tongues, feel annoyed by an acridity, and watch admiringly an old man's tenacity. The usual doctrine is that we can play sounds but not

[9] Cf. H. H. Price, *Thinking and Experience* (London, 1953), ch. I.

pitches, taste stuffs but not sweetness, be annoyed by smells but not by acridity, and observe an old man but not tenacity. But once we see that the reference of terms and of pointings is fixed by the identity criteria of the entity referred to, and once we see that there are identity criteria for universals as well as for particulars, there seems no reason at all to defend the dictum that only instances of universals can be perceived but not universals themselves. Psychologists, in speaking of brightness and loudness scales, have had the correct intuition.

Immediately associated with the view just considered is the belief, present in Western philosophy almost since its inception, that universals are indifferent to the buzz of space and time, composing a still and immutable world of their own. But this is equally mistaken; for if we can point to and perceive universals, then universals *must* be locatable. The basis of the traditional doctrine is, I suppose, a vague intuition of the fact that places and times play no role in determining the identity of universals. But of course it does not follow from this that universals are outside of space and time. Greenness *does* appear at certain times and places; the father in teaching his child says, "Here's green, and here's green, and here's green again." And though we would probably never ask, "Where is green?" men have asked "Where is virtue to be found?" and conductors have no doubt inquired "Where is that *F*-sharp coming from?"

So the usual dread of admitting the existence of universals is quite unfounded. They are quite as humdrum and quite as circumambient as particulars, differing just in the fact that the criteria for saying "This is the same universal as that" are different from those for saying "This is the same physical object as that."

5. We have seen, then, that both realism and nominalism can be given consistent and plausible interpretations. According to the nominalist, similarity is a relation holding among particulars, and we use it as the criterion for membership in quality-classes. According to the realist, similarity is a relation holding among qualities as well, and

we use it as the criterion for the identity of universals. Which theory, then, is correct? What statements do we make about qualities which show that the one interpretation is right and the other wrong?

(i) We might consider, first, the statements which gave the nominalist trouble previously—for example, "The color of this table is identical with the color of that table." Now the realist interprets this to mean that there is here one entity, a universal, shared by two particulars; and he holds that we establish the identity of this entity by comparing the color of this table with the color of that. And this is certainly a plausible interpretation. Unfortunately, however, the nominalist's interpretation is equally plausible. For he interprets the sentence to mean that there is here one entity, a class, of which these two particulars are members; and he holds that we establish the fact that they are members of the same class by comparing the two tables. So this sort of statement—statements asserting an identity of qualities—can be handled easily by both theories.

(ii) But there is another kind of statement which, prima facie at least, offers more promise. According to the nominalist, similarity holds only among particulars. Apparently all we need do then to refute nominalism is find statements asserting similarity among qualities. And such are immediately at hand; for instance, "Yellow is more like orange than like purple." But will this really turn the trick; is it impossible to give a nominalistic interpretation of this sentence? One paraphrase which the nominalist might suggest is this: take anything yellow, anything orange, and anything purple; then the yellow thing is more like the orange thing than like the purple thing. But there is no assurance that this statement is even true; for though, *in respect to color*, yellow things are more like orange things than like purple things, this may well not be true in general. The way around this objection, however, is just to make the paraphrase refer to aspects and not to concrete things, thus: for anything yellow and anything orange and anything purple, the color of the yellow thing is more similar to the color of the orange thing than to the color of the purple thing. And though this is by no means as straightforward an interpretation of our original statement as that which the realist can give, there seems to be no consideration which would show it to be actually mistaken.

So apparently there is no way of showing either theory to be incorrect. But it might still be felt that there are grounds for *preferring* one theory to the other. So let us consider various suggestions to this effect.

(i) Is there any way, for instance, of showing the one theory to be simpler than the other? I think not. For the realist assumes the existence of universals, whereas the nominalist assumes the existence of quality-classes. Consequently on this level they are precisely comparable. Furthermore, the definition of quality-classes does not seem to me significantly more or less complicated than that of universals. So the test of simplicity yields inconclusive results.

(ii) It has sometimes been argued that the criteria for the identity of classes are clearer than those for universals; and if this were true, it would certainly be a reason for preferring nominalism. But whether or not universals are *in general* vaguer entities than classes (and I suppose they are), they are certainly no more vague than quality-classes. For as we have already seen, both the realist and the nominalist make use of the notion of similarity; consequently any vagueness in the one theory will find its parallel in the other. So the criterion of clarity also gives no ground for preference.

6. My conclusion to this whole discussion, therefore, is that there is no ground whatever for preferring either realism or nominalism. Now in such a situation, the intuitive response of the contemporary philosopher is to suspect that the dispute is meaningless. But it is clear that this is not the case. For if the color of two tables is indistinguishable, the realist says the color of the one is *therefore* identical with the color of the other, whereas the nominalist says they are exactly similar and *therefore* belong to the same quality-class. But "is similar to" is not synonymous with "is identical with"; and regarding entities as identical if and only if they have the same members is not the same as regarding entities as identical if and only if they are exactly

similar. Hence we find that we have here the anomalous situation of a meaningful but pointless dispute.

To see more clearly the source of this anomaly, consider a hypothetical case in which the distinction between similarity and identity cannot, as a matter of fact, be drawn. Suppose, for instance, that identity of persons were determined by identity of memories; and imagine that I find a person with memories the same as mine in all respects. Are his memories then identical with mine, or are they merely exactly similar? I think it is easily seen that such a question cannot be answered. The distinction between the two senses of "the same" is here inoperative; for there is no defense which one could give of the contention that they are similar but not identical, but there is also no defense which one could give of the contention that they are not only similar but identical. The distinction between qualitative and numerical sameness is vacuous.

But the situation with respect to qualities is not quite like this, for the nominalist *can* point to something which will distinguish similarity from identity, namely, difference of place; and his contention is that, though x and y may be qualitatively similar, this does not prove that they are identical. So the issue here is not whether similarity *can* be distinguished from identity, but whether difference of place shall establish nonidentity. Now in the case of physical objects it does; all 1959 Fords may be qualitatively alike, but they are not identical. And if this were the only permissible criterion for the identity of entities, realism would be an impossible view; indeed, one could not even distinguish between the meaning and the criteria of identity. But suppose on the other hand that all our singular terms referred to universals. In this case nominalism would be an impossible view, and again there would be no way of distinguishing between the meaning and the criteria of identity. As a matter of fact, however, identity *can* be determined according to different criteria; and so the issue is joined. But it cannot be settled. For though the nominalist may insist on diversity of places as implying nonidentity, he can give no justification for his insistence; and though the realist may insist that nonidentity of places does not always determine nonidentity of entities, he too can give no reason for his insistence.

The debate is thus clear enough, and it may seem surprising that our language fails to reflect it. Still, it may *not* be so surprising. For in the first place, both theories regard similarity as, directly or indirectly, determining the identity of qualities. And secondly, in our existing language the reference of quality-descriptions is ambiguous, and it is this ambiguity which is fundamental to the whole issue. For though there are indeed some cases in which quality-descriptions cannot be interpreted as referring to particulars, we saw that the nominalist can, by using the notion of classes, still interpret them as referring *in a roundabout way* to particulars. Hence we end where we began.

Whatever be the reasons, though, it is clear that, given our actual language, there is no point in distinguishing senses of "this is the same as that" when dealing with qualities. For whatever our theory, we would all agree that a person knew what colors were if, upon being asked to bring something of the same color as the green thing I have, he always brought something green.[10]

[10] I have profited a great deal in writing this paper from conversations with Mr. Noel Fleming.

UNIVERSALS AND FAMILY RESEMBLANCES

Renford Bambrough

I believe that Wittgenstein solved what is known as "the
problem of universals", and I would say of his solution, as
Hume said of Berkeley's treatment of the same topic, that
it is "one of the greatest and most valuable discoveries that
has been made of late years in the republic of letters."

I do not expect these claims to be accepted by many
philosophers.

Since I claim that Wittgenstein solved the problem I
naturally do not claim to be making an original contribution
to the study of it. Since I recognise that few philosophers
will accept my claim that Wittgenstein solved it, I naturally
regard it as worth while to continue to discuss the problem. My purpose is to try to make clear what Wittgenstein's
solution is and to try to make clear that it is a solution.

Philosophers ought to be wary of claiming that philosophical problems have been finally solved. Aristotle and
Descartes and Spinoza and Berkeley and Hume and the
author of the *Tractatus Logico-Philosophicus* lie at the
bottom of the sea not far from this rock, with the skeletons
of many lesser men to keep them company. But nobody
suggests that their journeys were vain, or that nothing can
be saved from the wrecks.

In seeking for Wittgenstein's solution we must look
mainly to his remarks about "family resemblances" and

From *Proceedings of the Aristotelian Society*, Vol. LX (1960–61).
Copyright 1961, the Aristotelian Society. Reprinted by permission
of the author and the editor of the Aristotelian Society.

to his use of the example of games. In the *Blue Book* he speaks of "our craving for generality" and tries to trace this craving to its sources:

> This craving for generality is the resultant of a number of tendencies connected with particular philosophical confusions. There is—
>
> (*a*) The tendency to look for something in common to all the entities which we commonly subsume under a general term.—We are inclined to think that there must be something in common to all games, say, and that this common property is the justification for applying the general term "game" to the various games; whereas games form a *family* the members of which have family likenesses. Some of them have the same nose, others the same eyebrows and others again the same way of walking; and these likenesses overlap. The idea of a general concept being a common property of its particular instances connects up with other primitive, too simple, ideas of the structure of language. It is comparable to the idea that *properties* are *ingredients* of the things which have the properties; *e.g.*, that beauty is an ingredient of all beautiful things as alcohol is of beer and wine, and that we therefore could have pure beauty, unadulterated by anything that is beautiful.
>
> (*b*) There is a tendency rooted in our usual forms of expression, to think that the man who has learnt to understand a general term, say, the term "leaf", has thereby come to possess a kind of general picture of a leaf, as opposed to pictures of particular leaves. He was shown different leaves when he learnt the meaning of the word "leaf"; and showing him the particular leaves was only a means to the end of producing "in him" an idea which we imagine to be some kind of general image. We say that he sees what is in common to all these leaves; and this is true

if we mean that he can on being asked tell us certain features or properties which they have in common. But we are inclined to think that the general idea of a leaf is something like a visual image, but one which only contains what is common to all leaves. (Galtonian composite photograph.) This again is connected with the idea that the meaning of a word is an image, or a thing correlated to the word. (This roughly means, we are looking at words as though they all were proper names, and we then confuse the bearer of a name with the meaning of the name.) (Pp. 17–18).

In the *Philosophical Investigations* Wittgenstein again speaks of family resemblances, and gives a more elaborate account of the similarities and differences between various games:

66. Consider for example the proceedings that we call "games". I mean board-games, card-games, ball-games, Olympic games, and so on. What is common to them all?—Don't say: "there *must* be something common, or they would not be called 'games' "—but *look and see* whether there is anything common to all.—For if you look at them you will not see something that is common to *all,* but similarities, relationships, and a whole series of them at that. To repeat: don't think, but look!—Look for example at board-games, with their multifarious relationships. Now pass to card-games; here you find many correspondences with the first group, but many common features drop out, and others appear. When we pass next to ball-games, much that is common is retained, but much is lost.—Are they all "amusing"? Compare chess with noughts and crosses. Or is there always winning and losing, or competition between players? Think of patience. In ball-games there is winning and losing;

but when a child throws his ball at the wall and catches it again, this feature has disappeared. Look at the parts played by skill and luck; and at the difference between skill in chess and skill in tennis. Think now of games like ring-a-ring-a-roses; here is the element of amusement, but how many other characteristic features have disappeared! And we can go through the many, many other groups of games in the same way; can see how similarities crop up and disappear.

And the result of this examination is: we see a complicated network of similarities overlapping and criss-crossing: sometimes overall similarities, sometimes similarities of detail.

67. I can think of no better expression to characterise these similarities than "family resemblances"; for the various resemblances between the members of a family: build, features, colour of eyes, gait, temperament, etc. etc. overlap and criss-cross in the same way.—And I shall say: "games" form a family.

Wittgenstein expounds his analogy informally, and with great economy. Its power can be displayed in an equally simple but more formal way by considering a situation that is familiar to botanical taxonomists.[1] We may classify a set of objects by reference to the presence or absence of features *ABCDE*. It may well happen that five objects *edcba* are such that each of them has four of these properties and lacks the fifth, and that the missing feature is different in each of the five cases. A simple diagram will illustrate this situation:

e	d	c	b	a
ABCD	*ABCE*	*ABDE*	*ACDE*	*BCDE*

[1] I have profited from several discussions with Dr. S. M. Walters on taxonomy and the problem of universals. On the more general topics treated in this paper I have had several helpful discussions with Mr. R. A. Becher. Miss G. E. M. Anscombe kindly lent me the proofs of her essay on Aristotle, which is to appear in *Three Philosophers* by Miss Anscombe and Mr. P. T. Geach.

Here we can already see how natural and how proper it might be to apply the same word to a number of objects between which there is no common feature. And if we confine our attention to any arbitrarily selected four of these objects, say *edca,* then although they all *happen* to have *B* in common, it is clear that it is not in virtue of the presence of *B* that they are all rightly called by the same name. Even if the actual instances were indefinitely numerous, and they all happened to have one or more of the features in common, it would not be in virtue of the presence of the common feature or features that they would all be rightly called by the same name, since the name also applies to *possible* instances that lack the feature or features.

The richness of the possibilities of the family resemblances model becomes more striking still if we set it out more fully and formally in terms of a particular family than Wittgenstein himself ever did. Let us suppose that "the Churchill face" is strikingly and obviously present in each of ten members of the Churchill family, and that when a family group photograph is set before us it is unmistakable that these ten people all belong to the same family. It may be that there are ten features in terms of which we can describe "the family face" (high forehead, bushy eyebrows, blue eyes, Roman nose, high cheekbones, cleft chin, dark hair, dimpled cheeks, pointed ears and ruddy complexion). It is obvious that the unmistakable presence of the family face in every single one of the ten members of the family is compatible with the absence from each of the ten members of the family of one of the ten constituent features of the family face. It is also obvious that it does not matter if it happens that the feature which is absent from the face of each individual member of the family is present in every one of the others. The members of the family will then have no *feature* in common, and yet they will all unmistakably have *the Churchill face* in common.

This example is very artificial, and it may seem at first sight that its artificiality plays into my hands. But on the contrary, the more natural the example is made the more it suits my purpose. If we remember that a family face does

not divide neatly into ten separate features, we widen
rather than reduce the scope for large numbers of instances
of the family face to lack a single common feature. And
if we remember that what goes for faces goes for features
too; that all cleft chins have nothing in common except
that they are cleft chins, that the possible gradations from
Roman nose to snub nose or from high to low cheekbones
are continuous and infinite, we see that there could in
principle be an infinite number of unmistakable Churchill
faces which had no feature in common. In fact it now
becomes clear that there is a good sense in which *no two*
members of the Churchill family need have *any* feature
in common in order for *all* the members of the Churchill
family to have the Churchill face.

The passages that I have quoted contain the essence of
Wittgenstein's solution of the problem of universals, but
they are far from exhausting his account of the topic. Not
only are there other places where he speaks of games and
of family resemblances: what is more important is that
most of his philosophical remarks in *The Blue and Brown
Books* and in the *Philosophical Investigations* are concerned with such questions as "What is the meaning of a
word?" "What is language?" "What is thinking?" "What
is understanding?" And these questions are various forms
of the question to which theories of universals, including
Wittgenstein's theory of universals, are meant to be answers. There is a clear parallel between what Wittgenstein
says about games and what he says about reading, expecting, languages, numbers, propositions; in all these cases we
have the idea that there is a common element or ingredient, and Wittgenstein shows us that there is no such ingredient or element. The instances that fall under each of
these concepts *form a family*.

It is already clear that the point Wittgenstein made with
the example of games has a much wider range of application than that example itself. But exactly how wide is its
application meant to be? Wittgenstein's own method of
exposition makes it difficult to answer this question. In his
striving to find a cure for "our craving for generality," in
his polemic against "the contemptuous attitude towards

the particular case," he was understandably wary of expressing his own conclusions in general terms. Readers and expositors of Wittgenstein are consequently impelled to make use of glosses and paraphrases and interpretations if they wish to relate his work to philosophical writings and doctrines that are expressed in another idiom; that is to say, to most other philosophical writings and doctrines.

I believe that this is why Wittgenstein's solution of the problem of universals has not been widely understood, and why, in consequence, it has not been widely seen to be a solution.[2] In avoiding the generalities that are characteristic of most philosophical discussion he also avoided reference to the standard "problems of philosophy" and to the "philosophical theories" which have repeatedly been offered as answers to them. He talks about games and families and colours, about reading, expecting and understanding, but not about "the problem of universals." He practised an activity which is "one of the heirs of the subject which used to be called 'philosophy'", but he did not relate the results of his activity to the results of the enquiries to which it was an heir. He did not, for example, plot the relation between his remarks on games and family resemblances and the doctrines of those philosophers who had been called Nominalists and Realists.

When I claim that Wittgenstein solved the problem of universals I am claiming that his remarks can be paraphrased into a doctrine which can be set out in general terms and can be related to the traditional theories, and which can then be shown to deserve to supersede the traditional theories. My purpose in this paper is to expound such a doctrine and to defend it.

But first I must return to my question about the range of application of the point that is made by the example of games, since it is at this crucial first stage that most readers of Wittgenstein go wrong. When we read what

---

[2] Of recent writings on this topic I believe that only Professor Wisdom's *Metaphysics and Verification* (reprinted in *Philosophy and Psycho-analysis*) and Mr. D. F. Pears' *Universals* (reprinted in Flew, *Logic and Language,* Second Series) show a complete understanding of the nature and importance of Wittgenstein's contribution.

he says about games and family resemblances, we are
naturally inclined to ask ourselves, "With what kinds of
concepts is Wittgenstein *contrasting* the concepts of game,
language, proposition, understanding?" I shall consider
three possible answers to this question.

The first answer is suggested by Professor Ayer's remarks about games and family resemblances on pp. 10–12
of *The Problem of Knowledge*. Ayer contrasts the word
"game" with the word "red", on the ground that the former
does not, while the latter does, mark "a simple and straightforward resemblance" between the things to which the word
is applied. He claims that, "The point which Wittgenstein's
argument brings out is that the resemblance between the
things to which the same word applies may be of different
degrees. It is looser and less straightforward in some cases
than in others." Now this contrast between simple and
complicated concepts is important, and the games example is a convenient means of drawing attention to it,
but I am sure that this is not the point that Wittgenstein
was making with his example. In the *Brown Book* (p.
131) he asks, "Could you tell me what is in common
between a light red and a dark red?" and in the *Philosophical Investigations* (Section 73) he asks, "Which shade is
the 'sample in my mind' of the colour green—the sample
of what is common to all shades of green?" Wittgenstein
could as easily have used the example of red things as the
example of games to illustrate "the tendency to look for
something in common to all the entities which we commonly subsume under a general term." Just as cricket and
chess and patience and ring-a-ring-a-roses have nothing in
common *except that they are games,* so poppies and blood
and pillar-boxes and hunting-coats have nothing in common *except that they are red.*

A second possible answer is implied by a sentence in
Mr. P. F. Strawson's *Individuals:* "It is often admitted, in
the analytical treatment of some fairly specific concept, that
the wish to understand is less likely to be served by the
search for a single strict statement of the necessary and
sufficient conditions of its application than by seeing its
applications—in Wittgenstein's simile—as forming a fam-

ily, the members of which may, perhaps, be grouped around a central paradigm case and linked with the latter by various direct or indirect links of logical connexion and analogy." (p. 11). The contrast is not now between simple and complex concepts, but between two kinds of complex concepts: those which are definable by the statement of necessary and sufficient conditions and those which are not. But once again the contrast, although it is important, and is one which the family resemblances simile and the example of games are well able to draw, is not the point that Wittgenstein is concerned with. In the sense in which, according to Wittgenstein, games have nothing in common except that they are games, and red things have nothing in common except that they are red, *brothers have nothing in common except that they are brothers.* It is true that brothers have in common that they are male siblings, but their having in common that they are male siblings is their having in common that they are *brothers,* and not their having in common something in addition to their being brothers. Even a concept which can be explained in terms of necessary and sufficient conditions cannot be *ultimately* explained in such terms. To satisfy the craving for an ultimate explanation of "brother" in such terms it would be necessary to define "male" and "sibling", and the words in which "male" and "sibling" were defined, and so on *ad infinitum* and *ad impossibile.*

What then *is* the contrast that Wittgenstein meant to draw? I suggest that he did not mean to draw a *contrast* at all. Professor Wisdom has remarked that the peculiar difficulty of giving a philosophical account of universals lies in this: that philosophers are usually engaged in implicitly or explicitly comparing and contrasting one type of proposition with another type of proposition (propositions about minds with propositions about bodies, propositions of logic with propositions about matters of fact, propositions about the present and the past with propositions about the future, etc.) whereas propositions involving universals cannot be compared or contrasted with propositions that do not involve universals, since *all* propositions involve universals.[8] If we look at Wittgenstein's doctrine in the light of this remark we can understand it aright and can also see why it has been misunderstood in just those ways that I have mentioned. It is because of the very power of the ways of thought against which Wittgenstein was protesting that philosophers are led to offer accounts of his doctrine which restrict the range of its application. They recognise the importance of Wittgenstein's demonstration that *at least some* general terms can justifiably be applied to their instances although those instances have nothing in common. But they are so deeply attached to the idea that there must be something in common to the instances that fall under a general term that they treat Wittgenstein's examples as special cases, as rogues and vagabonds in the realm of concepts, to be contrasted with the general run of law-abiding concepts which *do* mark the presence of common elements in their instances.

Here we come across an ambiguity which is another obstacle to our getting a clear view of the problem of universals and of Wittgenstein's solution of it. Ayer remarks, in the passage to which I have already referred, that, "It is correct, though not at all enlightening, to say that what games have in common is their being games." It is certainly correct, but I strongly deny that it is unenlightening. It is of course trivially and platitudinously true, but trivialities and platitudes deserve emphatic affirmation when, as often in philosophy, they are explicitly or implicitly denied, or forgotten, or overlooked. Now the platitude that all games have in common that they *are* games is denied by the nominalist, who says that all games have nothing in common except that they are *called* games. And it is not only the nominalist, but also his opponent, who misunderstands the central importance of the platitude that all games have in common that they are games. When he is provoked by the nominalist's claim that all games have nothing in common except that they are called games, and rightly wishes to insist that games have something more in common than

---

[8] Professor Wisdom has pointed out to me that further discussion would be necessary to show that claims of the form "This is Jack" are not exceptions to this rule.

simply that they are called games, he feels that he must look for something that games have in common apart from *being* games. This feeling is entirely misplaced. The very terms of the nominalist's challenge require only that the realist should point out something that games have in common apart from *being called* games, and this onus is fully discharged by saying that they *are* games.

Although the feeling is misplaced, it is a very natural feeling, as we can see by considering the kinds of case in which we most typically and ordinarily ask what is in common to a set of objects. If I ask you what these three books have in common, or what those four chairs have in common, you will look to see if the books are all on the same subject or by the same author or published by the same firm; to see if the chairs are all Chippendale or all three-legged or all marked "Not to be removed from this room." It will never occur to you to say that the books have in common that they are books or the chairs that they are chairs. And if you find after close inspection that the chairs or the books do not have in common any of the features I have mentioned, and if you cannot see any other specific feature that they have in common, you will say that as far as you can see they have nothing in common. You will perhaps add that you suppose from the form of my question that I must know of something that they have in common. I may then tell you that all the books once belonged to John Locke or that all the chairs came from Ten Rillington Place. But it would be a poor sort of joke for me to say that the chairs were all chairs or that the books were all books.

If I ask you what *all* chairs have in common, or what *all* books have in common, you may again try to find a feature like those you would look for in the case of *these three* books or *those four* chairs; and you may again think that it is a poor sort of joke for me to say that what all books have in common is that they are books and that what all chairs have in common is that they are chairs. And yet this time it is not a joke but an important philosophical truth.

Because the normal case where we ask "What have all *these* chairs, books or games in common?" is one in which we are not concerned with their all being chairs, books or games, we are liable to overlook the extreme peculiarity of the *philosophical* question that is asked with the words "What do *all* chairs, *all* books, *all* games have in common?" For of course games *do* have something in common. They *must* have something in common, and yet when we look for what they have in common we cannot find it. When we try to say what they have in common we always fail. And this is not because what we are looking for lies deeply hidden, but because it is too obvious to be seen; not because what we are trying to say is too subtle and complicated to be said, but because it is too easy and too simple to be worth saying: and so we say something more dramatic, but something false, instead. The simple truth is that what games have in common is that they are games. The nominalist is obscurely aware of this, and by rejecting the realist's talk of transcendent, immanent or subsistent forms or universals he shows his awareness. But by his own insistence that games have nothing in common except that they are called games he shows the obscurity of his awareness. The realist too is obscurely aware of it. By his talk of transcendent, immanent or subsistent forms or universals he shows the obscurity of his awareness. But by his hostility to the nominalist's insistence that games have nothing in common except that they are called games he shows his awareness.

All this can be more fully explained by the application of what I will call "Ramsey's Maxim." F. P. Ramsey, after mapping the course of an inconclusive dispute between Russell and W. E. Johnson, writes as follows:

> Evidently, however, none of these arguments are really decisive, and the position is extremely unsatisfactory to any one with real curiosity about such a fundamental question. In such cases it is a heuristic maxim that the truth lies not in one of the two disputed views but in some third possibility which has not yet been thought of, which we can only discover by rejecting something as-

sumed as obvious by both the disputants. (*The Foundations of Mathematics,* pp. 115–16.)

It is assumed as obvious by both the nominalist and the realist that there can be no objective justification for the application of a general term to its instances unless its instances have something in common over and above their having in common that they *are* its instances. The nominalist rightly holds that there is no such additional common element, and he therefore wrongly concludes that there is no objective justification for the application of any general term. The realist rightly holds that there is an objective justification for the application of general terms, and he therefore wrongly concludes that there *must* be some additional common element.

Wittgenstein denied the assumption that is common to nominalism and realism, and that is why I say that he solved the problem of universals. For if we deny the mistaken premiss that is common to the realist's argument and the nominalist's argument then we can deny the realist's mistaken conclusion and deny the nominalist's mistaken conclusion; and that is another way of saying that we can affirm the true premiss of the nominalist's argument and can also affirm the true premiss of the realist's argument.

The nominalist says that games have nothing in common except that they are called games.

The realist says that games must have something in common, and he means by this that they must have something in common other than that they are games.

Wittgenstein says that games have nothing in common except that they are games.

Wittgenstein thus denies at one and the same time the nominalist's claim that games have nothing in common except that they are called games and the realist's claim that games have something in common other than that they are games. He asserts at one and the same time the realist's claim that there is an objective justification for the application of the word "game" to games and the nominalist's claim that there is no element that is common to all games. And he is able to do all this because he denies the joint claim of the nominalist and the realist that there cannot be an objective justification for the application of the word "game" to games unless there is an element that is common to all games (*universalia in rebus*) or a common relation that all games bear to something that is not a game (*universalia ante res*).

Wittgenstein is easily confused with the nominalist because he denies what the realist asserts: that games have something in common other than that they are games.

When we see that Wittgenstein is not a nominalist we may easily confuse him with the realist because he denies what the nominalist asserts: that games have nothing in common except that they are called games.

But we can now see that Wittgenstein is neither a realist nor a nominalist: he asserts the simple truth that they both deny and he also asserts the two simple truths of which each of them asserts one and denies the other.

I will now try to put some flesh on to these bare bones.

The value and the limitations of the nominalist's claim that things which are called by the same name have nothing in common except that they are called by the same name can be seen if we look at a case where a set of objects literally and undeniably have nothing in common except that they are called by the same name. If I choose to give the name "alpha" to each of a number of miscellaneous objects (the star Sirius, my fountain-pen, the Parthenon, the colour red, the number five, and the letter Z) then I may well succeed in choosing the objects so *arbitrarily* that I shall succeed in preventing them from having any feature in common, other than that I call them by the name "alpha." But this imaginary case, to which the nominalist likens the use of all general words, has only to be described to be sharply contrasted with the typical case in which I apply a general word, say "chair", to a number of the instances to which it applies. In the first place, the *arbitrariness* of my selection of alphas is not paralleled in the case in which I apply the word "chair" successively to the chair in which I am now sitting, the Speaker's Chair in the House of Commons, the chair used at Bisley for carrying the winner of the Queen's Prize, and one of the deck chairs on the beach at Brighton. In giving a list of chairs I cannot just mention anything that happens to come into my head, while this is exactly what I do in giving my list of alphas. The second point is that the class of alphas is a *closed* class. Once I have given my list I have referred to every single alpha in the universe, actual and possible. Although I *might* have included or excluded any actual or possible object whatsoever when I was drawing up my list, once I have in fact made my arbitrary choice, no further application can be given to the word "alpha" according to the use that I have prescribed. For if I later add an object that I excluded from my list, or remove an object that I included in it, then I am making a different use of the word "alpha." With the word "chair" the position is quite different. There are an infinite number of actual and possible chairs. I cannot aspire to complete the enumeration of all chairs, as I can arbitrarily and at any point complete the enumeration of all alphas, and the word "chair," unlike the word "alpha", can be applied to an infinite number of instances without suffering any change of use.

These two points lead to a third and decisive point. I cannot teach the use of the word "alpha" except by specifically attaching it to each of the objects in my arbitrarily chosen list. No observer can conclude anything from watching me attach the label to this, that, or the other object, or to any number of objects however large, about the nature of the object or objects, if any, to which I shall later attach it. The use of the word "alpha" cannot be learned or taught as the use of a general word can be learned or taught. In teaching the use of a general word we may and must refer to characteristics of the objects to which it applies, and of the objects to which it does not apply, and indicate which of these characteristics count for the application of the word and which count against it. A pupil does not have to consult us on every separate occasion on which he encounters a new object, and if he did consult us every time we should have to say that he was not *learning* the use of the word. The reference that we make to a finite number of objects to which the word applies, and to a finite number of objects to which the word does not apply, is capable of equipping the pupil with a capacity for correctly applying or withholding the word to or from an infinite number of objects to which we have made no reference.

All this remains true in the case where it is not I alone, but a large number of people, or all of us, who use the word "alpha" in the way that I suggest. Even if everybody always called a particular set of objects by the same name, that would be insufficient to ensure that the name was a general name, and the claim of the name to be a general name would be defeated by just that necessity for reference to the arbitrary choices of the users of the name that the nominalist mistakenly claims to find in the case of a genuinely general name. For the nominalist is right in thinking that if we always had to make such a reference then there would be no general names as they are understood by the realist.

The nominalist is also right in the stress that he puts on the role of human interests and human purposes in determining our choice of principles of classification. How this insistence on the role of human purposes may be reconciled with the realist's proper insistence on the objectivity of the similarities and dissimilarities on which any genuine classification is based can be seen by considering an imaginary tribe of South Sea Islanders.

Let us suppose that trees are of great importance in the life and work of the South Sea Islanders, and that they have a rich and highly developed language in which they speak of the trees with which their island is thickly clad. But they do not have names for the species and genera of trees as they are recognised by our botanists. As we walk round the island with some of its inhabitants we can easily pick out orange-trees, date-palms and cedars. Our hosts are puzzled that we should call by the same name trees which appear to them to have nothing in common. They in turn surprise us by giving the same name to each of the trees in what is from our point of view a very mixed plantation. They point out to us what they called a mixed plantation, and we see that it is in our terms a clump of trees of the same species. Each party comes to recognise that its own classifications are as puzzling to the other as the other's are puzzling to itself.

This looks like the sort of situation that gives aid and comfort to the nominalist in his battle against the realist. But if we look at it more closely we see that it cannot help him. We know already that our own classification is based on similarities and differences between the trees, similarities and differences which we can point out to the islanders in an attempt to teach them our language. Of course we may fail, but if we do it will not be because we *must* fail.

Now *either* (*a*) The islanders have means of teaching us their classifications, by pointing out similarities and differences which we had not noticed, or in which we had not been interested, in which case *both* classifications are genuine, and no rivalry between them, of a kind that can help the nominalist, could ever arise;

or (*b*) Their classification is arbitrary in the sense in which my use of the word "alpha" was arbitrary, in which case it is not a genuine classification.

It may be that the islanders classify trees as "boat-building trees," "house-building trees," etc., and that they are more concerned with the height, thickness and maturity of the trees than they are with the distinctions of species that interest us.

In a particular case of *prima facie* conflict of classifications, we may not in fact be able to discover whether what appears to be a rival classification really *is* a classification. But we can be sure that *if* it is a classification *then* it is backed by objective similarities and differences, and that if it is *not* backed by objective similarities and differences then it is merely an arbitrary system of names. In no case will it appear that we must choose between rival systems of genuine classification of a set of objects in such a sense that one of them is to be recognised as *the* classification for all purposes.

There is no limit to the number of possible classifications of objects. (The nominalist is right about this.)[4]

There is no classification of any set of objects which is not objectively based on genuine similarities and differences. (The realist is right about this.)

The nominalist is so impressed by the infinite diversity of possible classifications that he is blinded to their objectivity.

The realist is so impressed by the objectivity of all genuine classifications that he underestimates their diversity.

Of course we may if we like say that there is one complete system of classification which marks all the similarities and all the differences. (This is the realist's summing up of what we can learn by giving critical attention to the realist and the nominalist in turn.)

Or we may say that there are only similarities and differences, from which we may choose according to our purposes and interests. (This is the nominalist's summing up.)

In talking of genuine or objective similarities and differences we must not forget that we are concerned with similarities and differences between *possible* cases as well as between actual cases, and indeed that we are concerned with the actual cases only because they are themselves a selection of the possible cases.

Because the nominalist and the realist are both right and both wrong, each is driven into the other's arms when he tries to be both consistent and faithful to our language, knowledge and experience. The nominalist talks of resemblances until he is pressed into a corner where he must acknowledge that resemblance is unintelligible except as resemblance *in a respect,* and to specify the respect in which objects resemble one another is to indicate a *quality* or *property*. The realist talks of properties and qualities until, when properties and qualities have been explained in

---

[4] Here one may think of Wittgenstein's remark that "Every application of every word is arbitrary," which emphasises that we can always find *some* distinction between any pair of objects, however closely similar they may be. What might be called the principle of the diversity of discernibles guarantees that we can never be *forced* to apply the same word to two different things.

terms of other properties and other qualities, he can at last do nothing but point to the *resemblances* between the objects that are said to be characterised by such and such a property or quality.

The question "Are resemblances ultimate or are properties ultimate?" is a perverse question if it is meant as one to which there must be a simple, *single* answer. They are both ultimate, or neither is ultimate. The craving for a single answer is the logically unsatisfiable craving for something that will be the ultimate terminus of explanation and will yet itself be explained.

UNIVERSALS AND METAPHYSICAL REALISM

Alan Donagan

'The point of philosophy is to start with something so simple as not to seem worth stating, and
end with something so paradoxical that no one
will believe it.'

—Bertrand Russell, *The Monist* (1918)

The late Friedrich Waismann once remarked that, while
you may confute and kill a scientific theory, a philosophy
dies only of old age. The realist theory of universals,
which G. E. Moore and Bertrand Russell revived in the
brilliant fifteen years which preceded the first World War,[1]
seems to have aged more rapidly than its authors, and to
have died, or fallen into oblivion, during the 'forties. In
the United States, the very different conception of realism
propounded by Professors Quine and Goodman,[2] and nick-

Reprinted from *The Monist*, Vol. 47, No. 2, 1963, with permission
of the author and the Open Court Publishing Company, La Salle,
Illinois.

[1] G. E. Moore, 'The Nature of Judgment', *Mind*, 8 (1899), esp.
pp. 178–83; 'Identity', *Proc. Aris. Soc.*, 1 (1900–1), esp. pp. 105–15;
Some Main Problems of Philosophy (London, 1953), hereafter cited
as *Main Problems*, pp. 301–5, 312–77 (composed in 1910–11); and
Bertrand Russell, 'On the Relations of Universals to Particulars'
(composed 1911) in *Logic and Knowledge*, ed. Robert C. Marsh
(London, 1956); *The Problems of Philosophy* (London, 1912), chs.
8–10.
[2] W. V. Quine, *From a Logical Point of View* (Cambridge, Mass.,
1951), chs. 1, 6; Nelson Goodman, *The Structure of Appearance*
(Cambridge, Mass., 1951), ch. 2.

named by Quine 'Plato's Beard', has displaced it, leaving Professor Bergmann almost alone to defend it.[3] In Britain, a polished essay by Mr. Pears seems to have been received as its epitaph.[4] In this paper I propose to re-examine Moore's and Russell's principal argument for the reality of universals, in order to determine whether any spark of life remains in it. Is it truly dead, or only neglected?

I

Russell's *The Problems of Philosophy* is a convenient and familiar point of departure. Lucidly and simply, it states the position which Moore and Russell held, and their reason for holding it. In its eighth chapter, Russell wrote this:

> Suppose, for instance. that I am in my room. I exist, and my room exists; but does "in" exist? Yet obviously the word "in" has a meaning; it denotes a relation which holds between me and my room. This relation is something, although we cannot say that it exists *in the same* sense in which I and my room exist. The relation "in" is something which we can think about and understand, for, if we could not understand it, we could not understand the sentence "I am in my room."[5]

The conclusion that we are to investigate is that the relation denoted by 'in' *is*, or is real. Russell's distinction between being and existence, according to which the relation denoted by 'in' has being (*is* or is real) but does not exist, is notoriously difficult, and we shall defer investigating it.

[3] Gustav Bergmann, *Meaning and Existence* (Madison, Wis. 1959), esp. chs. 4, 13. My debts in this essay to Professor Bergmann, particularly in what I say about the attempts of Professors Quine and Goodman to shave Plato's Beard, are heavy and obvious, though no doubt he would reject most of my conclusions.

[4] D. F. Pears, 'Universals', in *Logic and Language*, 2nd series, ed. Antony Flew [reprinted in this anthology].

[5] Bertrand Russell, *The Problems of Philosophy* (London, reset edn. 1946), hereafter cited as *Problems*, p. 90.

Yet, even apart from that distinction, Russell's argument and conclusion are puzzling.

His reasoning seems to have been as follows:

(i) Some propositions of the form *x is in y*, where '*x*' and '*y*' deputize for names or descriptions of things which in a familiar sense exist, can be thought about and understood.

(ii) They could not be thought about or understood unless the word 'in' were thought about and understood; *i.e.* 'in' is not redundant.

(iii) Some propositions of the form *x is in y* are true. (I take this to be presupposed in Russell's opening injunction: 'Suppose, for instance, that . . .')

(iv) The non-redundant elements of true propositions denote things that are real or have being, if not things that exist.

(v) Therefore, 'in' denotes something which *is* or is real, if not something which exists; and since if 'in' denotes anything at all it is a relation, it follows that at least one relation *is* or is real.

If relations are real, then universals are real: for 'a *universal* will be anything which may be shared by many particulars';[6] and at least two pairs of particulars, namely, Russell and his room, and Moore and his room, may share the relation denoted by 'in'.

Neither Russell nor Moore believed that all universals were relational. In *The Problems of Philosophy* Russell had much to say of justice and whiteness, which he considered to be non-relational qualities; and in *Some Main Problems of Philosophy* Moore strove to demonstrate that in some sense *whiteness* is a universal which is neither a relation (like *in*) nor a relational property (like *in Russell's room*). Yet both Moore and Russell considered the being of relations and relational properties to be far more evident than that of non-relational (qualitative) univer-

---

[6] Russell, *Problems*, p. 93 [p. 16 in this anthology]; cf. Moore, *Main Problems*, p. 304.

sals; and both ascribed the nominalist tendencies in the work of Berkeley and Hume to their error that, unlike qualities, relations are evidently the work of the mind.[7] Russell plainly agreed with Moore that 'it is . . . comparatively easy to distinguish universals of both these two sorts [relations and relational properties]; and if it were quite clear that they were the only sorts, the whole question about universals would be . . . comparatively simple.'[8]

Simple or not, it is the question we are to investigate. In doing so, I shall assume that Moore and Russell were in the right when they declared that whether or not there are qualities which are irreducible to relational properties has not the slightest bearing on whether or not there are universals.

Despite Russell's lucidity, there are obscurities in his argument as I have analysed it. It only applies to expressions which are non-redundant, i.e. which must be thought about and understood if the meaning of the sentences in which they occur is to be thought about and understood. Clearly if, instead of saying 'I am in my room', Russell had added some expletive to 'room', e.g. 'God-forsaken', that expletive would have been redundant, and his argument would not have shown that there is something which 'God-forsaken' denotes. To show that, it would be necessary to produce a true statement in which 'God-forsaken' was not redundant. But is it enough to exclude redundant expressions? Some expressions, for example in mathematics, are rigorously defined. If the definition of 'triangle' were substituted for the word 'triangle' in a theorem of Euclid, the meaning of that theorem would remain unchanged. Are we to interpret Russell's argument as showing that there is a universal denoted by 'triangle', *as well as* those denoted by 'figure', 'plane', and 'three-sided'? In his later work Russell construed his argument as applying only to expressions which are primitive. Hence, the fact that you can think about and understand the expression 'in' shows

[7] Russell, *Problems*, pp. 95–97 [pp. 19–20 in this anthology]; Moore, *Main Problems*, pp. 305, 313–14.
[8] Moore, *Main Problems*, p. 353; cf. Russell, *Problems*, pp. 93–94, 97 [pp. 19–20 in this anthology].

either that 'in' denotes something that is real or has being, *or* that 'in' is definable, and that the primitive expressions by which it is ultimately to be defined denote things that are real or have being.

Even after this clarification, the scope of Russell's argument remains obscure. Suppose that the sentences with which Russell began were, 'You are *or* I am in my room' or 'I am an *individual* (or a *particular*).' The expressions 'or' and 'individual' (or 'particular') are, in Russell's own view, not redundant. Once more, we must turn to his later works for guidance. If all logical connectives such as 'and', 'or', 'if . . . then' be interpreted truth-functionally, then they must be excluded from the fundamental propositions from which compound propositions are constructed. It must be conceded that a difficulty remains about the sentence, ' "I am in my room" is true'. To understand that sentence, it is necessary to understand the expression 'true'; and if truth-functional analyses of the logical connectives are to be admitted, such sentences must be indispensable. However, Russell might plead that the expressions 'true' and 'false', which signify, not properties of objects, but properties of propositions about objects, call for separate elucidation and interpretation. I shall therefore assume that his argument applies neither to them nor to their derivatives.

Expressions like 'individual', 'particular', and 'universal' must also be treated separately. Frege's technique of quantification enables us to dispense with them as they most commonly occur, in such sentences as, 'Some individual both took office under Caesar and conspired to murder him', by replacing them with variables, *e.g.* 'For some value of "x", "x took office under Caesar and x conspired to murder Caesar" is true'. As for sentences which cannot be so analysed, *e.g.* 'Brutus is an individual', what they say is *shown* by allowing certain expressions, *e.g.* 'Brutus', to be substituted for certain variables, *e.g.* 'x' in the above function; and it may be expressed in the formal mode by such sentences as, 'The expression "Brutus" is a legitimate value of the variable "x".' Russell was to accept Wittgenstein's view that expressions like 'individual', 'particular', and 'universal', which can be eliminated by such devices, signify formal concepts,[9] and should not be mistaken for predicates signifying properties which a thing may or may not possess.

These elucidations affect only the scope of Russell's argument. What of its nature? If our analyses and clarifications are sound, it asserts that the reality of the universal *in* follows from three facts: (i) that the sentence 'I am in my room' can be thought about and understood; (ii) that on the occasion when Russell wrote it he expressed a true proposition; and (iii) that the word 'in' is neither definable nor is a logical connective nor signifies a formal concept, and is predicable of many particulars (henceforth I shall call such expressions 'primitive predicates'). That universals are real is held to follow from these facts by the general principle that the non-redundant elements of true propositions denote things that are real or have being. That principle, however, applies to proper names as well as to predicates. Russell's argument requires only a narrower principle, which I shall henceforth call 'the Realist Principle'; namely, that primitive predicates occurring nonredundantly in true propositions denote real things, or, as Moore liked to say, 'real constituents of the world'. It is plain why Russell and Moore adhered to this Principle. They could not conceive how otherwise propositions containing primitive predicates could state facts about the world.[10] And certainly this consideration is weighty. If the ultimate non-logical and non-formal constituents of true propositions refer to nothing in the world, in what can the truth of such propositions consist?

Before proceeding to consider objections to Russell's argument one more elucidation is called for. While it presupposes that there are true propositions containing expressions which stand for universals, it does not stipulate that those propositions must assert that those universals are exemplified. In his example Russell laid it down that the

[9] Ludwig Wittgenstein, *Tractatus Logico-Philosophicus* (London, 1922), 4.126-4.12721.

[10] Russell, *Problems,* pp. 90 (cf. 80–88), 97–98 [pp. 20–23 in this anthology]; Moore, *Main Problems,* pp. 303–5.

relation *in* was supposed to be exemplified; for he invited
his readers to suppose that he was in his room. But, since
'in' is as much a constituent of the negative proposition
'Russell is not in his room', as of the affirmative one, 'Russell is in his room', the reality of the relation *in* would seem
to follow from the truth of either one'.

This point can be generalized. Let '. . . R . . .' signify
a relational expression, and let the only true propositions
containing '. . . R . . .' be of the form $\sim R(x,y)$ or
$\sim xRy$. In other words, let it be true that $\sim (\exists x,y)\ xRy$.
Six years after writing *The Problems of Philosophy*, Russell stoutly maintained the possibility that there are negative facts, *i.e.* that there are facts expressible by propositions of the form $\sim fx$, which cannot be reduced to facts
expressible by propositions that contain no sign of negation.[11] If that is possible, then it is logically possible that
the only true propositions containing a given predicative
expression, whether 'F . . .', or 'R (. . , . . .)' or some
other, should be negative. By Russell's argument, such an
unexemplified universal would have exactly the same claim
to being or reality as exemplified ones.

Both in *The Problems of Philosophy* and 'The Philosophy of Logical Atomism' Russell avoided admitting
this by adopting the Principle of Acquaintance, namely,
that 'in every proposition that we can apprehend (*i.e.* not
only in those whose truth and falsity we can judge of,
but in all that we can think about) all the constituents are
really entities with which we have immediate acquaintance.'[12] It follows that we cannot think about any proposition the primitive expressions in which do not stand for
constituents with which we are acquainted; and we can
be acquainted with the constituent denoted by a qualitative or relational expression only if that constituent is exemplified and we are acquainted with an instance of it. In
short, we cannot even think about a negative proposition
containing '. . . R . . .', *e.g.* '$\sim aRb$', unless we have been

---

[11] Russell, *Logic and Knowledge*, pp. 211–16, esp. 213.
[12] Russell, *Problems*, p. 58; *Logic and Knowledge*, pp. 195, 270–80.
For a criticism of the Principle of Acquaintance see Max Black, *Language and Philosophy* (Ithaca, 1949), pp. 130–34.

acquainted with a state of affairs asserted by a proposition of the form xRy.

The metaphysical problem, however, cannot be dodged in that way. First, the question whether universals have being or are real is quite distinct from the question whether every universal of which we have formed a concept has been exemplified somewhere at some time. Nothing in Russell's argument confines its application either to affirmative propositions, or to propositions we know. Of course, he might stipulate that its application be so confined; but such an arbitrary stipulation would carry no weight. Secondly, the problem of unexemplified universals can be propounded even if the Principle of Acquaintance be accepted. That Principle entails neither that any given language, English say, contains expressions for all exemplified qualities and relations, nor that speakers of English are acquainted with instances of all of them. It cannot, therefore, forbid a speaker of English to opine that two objects, say the Atlantic and the Pacific Oceans, stand to each other in some relation with which he is not acquainted. It follows that somebody who said, in English, '($\exists R$) the Atlantic Ocean R the Pacific Ocean, and I am not acquainted with R', would make an intelligible statement.

Now if you can opine that a pair of objects exemplifies a relation with which you are not acquainted, you can equally opine that it does not. For example, you might intelligibly say:

(1) '($\exists R$) $\sim R$ (the Atlantic Ocean, the Pacific Ocean) and I am not acquainted with R.'

Having said that, you might generalize it:

(2) '($\exists R$)(x,y) $\sim R(x,y)$ and I am not acquainted with R.'

If (2) were true, an infinite number of statements of the form $\sim R(x,y)$ would be true, in each of which the value of the variable 'R' would signify an unexemplified relation. The Principle of Acquaintance entails, not that there is no such relation, but that no language contains a predicate denoting it. Although the limits of my language may be the limits of *my* world, they are not the limits of *the* world.

Since I am not tempted to endorse any metaphysical Principle of Plenitude, I am inclined to think the proposition (2) above to be true. If it is, then there are innumerable negative facts which, if the Principle of Acquaintance be true, nobody will ever know. From that, if Russell's argument is sound, it follows that an unexemplified relation is a real constituent of the world. Those who countenance Russell's argument can escape this conclusion in only two ways: either by demonstrating that unexemplified universals are impossible (not merely that they cannot be directly known), or by demonstrating that all negative propositions are reducible to affirmative ones. Up to now, neither has been established.

II

Realist arguments like Russell's have been rejected for such a variety of reasons that I cannot here examine them all. I shall, therefore, select those few which I judge to be cardinal. I cannot even justify my selection; for to do so it would be necessary to show that none of the objections I do not discuss has more weight than any of those I do.

The four objections I have selected are: (1) the classical difficulty, with which Plato struggled, that the very concept of a unitary universal which is 'shared by' many particulars appears to be self-contradictory; (2) that although some realist principle may be true, the Realist Principle which Russell held is false; (3) that Russell's argument depends on features peculiar to certain languages, which may be dispensed with in an artificial language, and perhaps is in some natural languages; (4) that Russell's theory of universals, as a whole, is 'circular and uninformative'.

(1) *The Classical Difficulty.* In the *Philebus* Plato drew attention to two difficulties in his theory of forms: if there are many things in which a form may be said to be present,

it would seem that 'we must think [either] that [the form] is dispersed and has become many', or 'that it is still entire and divided from itself, which latter would seem to be the greatest impossibility of all' (*ibid.* 15B). Russell's theory appears to avoid the first difficulty, but not the second. He recognized a universal denoted by 'in' which may be 'shared' or, to avoid metaphor, 'exemplified' by, many pairs of particulars, *e.g.* by Russell and his room, and by Moore and his. However, he did not think that only part of the universal *in* would be exemplified by each pair that exemplifies it: that is, he did not think that it could be 'dispersed' among those pairs, and so 'become many'. A universal remains unitary. Yet, since Russell did think that Moore could be in his room at the very same time as he was in his, the two rooms being necessarily at different places, he could not avoid concluding that at the same time the unitary universal *in* could be exemplified at different places. Does that not imply what to Plato seemed 'the greatest impossibility of all', that it is 'still entire and yet divided from itself'?

A tempting way out of this difficulty is to deny that because the *in* is exemplified by Russell and his room, both of which are at a certain place, the universal itself must be at that place, or at any place. Yet that way lies destruction. It is true that the question form, 'Where is the universal?' has no established use in non-philosophical discourse. But then, neither has the term 'universal' such a use; and questions of the impugned form naturally arise out of Russell's theory. Moreover, there is a strong reason for thinking that if universals are exemplified in space and time, they are where they are exemplified. You can verify the statement that Russell is in his room by looking into it and seeing him there. When you look, you see not only him and his room, but also that he is in it. It is true that it is not good English to say that you see *in*, along with Russell and his room: but, as the late J. L. Austin once pointed out, neither is it good English to say that you do not see it, or that you intuit it. 'I [see] what in English is described by means of two demonstrative pronouns and an adverbial phrase. To look for an isolable entity corresponding to the

latter is a bad habit . . .'[13] Now, if what you see includes
what is described by the adverbial phrase '. . . is in . . .',
i.e. a universal, must it not be where you are looking? And
if one man was to see that Russell was in his room at the
same time as another was to see Moore in his, would it
not follow that the universal *in* was in the two different
places where the two were looking? If so, would not the
universal *in* be both 'entire and yet divided from itself'?

At this juncture, realists should act on the principle
that the best defense is attack, and protest that *by its very
nature* a universal is the sort of thing that can be exemplified by particulars in different places at the same time.
To say that it is 'entire and yet divided from itself' is objectionable, because it presupposes that to be exemplified
in two different places at once implies being divided. It is
true that a *particular* can only be in two places at once if
one part of it is at one place, and another part at the other;
but, by their very nature, universals are not divisible into
parts. Exasperated, the objector may retort that what is
seen to be exemplified at two different places is seen at
those places; and that, since what is seen at one place is not
what is seen at the other, the *in* which is seen to be exemplified in Russell's room cannot be the same as the *in* which
is seen to be exemplified in Moore's room. In his turn, a
realist may reply that the second premise of this argument,
namely that what is seen at one place is not what is simultaneously seen at the other, holds for particulars but not for
universals. If he is asked how that can be, he need not
hesitate to reply that you cannot explain what is fundamental. At a certain time Russell is in his room and Moore
is in his; and one and the same relation, namely that denoted by 'in', is a constituent of both facts. If that is impossible, then all discourse is impossible.

Even this resounding affirmation may not silence the
objector. We have supposed that realists may avoid meta-
phorical expressions like 'share' and 'participate in' when
speaking of the connexion between particulars and universals, and have employed instead the non-metaphorical

[13] J. L. Austin, *Philosophical Papers* (Oxford, 1961), p. 18.

'exemplify'. But what does 'exemplify' denote? In his 1911 essay 'On the Relations of Universals and Particulars', Russell wrote that,

> . . . according to the theory which assumes particulars, there is a specific relation of subject to predicate . . . [O]rdinary sensible qualities will be predicates of the particulars which are instances of them . . . Predication is a relation involving a fundamental logical difference between its two terms . . . [T]he question whether predication is an ultimate simple relation may be taken as distinguishing the two theories [i.e. that there are particulars and that there are not]; it is ultimate if there are particulars (*Logic and Knowledge*, p. 123).

Plainly Russell's 'predication' has the same sense as our 'exemplification' ('exemplification' is better because it is convenient to reserve 'predication' for the relation between a linguistic expression and what it is predicated of); and Russell is saying that predication (or exemplification) itself is an 'ultimate simple relation.'

In the first of his articles on Plato's *Parmenides*, Professor Ryle showed that there cannot be such a relation.[14] By Russell's own exposition, it would be anomalous. Whereas ordinary relations relate particulars (John is *to the left of* James) or universals (Yellow *is lighter than* red), exemplification is supposed to relate particulars *to* universals. Suppose, nevertheless, that there is such a relation. Applying this supposition to Russell's example, exemplification will relate the two particulars, Russell and his room, to the relation *in*, and the two particulars, Moore and his room, to the same relation. It follows that exemplification is a universal. For, although Russell defined a universal as 'anything which may be shared by many particulars,' by explicitly acknowledging that 'predicates them-

---

[14] Gilbert Ryle, 'Plato's *Parmenides* (I)', *Mind*, 48 (1939), pp. 137–38; reprinted in R. E. Allen (ed.), *Studies in Plato's Metaphysics* (London, 1965), pp. 106–7.

selves may have predicates'[15] *i.e.* that there may be universals which are exemplified only by universals, he showed that he considered it a sufficient condition of universality that a thing be predicable of or exemplifiable by many other things whether particulars or not.

The ultimate simple relation of exemplification is then a constituent of each of the two facts:

> (i)   The relation *in* is exemplified by Russell and his room;
>
> (ii) The relation *in* is exemplified by Moore and his room.

It follows that,

> (ia) The relation of exemplification is exemplified by Russell, his room, and the relation *in,*

and that,

> (iia) The relation of exemplification is exemplified by Moore, his room, and the relation *in.*

But the facts (ia) and (iia) are stated in sentences which contain the expression 'is exemplified by'. What does that expression denote? It cannot denote the relation of exemplification which is said to be exemplified, because a relation cannot relate anything to itself. It must therefore denote either nothing at all or a second-order relation of exemplification. It cannot denote nothing at all, if the first-order relation of exemplification is genuine, as it must be if universals are related to what they exemplify by an ultimate simple relation. Hence it must denote a second-order relation of exemplification. Manifestly, this regress is interminable and vicious. For, since second-order exemplification must in turn be a genuine universal, exem-

---

[15] *Logic and Knowledge*, p. 123; cf. *Problems*, pp. 102–3.

plified by Russell, his room, the relation *in,* and first-order exemplification, there must be a third-order relation of exemplification, and so *ad infinitum.*[16]

Since vicious infinite regresses cannot be stopped, they must not be allowed to start. Once you concede to the Platonic imp that particulars and universals need a further universal, and an anomalous one at that, to relate them, you cannot deny that that further universal requires yet a further one, and so *ad infinitum.* Nor will it help to plead that the relation of exemplification is unique. It is *not* unique in the only respect that matters: namely, that many sets of universals and particulars share it or exemplify it.

Why did Russell postulate a relation of exemplification at all? Presumably because he perceived that even if he and his room are real particulars, and the relation *in* a real universal, it does not follow that he is in his room, any more than it follows that he is not in his room. The relation *in* is a constituent of both the positive and the negative fact. What is the difference between those facts? It is natural to suggest that in the positive fact the relation *in* is tied to Russell and his room by an ultimate simple relation, and that in the negative fact it is not. But by accepting that suggestion, you generate Ryle's regress.

The only possible escape is to deny that the statement 'Russell is in his room' asserts any relation, whether ultimate or not, between the relation *in* and the particulars it is said to relate. The relation *in* may relate Russell and his room, or it may not; but, supposing it does relate them, it does not follow that some further relation relates it to them. In the same way, a certain rose may be red or not; but, supposing it is red, it does not follow that *being red* is related to it.

Ryle's regress can only be forestalled by conceiving

---

[16] Ryle truly observed that his regress is not the same as F. H. Bradley's celebrated regress of relations, 'though reminiscent of it' (*loc. cit.* p. 138). The question which generated Bradley's regress, namely, How can 'a more or less independent' relation relate its terms? arises from Bradley's doctrine that a relation between *A* and *B* 'implies really a substantial foundation within them' (*Appearance and Reality,* Oxford, 1946, pp. 17–18). Neither Russell nor Ryle saw any difficulty in the 'independence' or externality of relations.

the exemplification of a universal by a particular or set of particulars as non-relational. Language inevitably misleads us here. Having recognized that expressions like '. . . is red' and '. . . is in . . .' denote constituents of facts, it is tempting to think that the difference between the facts asserted by the pairs of sentences:

'*a* is red' and '*a* is not red',
'*a* is in *b*' and '*a* is not in *b*',

must be found in the presence or absence of some further constituent, the relation of exemplification. That would be a mistake. The fact, if it be a fact, that *a* is red, has exactly the same constituents as the fact, if it be a fact, that *a* is not red. There is an ultimate difference between the two facts, but it is not a difference in their constituents.

I have argued: (1) that Plato's objection to the realist theory of universals does not arise if it is presupposed that a universal may be simultaneously exemplified by many particulars without being divided from itself; and (2) that Ryle's regress cannot begin if it is presupposed that the difference between the facts asserted by propositions of the forms $f(x)$ and $\sim f(x)$ is not a difference in their constituents, *i.e.* is not a relational difference. Neither presupposition seems to me to be inconsistent. Whether or not Russell's Realist Principle is true, Plato's objection does not refute it.

(2) *Even if some realist principle is true, must it be Russell's?* It is well-known that, ever since the Nominalist controversy vexed the medieval Schools, most of those who have claimed to be realists have adopted a position less extreme than Russell's.

The most familiar form of 'moderate' realism is that commonly ascribed to Aristotle. According to it, while something in the world must correspond to a true proposition, that correspondence need not be point for point. As Aquinas urged, *'Alius est enim modus intellectus in intelligendo quam rei in essendo'*. If 'Russell is in his room' is true, then something in the world must correspond to that proposition; but there need not be a constituent in the world for each constituent of the proposition. If we take the true propositions 'Socrates is a man', and 'Plato is a man', there must once have been something in the world corresponding to each of them. But it was not that the particulars Socrates and Plato each exemplified the universals denoted by the primitive predicates into which 'is a man' is supposedly analysable. (Nor was it that the particulars of which the complex particulars Socrates and Plato are supposedly composed exemplified the universals denoted by certain primitive predicates.) Rather, it was that the essence *man,* which in itself is neither universal nor particular, was *in rerum natura* individuated in Socrates and Plato, as well as in other men. *In rerum natura* the same essence may therefore be multiplied. However, when somebody forms the proposition that Socrates is a man, or that Plato is a man, he does so by abstracting the individuated essence both from the different parcels of matter which it informed and from the accidents with which it was associated. Since the abstracted essence of Socrates is the same as that of Plato or of any other man, it is universal. It follows that an essence exists in two distinct ways: *in rerum natura* as a many, and in the mind as a one. The universal term 'man' stands for the essence *man* as it exists in the mind abstractly. The essence itself, being neutral with respect to universality and particularity, can exist *in rerum natura* as individuated in Socrates, Plato, and other men.[17]

Against this theory, Russell would presumably argue that it is unintelligible to suppose that a neutral essence should be capable of existing both as many individuals, and as an abstract unitary universal. In what sense can the same neutral thing exist as both a many and a one? An Aristotelian would retort that this seems absurd only because of the dogma that everything is either universal or particular. If Russell may protest that universals are uni-

[17] The traditional Aristotelian doctrine is clearly explained by Henry B. Veatch in *Intentional Logic* (New Haven, 1952), pp. 105–13, esp. 111–13. Fr. Joseph Owens, C.S.S.R., has argued that the 'Aristotelian' doctrine really was Aristotle's: see *The Doctrine of Being in the Aristotelian Metaphysics* (2nd edn., Toronto, 1963), pp. 367–74, 386–95.

tary and yet exemplified by many things, why may not an Aristotelian protest that essences, while neither universal nor particular, may exist in the world as many particulars and in the mind as unitary universals?

Set against Russell's, the Aristotelian theory has two drawbacks. First, it postulates not merely one problematic entity, as Russell's does, but one problematic entity and two problematic forms of existence for it. By Ockham's Razor, Russell's theory, if tenable at all, is preferable. Secondly, the question cannot be suppressed: If the essence *man* is individuated in Socrates and Plato, are Socrates and Plato nothing but two individuals? Are they not both men? And if they are both men, can you stop short with saying that the essence *man* is individuated? Must you not add that the individuals, Socrates and Plato, exemplify the same thing, namely man?

A very different criticism of Russell's Realist Principle has been made by Goodman and Quine.[18] Like Russell, they hold that in some way true statements correspond in their structure to the structure of the world, but they altogether reject Russell's doctrine that there must be real universals which correspond to the primitive predicates of true propositions. In their view, only one part of any statement carries ontological commitment: its quantified variables. To find out what a man's ontological commitments are, you must find over what variables the statements he believes to be true compel him to quantify. 'Entities of a given sort', Quine wrote, are ontologically assumed by a theory 'if and only if some of them must be counted among the values of the variables in order that the statements affirmed in the theory be true'.[19]

On this view, if in the proposition, 'Russell is in his room', you permit 'Russell' and 'his room' to be replaced by the non-predicative name variables 'x' and 'y', and those variables to be quantified, *i.e.* if you assert that $(\exists x,y)$ x is in y, you commit yourself to a world con-

---

[18] W. V. Quine, *From a Logical Point of View*, pp. 9–14, 102–29, esp. 122–24; Nelson Goodman, *The Structure of Appearance*, pp. 33–41.

[19] Quine, *op. cit.* p. 103.

taining individuals, but not to the reality of the relation *in*. It is true that in (∃ x,y) x is in y, you use the word 'in', and presuppose that it has meaning. But Quine has insisted that 'there is a gulf between *meaning* and *naming*'.[20] In the same spirit, Goodman has defined nominalism as 'the refusal to countenance any entities other than individuals', while at the same time allowing 'the nominalist's language' to contain 'one-place and many-place predicates of individuals'.[21] He can consistently do so, because, like Quine, he does not consider predicates to stand for any entity.[22] In the opinion of both Goodman and Quine, then, a philosopher would commit himself to rejecting nominalism only if he were to allow '. . . is in . . .' to be replaced by a variable, and that variable to be quantified, as in '(∃ R) Russell R his room'; for only by doing so would he expressly assert that there is some relation (and relations are universals) in which Russell stands to his room.

This position can be assailed from several directions. Professor Sellars, for example, has forcibly argued that to quantify over a variable does not commit you to accepting the values of that variable as denoting anything real.[23] Russell would approach the matter from another quarter. Holding, as he does, that what you quantify over has no special ontological significance, he might nevertheless urge that the alleged gulf between admitting predicates of individuals and quantifying over predicate variables is imaginary. Of course a logician may for his own convenience eschew such quantification. Russell himself discovered that unrestricted quantification over predicate variables generates the paradox which bears his name, nor could he deny force to Quine's charge that 'our precautions against [such] contradictions [*e.g.* Russell's Theory

[20] *Ibid.* p. 9.
[21] Goodman, *op. cit.* pp. 33–34.
[22] *Ibid.* pp. 34–35.
[23] W. S. Sellars, 'Grammar and Existence: A Preface to Ontology', *Mind,* 69 (1960), esp. pp. 499–503, 507–17. Although my position in this paper is reactionary while his is revolutionary, my debt to Sellars' writings and conversation is too great to be indicated in detail: in particular, his criticism over many years at Minnesota showed me that realism is still an issue, and that Russell's and Moore's views deserve serious consideration.

of Types] are *ad hoc* devices, justified only in that, or in so far as, they seem to work'.[24]

Yet he might rejoin that to prohibit *all* quantification over predicate variables because unrestricted quantification gives rise to contradiction would be a remedy worse than the disease. Quine himself admits such facts as that more than one dog is white, and that roses and sunsets are red. Well, if it is true both that Fido is white and that Rover is white, must it not also be true that there is some colour which Fido and Rover both have? More generally, if Fa and Fb are both true, must it not be true that $(\exists f)(fa$ and $fb)$? It will not do for a logician to say: in my system, quantification over predicate variables is forbidden. The device of quantification is not private property; and any logician may be called upon to answer whether the result of a particular quantification is or is not true. Prima facie, that Fido and Rover are both white is a sufficient condition of the truth of the proposition that $(\exists f)[f(\text{Fido})$ and $f(\text{Rover})]$; and if any proposition expressed by means of quantification over predicates is true, then *some* quantification over predicates is legitimate, and no considerations of elegance or convenience can justify prohibiting it.

By arguing against Quine in this way, Russell would not surrender to Quine's criterion of ontological commitment. He might continue to hold the Realist Principle that the primitive predicates of true propositions must each denote something real. He would overcome Quine's criterion by showing that, rightly employed, it yields exactly the same results as his own. If by asserting the truth of a proposition containing a primitive predicate you oblige yourself to assert the truth of a proposition containing a quantified predicate variable, then quantified variables are not unique in disclosing ontological commitments.

Yet Quine has another argument. 'We may say', he wrote, 'that some dogs are white and not thereby commit ourselves to recognizing either doghood or whiteness as

---

[24] Russell did not, however, plead guilty. 'The theory of logical types', he wrote, '. . . has also a certain consonance with common sense which makes it inherently credible' (*Principia Mathematica* (2nd ed., Cambridge, 1927), p. 37).

entities. "Some dogs are white" says that some things that are dogs are white; and in order that this statement be true, the things over which the bound variable "something" ranges must include some white dogs, but need not include doghood or whiteness'.[25] Russell of course knew that in the proposition 'Something is white', the bound variable 'something' does not range over a class of things which includes whiteness; and wisely, he did not couch his argument in terms of abstract nouns like whiteness or doghood. His rejoinder to Quine would be: If some things that are dogs are white, is there not some quality which things that are dogs have? Otherwise how do white dogs differ from those which are not white? How can it be a fact that this dog and that are white, if the predicate '. . . is white' does not stand for something which dogs can either be or not be?

(3) *Does Russell's argument depend on features peculiar to certain languages?* Russell began by defining a universal as 'anything which may be shared by many particulars'. Now it is manifest that in English, as in all modern European languages, innumerable true propositions can be expressed by joining predicative expressions like verbs, adjectives, and common nouns, to proper names or demonstrative pronouns; and that in many of the sentences so constructed the same predicative expression, used in the same sense, is joined to a variety of proper names and demonstrative pronouns. Inasmuch as those propositions are faithfully reflected in English (or French, or German, or Italian) sentences which express them, there must by the Realist Principle be universals corresponding to those predicative expressions. Russell evidently recognized this; for he wrote that, 'broadly speaking, proper names stand for particulars, while other substantives, adjectives, prepositions, and verbs stand for universals'.[26]

But what if the very same propositions which are expressed in English by predicative expressions can be expressed in some other language, whether artificial or not, without them? A suggestion with which Russell toyed in *An Inquiry into Meaning and Truth* is to the point here.

[25] Quine, *op. cit.* p. 13 [p. 27 in this anthology].
[26] Russell, *Problems*, p. 93 [p. 16 in this anthology].

Imagine a language in which what is expressed in English by 'That wall is white' is expressed, not by a predicative expression corresponding to '. . . is white', but by a proper name, say 'White', which is taken to be the name of a spatially and temporally discontinuous particular. This particular can be said to be wherever any part of it is, much as a salesman can be said to be in a house if he has his foot in the door. Instead of saying, as in English, 'That wall is white', speakers of our imaginary language would say 'White is there', pointing to that wall (or possibly, 'White and Wall are there').

In *An Inquiry into Meaning and Truth* (London 1940), Russell proposed a similar interpretation of many statements in modern European languages. 'I wish to suggest', he wrote, 'that "this is red . . ." is not a subject-predicate proposition, but is of the form "redness is here"; [and] that "red" is a name, not a predicate . . .' (p. 97). In *Three Philosophers,* Miss G. E. M. Anscombe attributed an apparently similar view to Aristotle. 'It would be closer to [Aristotle's] view,' she wrote, 'if we ascribed to him an alternative that Plato proposes: namely, that a single form is divided up and becomes many. . . . Thus if there were only one large lump of [gold] in the world, the division of it would make gold, which had been only one thing, become many' (pp. 31–32).

Prima facie, an expression like 'White' in this imaginary language would not denote anything which may be shared by many particulars. It is not shared by many places; for while White is in many places, a different part of it is at each of them. And although it would seem very strange to us to speak of In, say, as being where Russell and his room are, it is not obviously impossible that a language could be constructed in which even relational predicates like '. . . is in . . .' would be replaced by proper names of discontinuous particulars. If this could be done, there would be no reason to suppose that there are any constituents of reality which may be exemplified by many particulars. That supposition would be dismissed as an illusion created by the structure of certain languages. It could not survive the discovery that non-predicative structures are possible.

Unfortunately, not even in imaginary languages can predicative expressions be completely replaced by names of particulars. Suppose there to be a language in which everything said in English about what is white or not white is said by means of a proper name 'White' of the kind I have described, *i.e.* the name of a spatially and temporally discontinuous particular. We may then inquire how saying that this particular is in two places is synonymous with saying that two different regions are white. Obviously, if the discontinuous particular 'White' were many-coloured, the two could not be synonymous. "The particular White is both here and there' could express the same proposition as 'This region and that region are white', only if the particular White were of one colour, and that colour were white. But that condition cannot even be stated in our imaginary language. Manifestly, to introduce a further discontinuous particular, Albus say, and to lay it down that Albus is wherever White is, would only put off the evil day; for the regions where Albus is need not be white unless Albus itself is white all over.

Neither the belief that predicative expressions could be replaced names of discontinuous particulars, nor Russell's notion that logically 'This is white' is 'not a subject-predicate proposition, but is of the form "[Whiteness] is here",'[27] would be tempting were not the predicative expression itself, or one of its derivatives, used as the name of the discontinuous particular. Suppose that particular to be named 'Jack'. The proposition 'Jack is here' can only express the same proposition as 'This is white' if Jack fulfills certain conditions. Those conditions can be stated in English, by means of the predicative expression, '. . . is white'; but I cannot conceive how they could be stated except by predicative expressions or their equivalents, *i.e.* by combining the same linguistic element used in the same sense with a number of other linguistic elements, in order to say the same thing about the things for which those other linguistic elements stand. The nature of the elements and the modes of combining them fall within the province of grammar,

---

[27] Russell. *An Inquiry into Meaning and Truth*, p. 97.

and Russell placed no limitation on their variety. He presupposed only that any language in which what can be said in modern European languages can be said, must contain predicative expressions or their equivalents. That presupposition has not been shown to be false by any argument known to me.

(4) *The objection that Realism is 'circular and uninformative'*. Having survived the objections of candid friends like Plato, and of nominalist foes like Goodman and Quine, it would be an anti-climax if realism should succumb to the objection, not that it is inconsistent, but that it is trivial. Yet Mr. D. F. Pears has put that objection vigorously:

> [R]ealism is necessarily a circular explanation of naming . . . [U]ltimately there must be some exit from the maze of words, and, whenever this exit is made, it will be impossible to give an informative reason except by pointing . . . [It is true that] at the place where the exit is made it is always possible to give a detailed reason like 'we are able to call things red because they are red', . . . [but that] is too obviously circular to look informative . . . What philosophers who propose the existence of universals do is to propose a general reason which looks informative because it shifts to another level, but unfortunately it is not. It merely marks time . . .[28]

The form of realism which Pears chose to attack is not precisely Russell's. Russell's premise was not that we are able to call things red, but that some propositions containing the primitive predicate '. . . is red' are true; and his argument did not purport to explain such truths, but only to exhibit a necessary condition of their existence. However, it is beyond doubt that Pears would be willing to adapt his objection to Russell's theory.

In one respect, Pears is less than clear. He accuses realists like Russell of proposing a 'reason which looks in-

[28] D. F. Pears, 'Universals' in *Logic and Language*, 2nd series, ed. Antony Flew pp. 53–54 [pp. 37–38 in this anthology].

formative because it shifts to another level, but unfortunately it is not'. Literally, this means that, because it shifts to a new level, Russell's reason *looks* informative, although in fact it is not. In other words, Russell argued that a necessary condition of the truth of propositions of the form 'x is red' is that the universal *red* be real: this 'shifts to another level', *i.e.* shifts from the level of words like '. . . is red' to the level of real beings, and so looks informative. Pears, however, contends that it is not. But if Russell's argument does shift to a new level, is it not informative? To be told that real beings correspond to the primitive predicates of true propositions—is not that information?

A second interpretation of Pears' objection is possible. If the clause 'because it shifts to another level' falls within the scope of the verb 'looks', then what Pears meant is that Russell's 'reason' only *seems* to shift to another level, and so is not informative, although it seems so. Pears' example of a detailed realist 'reason' supports this interpretation: 'it is always possible to give a detailed reason like "We are able to call things red because they are red".' Observe that he does not write, 'we are able to call things "red" because they are red'; for, if he had, he could not have added that this 'is too obviously circular even to look informative'. By placing quotation marks around the word 'red', he would have shown that his realist is looking to a fact about the world to explain a fact about language, *i.e.* that he does 'shift to another level'.

Pears did not leave the matter there. He went on to dismiss as vain all realist efforts to escape from the maze of words by postulating real entities corresponding to primitive predicates, on the ground that entities so postulated would be no more than 'shadows' of their corresponding predicates.[29] Realism is 'like a dream'—a dream the 'manifest content [of which] is little more than a harmless caprice, but . . . [the] latent content [of which] is a serious error'.[30] I doubt whether I understand what Pears meant by this simile; but I interpret him as meaning that a universal is like a dream-object, an unreal image con-

[29] *Ibid.* p. 54 [p. 38 in this anthology].
[30] *Ibid.* p. 58 [p. 42 in this anthology].

structed in the realist's mind, which, since it merely re-
produces a fact about the objects from which it has been
derived, *i.e.* that they are called by the same name, 'taken
literally . . . seems to be of little importance'.[81] Its manifest content is therefore harmless. But, since it easily passes
over into full-blown Platonism, thus becoming both important and false, its latent content is dangerous.

This criticism is odd, not because it affirms anything
paradoxical, but because it affirms nothing (so far as its
'manifest content' goes) which Russell need deny. Russell
himself would reject full-blown Platonism,[82] *i.e.* the doctrine that only universals are real, and that objects in the
world of sights and sounds are 'between unbeing and
being'. Nor would he deny that universals are 'shadows' of
primitive predicates in the sense that the reality of universals
is inferred from the fact that primitive predicates are irreducible components of true propositions. Of course he
would deny that universals are shadows of primitive
predicates in the sense that if the predicates had never
been conceived, then the universals would not be real. That
universals are in that sense shadows is the harmful
latent content of Pears' simile.

Let it be conceded that the latent content of realism is
false: to Russell, that was never in question. Is its manifest content, Russell's theory as I have elucidated it, also
false? Pears' only objection to that manifest content, namely,
that it is circular, that it only seems to escape from the maze
of words, I think I have shown to be false. Realism asserts
that something in the world corresponds to, and in that
sense is a shadow of, every primitive predicate; but that
assertion is neither circular nor uninformative.

III

Wise philosophers defer to plain men; but a plain man
who has accompanied us so far will hardly contain his

---

[81] *Ibid*. p. 58 [p. 42 in this anthology].

[82] 'These mystical developments [i.e. Platonism] are very natural,
but the basis of the theory is in logic, and it is as based in logic that
we have to consider it' (Russell, *Problems*, p. 92) [p. 16 in this
anthology].

derision. To swallow the doctrine that universals are constituents of the world, just as a certain morsel of flour is a constituent of a pudding mixture, is painful, even when it is stipulated that the universals in question be exemplified. But that unexemplified universals are as much constituents of the world as exemplified ones! Is not that as though you were to say that flour is a real constituent of ice-cream because it is true that ice-cream is *not* made of it?

Should our plain man turn for aid and comfort to Moore's *Some Main Problems of Philosophy,* he would be confirmed in his outrage. Moore there invited his readers to distinguish two kinds of objects we can think about: 'those which do have *being,* and those which simply have not got it, are purely imaginary, and don't belong to the Universe at all'. To the second class he assigned 'pure fiction[s]' like griffins and chimaeras. He then proceeded:

> If you fix clearly in your mind the sense in which
> there certainly are no such things as griffins and
> chimaeras, . . . it seems to me quite plain . . .
> that universals are not in any way to be classed
> with griffins and chimaeras; that, on the contrary,
> there is *the* most fundamental difference in the
> world between the two, a difference ever so much
> more important than that which separates uni-
> versals from particulars (p. 373).

At this, any plain man who has learned a little Russellian logic will protest: 'The fictitiousness, the non-being, of griffins and chimaeras consists in the fact that nothing is a griffin or a chimaera; but in your argument that universals are real you don't even attempt to show that they are all exemplified: in fact, it has been urged that your argument proves that unexemplified universals are as much constituents of the world as exemplified ones.'

Such a protest is certainly justified. Moore himself, in his essay 'The Conception of Reality', later accepted Russell's and Frege's view that the question whether or not griffins and chimaeras are real is the same as the question whether or not the predicates '. . . is a griffin' and '. . . is a chimaera' are each truly predicable of something.[33] And it is quite clear that the Realist Principle on which Russell's argument for the reality of universals depends, namely, that primitive predicates occurring non-redundantly in true propositions denote real constituents of the world, does not mean that such predicates are truly predicable of something. To show this, it is not necessary, although it is sufficient, to demonstrate that nothing in Russell's argument precluded its application to negative facts involving unexemplified universals. One need only point out that Russell began by supposing that he was in his room, *i.e.* that the relational predicate '. . . is in . . .' was truly predicable of something, namely, himself and his room. It follows that if by his conclusion that the relation *in* is a real constituent of the world he had meant no more than that it is exemplified, then his argument would have been a gross *petitio principii*. To attribute such a blunder to Russell would be ridiculous.

Moore, then, was simply wrong when he implied that the sense in which realists claim to prove that universals are real constituents of the world is the sense in which griffins and chimaeras are not. Whether universals are real or have being in the sense of Russell's (and Moore's) proof is a question altogether distinct from the question whether they are or are not exemplified.

We may go further. Expressions like 'real constituent of the world', and descriptions of the task of Philosophy or Ontology as being 'to give a general description of the *whole* of the Universe, mentioning all the most important kinds of things which we *know* to be in it',[34] inevitably suggest that philosophers are looking for the ingredients of which the world is composed, much as a chemist looks for the ingredients of a chemical mixture, or perhaps a zoologist for the species of fauna inhabiting a given region. Plain men are led to expect that philosophers will place before them a list of distinct ingredients or species, like flour and sugar, or lions and antelopes, although of course it is not required that they be material or even ob-

---

[33] G. E. Moore, *Philosophical Studies* (London, 1922) p. 212.
[34] Moore, *Main Problems*, p. 1.

servable. And indeed some philosophers, for example the neo-Platonists and Aristotle and his medieval followers, with their hierarchies of beings, have done something like that. For example, Aquinas's catalogue—God or *Esse subsistens,* the Separate Substances or pure subsisting forms, and material substances or beings whose forms actualize matter—together with his account of their ordering with respect to one another, is in the ordinary sense a general description of the whole Universe, mentioning all the most important kinds of things which Aquinas believed he knew to be in it.

Since the sense in which Aquinas believed God and the Separate Substances to be 'in the Universe' (he would not, of course, have used that phrase) is the same as that in which Moore believed griffins and chimaeras *not* to be in it, namely that the predicates '. . . is God' and '. . . is a Separate Substance' are each truly predicable of something, we have already shown that Russell did not even profess to prove that universals are real in that sense. In what sense, then, did he profess to prove it? According to his Realist Principle, the non-redundant primitive predicates of true propositions denote things that are real or have being: but how are the expressions 'things that are real', 'things that have being' to be understood? If Moore, who in 1910 was as close to Russell as any man was, nevertheless misunderstood, have we any hope of doing better?

Wittgenstein once alleged that 'nothing is more likely than that the verbal expression of the result of a mathematical proof is calculated to delude us with a myth';[35] and whether he was right or wrong about mathematics, his remark holds good of Russell's proof of the reality of universals. Wittgenstein's prescription for getting rid of such delusions was to look at the proof. '[T]he *sense* of the result is not to be read off from [the result] by itself, but from the *proof.*'[36]

Why did Russell accept his Realist Principle? What

[35] Ludwig Wittgenstein, *Remarks on the Foundations of Mathematics* (Oxford, 1956), II, 26 (p. 77).
[36] *Ibid.* II, 25 (p. 76).

proof did he give of it? He seems to have thought that a proof of it would fall into two parts. First, it would be necessary to show that predicative expressions could not all be analysed into non-predicative ones. Both Russell and Moore held that traditional nominalism, *e.g.* that of Berkeley and Hume, had attempted such analyses, and had failed, because it had not been able to dispense with the relational predicate '. . . is similar to. . . .'[37] Secondly, it would be necessary to show that whether or not a proposition is true depends on how the world is, and not on how anybody, plain or scientific, chooses to think about it. If '*F*' and '*G*' are primitive predicates, then what '*Fa*' says about the world is different from what '*Ga*' says about it. The difference in what they say can only arise from the difference of their predicates. Suppose both to be true: then the world is as they say it is, and what they say it is depends in part on their predicates. Suppose either or both to be false, then the world will be as the negatives of either or both say it is, and that too depends in part on their predicates. This argument does not show that any bit of the world is named by '*F*' or '*G*'; for it is not about the elements or ingredients of the world in the way in which a chemical analysis is about the elements or ingredients of a chemical compound or mixture. But it does show that '*F*' and '*G*' refer to the world in the sense that they are descriptive and not merely formal parts of statements about it, the truth of those statements being determined by how the world is. And since, for any predicate *f* and any individual *x*, it is true either that *fx* or that $\sim fx$, every primitive predicate must be a descriptive and not merely a formal part of a true full description of the world, the truth of that description being determined by how the world is. That, if anything, is what Russell's proof proves; and that is what I think he meant when he asserted that a universal like *in* 'is something, although we cannot say that it exists *in the same sense* in which I and my room exist'.[38]

Russell confirmed this interpretation of his theory of uni-

[37] Russell, *Problems*, pp. 95–97 [pp. 19–20 in this anthology]; Moore, *Main Problems*, pp. 313–17.
[38] Russell, *Problems*, p. 90.

versals in an almost mocking remark in his 'Reply to Criticisms' in P. A. Schilpp's *The Philosophy of Bertrand Russell*.

> If it is true [he wrote], as it seems to be, that the world cannot be described without the use of the word 'similar' or some equivalent [i.e. without the use of predicates], that seems to imply something about the world, though I do not know exactly what. This is the sense in which I still believe in universals (p. 688).

In this passage, Russell took the realist theory of universals to consist in repudiating two errors: the nominalist error that predicates can be dispensed with in a true description of the world; and what we may call the 'idealist" error that the repudiation of the nominalist error implies nothing about the world, because the truth of a description depends, not on how the world is, but on how thinkers think.

Even if I have interpreted Russell's theory correctly, I have not shown that it is true; for I have proved neither that predicates cannot be dispensed with in a true description of the world, nor that whether a description of the world is true depends on how the world is. However, Moore's and Russell's criticism of Berkeley and Hume, and the difficulties I have pointed out in the proposal to replace qualitative predicates by the names of discontinuous particulars, show how difficult it is to carry out the nominalist programme. As for what I have called 'the idealist error', like Moore and Russell I consider it to merit exposure rather than refutation.

A plain man might accept all my explanations, and yet object that the realist theory of universals, although true, is of little importance. In one respect, he would be right. The major questions of metaphysics are either about the substance of the world (*e.g.*, what sorts of individuals does it contain? What are the space and time in which some, if not all, of them exist? Do they persist through time? Are they substances or processes? Are any or all of them phenomenal?) or about mind and knowledge (*e.g.*, what is a mind? How are minds related to bodies? Is thinking a physical process? How can we think of individuals, their kinds, and their properties? How is thinking related to perceiving?). The realist theory of universals does not lead to a solution of any of these problems. Its importance, like its character, is negative. If you reject it, that is, if you accept the nominalist or the idealist theories that conflict with it, you cannot avoid serious errors when you try to answer the major questions. Although negative, it is fundamental.[39]

[39] Although I doubt whether any of them will agree with most of my conclusions, this essay originated in conversations with my former colleagues: Herbert Hochberg, Reinhardt Grossmann, Henry B. Veatch, and Roger C. Buck. Both in design and in particular points it is heavily indebted to them.

ON THE NATURE OF UNIVERSALS

Nicholas Wolterstorff

Suppose that one distinguishes between those entities which can be predicated of something and those which cannot be, calling the former "predicables," and the latter "non-predicables." Then, for example, the property of being courageous would be a predicable, for one can predicate this of someone, say, of Napoleon. But Napoleon himself would be a non-predicable, for he cannot be predicated. In general, properties and actions would be predicables, whereas persons, events, and physical objects would be non-predicables. Likewise poems, symphonies, classes, groups, organizations, stuffs and propositions would be non-predicables. For though, to give but one example, one can predicate *being Bartok's Fifth Quartet* of something, one cannot predicate Bartok's Fifth Quartet itself. The class of non-predicables is clearly a very mixed bag of things.

Now among predicables one can distinguish between those which would traditionally be called "universals" and those which would not be so called. The distinction is that between those which can be truly predicated of more than one thing and those which cannot be truly predicated of more than one thing; or, equivalently, between those which can have more than one instance and those which cannot. *Being identical with Napoleon* is a non-universal, as is *being a round square;* whereas, *being identical with someone named "Napoleon"* is a universal, for it is possible that it should be truly predicated of more than one thing.

Just as there can be many instances of a single predicable, so, analogously, there can be many copies, and many recitations, of a single literary work (e.g., of "Sailing to Byzantium"). There can be many performances of a single musical work (e.g., of Bartok's Fifth). There can be many copies, and many showings, of a single film (e.g., of *Blow-up*). There can be many inscriptions, and many utterances, of a single word or sequence of words. There can be many impressions of a single art print (e.g., of Rembrandt's "Hundred Guilder Print"). There can be many performances of a single dance (e.g., of the Zuñi Rain Dance). There can be many castings of a single sculpture (e.g., of Rodin's "The Thinker"). There can be many productions of a single car model (e.g., of the '32 Ford Victoria), of a single house model (e.g., of the Tech-Bilt House), of a single chair model (e.g., of the Barcelona Chair), of a single flag (e.g., of the American Flag). There can be many playings of a single game (e.g., of Baseball). There can be many copies, and many productions, and many performances, of a single drama. There can be many issues of a single newspaper (e.g., of the Grand Rapids *Press*), many numbers of a single journal, many editions of a single book. There can be many executions of a single play or move in a game (e.g., of the Draw Play). There can be many doings of a single exercise (e.g., of Push-ups). There can be many uses of a single argument. There can be many printings of a single stamp. There can be many mintings of a single coin (e.g., of the Buffalo-Head Nickel). There can be many examples of a single genus or species (e.g., of the Lion). There can be many cases of a single disease.

In all these cases one feels, I think, a strong analogy between the fact cited and the fact that there can be many instances of a single predicable. Now in every such case there is present, of course, a one-many contrast. But the feeling of analogy must have deeper roots than this. For everything whatsoever is such that it bears *some* relation to many things. A painting, for example, can have many reproductions, a father, many children, a house, many doors; but we do not feel any strong analogy between these facts and the fact that a predicable can have many instances. Nor, I think, do we feel any especially strong analogy between this fact and the facts that a class can have many members, that a group or organization can have many members, and that a stuff can have many quantities of it.

It is well-known that more sorts of things than predicables have been called universals. Contemporary philosophers have frequently also cited such things as literary works and musical works as examples of universals. Presumably their ground for doing so is that they feel some significant analogy between the relation of a predicable to its many instances, on the one hand, and, on the other, the relation of a literary work to its many copies, a musical work to its many performances, etc. There have been, however, surprisingly few attempts to explain what this felt analogy might be. What attempts there have been, have mostly been attempts to show that predicable and non-predicable universals fit into space and time in similar fashion. Without here making any assessment of these particular attempts, I wish, in what follows, to strike out in a different direction in attempting to uncover the basis of our feeling that certain non-predicables bear a close enough analogy to predicable universals to justify us in calling them universals as well.

2. A key concept in our discussion will be the concept of a *kind* (type, sort). So to lay the groundwork for arriving at our conclusion, let us elucidate some features of this concept.

The recognition of kinds is, of course, by no means foreign to the thought of practical life. We are all aware of the fact that there are countless different kinds of things, the things being examples of the kinds. For instance, we recognize that there are various different kinds of cows, the Hereford being one of them; that there are various different kinds of animals, the Lion being one of them; that there are various different kinds of plants, the Lily being one of them; that there are various different kinds of people, the Negro being one of them. Some, but not all, cows we recognize to be examples of the Hereford; some animals, to be examples of the Lion; some plants, to be examples of the Lily; some people, to be examples of the Negro.

In practical life, we not only recognize the existence of kinds, we also, in ordinary speech, name and refer to them. I have just referred to four: the Hereford, the Lion, the Lily, and the Negro. The linguistic structure manifested by the names I have used is this: The name of the kind was composed by prefacing common nouns true of examples of the kinds ("Hereford," "lion," "lily," "Negro") with the word "the." And this is a thoroughly standard way, in English, of forming names of kinds. It is also, though, a standard way in English of forming definite descriptions. Suppose, for example, that I begin a story to my children thus: "Once upon a time a boy and a lion were walking in a woods. The boy, as boys will do, was teasing the lion. And the lion, as lions will do, was growling in annoyance." Here the expressions "the boy" and "the lion" are not functioning as names of kinds, but rather as definite descriptions. The expression "the boy" is being used to refer to a particular boy, real or imaginary, the one the speaker had in mind in his first sentence when he spoke of *a* boy; and the expression "the lion" is being used to refer to a particular lion, real or imaginary, the one the speaker had in mind when earlier he spoke of *a* lion. Thus, to tell whether such an expression as "the lion" is being used to refer to the kind, Lion, or is being used to refer to an example of this kind, we must look at how the expression is functioning. Form alone will not tell us.

It must be added that by no means are all names of kinds in English of the form just discussed. "Man," not "the Man," is correct; and the taxonomist does not preface his Latinate names of biological kinds with "the." He says simply, for example, *"Quercus imbricaria."*

Just as common nouns prefaced with "the" can be used both to refer to kinds and to refer to examples of the kinds, so, similarly, common nouns themselves are, in standard usage, true both of kinds and of examples of the kinds. The word "plant," or "a plant," for example, is true both of plant-examples and of plant-kinds. This is most clearly seen, perhaps, by noticing the ambiguity in such a question as "How many different plants do you have in your garden?" This may mean either: *How many different plant-examples do you have in your garden?* or *How many different plant-kinds do you have in your garden?* And, depending on what is meant, different answers may be correct. Suppose, for example, that my entire garden consists of one rosebush and two lily corms. Then to the question "How many different plants do you have?" I can answer, truly, either "two" or "three." The matter can be put thus: One can point in the direction of two different plants and say, truly and appropriately, "This is the same plant as that."

Underlying the fact that these two different correct answers can be given, is the fact that there are two different, equally correct, ways of counting what I have in my garden. I can count either plant-kinds, or examples of plant-kinds. Of course, in some situations there may be even more than two ways of counting plants. For example, if it were the case that I had three lily corms and one rosebush in my garden, the lilies being of two different species, then I could correctly say that I had three plants in my garden, as well as two or four. For plant-species can be counted as well as plant-particulars and plant-genera. Kinds are what are counted when, in the situation last indicated, we arrive at the conclusion, after counting correctly, that there are either two or three plants in the garden.

Thus far we have cited, by way of example, only natural, as opposed to man-made, kinds: the Hereford, the Lion, the Lily, the Negro. Further, the kinds we have cited are all ones whose examples are objects. But there are also natural kinds of other sorts—for example, the Bee's Honey-Dance, and the Wren's Song. Many honey-dances can be performed by bees, all of them examples of the Bee's Honey-Dance; and many songs can be sung by wrens, all of them examples of the Wren's Song. Both of these are kinds whose examples are occurrences. The linguistic form for speaking of such kinds is the same as that available for speaking of the other sort of natural kinds. For example, the name of the Wren's Song is obtained by prefacing the common noun "wren's song" with the word "the"; and the common noun "a wren's song" is ambiguous, true both of wren's song-kinds and wren's song-examples. The question "How many different wren's songs did you hear?" may be an invitation to count wren's song-examples or wren's song-kinds.

The recognition of kinds in practical life is by no means limited, however, to natural kinds. It includes man-made and man-performed kinds. The American Flag and the Barcelona Chair, for instance, are familiar kinds whose examples are objects; and the Draw Play and the Zuñi Rain Dance are kinds whose examples are occurrences. There can be many American flags, all of them examples of the American Flag; there can be many Barcelona chairs, all of them examples of the Barcelona Chair. Many draw plays can be executed, all of them examples of the Draw Play; many Zuñi rain dances can be performed, all of them examples of the Zuñi Rain Dance. Names of these kinds are formed in the now familiar manner. And just as "plant" is ambiguously true both of examples and kinds, so too "flag" and "chair" and "play" and "dance" are true both of kinds and of examples of those kinds. Suppose, for instance, that someone asks, referring to a football game: "How many different plays were used in the game?" This is ambiguous in a way which we have found to be typical. It may be that the Draw Play, if used at all, is to count as one play, or it may be that every *use* of the Draw Play is to count as one play. Thus different answers will be correct depending on what is actually being asked. So, too, the owner of a furniture store can count the different chairs he has in stock either by counting chair-kinds or by counting chair-examples.

So far we have done nothing more than cite, by way of example, various familiar kinds, and point to some features of the language used for talking about kinds. Let us now look briefly at the nature of kinds.

Perhaps a good way to begin is by pointing out some of the differences between kinds and classes; for it is classes that kinds are most naturally confused with. And certainly the two are similar. The relation of a class to its members is much like that of a kind to its examples; in fact, it does not seem incorrect to say that the examples of a kind are *members* of the kind. And there can be kinds of kinds, just as there can be classes of classes.

But in spite of their close similarities, kinds are not the same thing as classes—the decisive differences being these two: No class can have had different members from those it does have, whereas many kinds can have had different examples from those they do have; and classes are necessarily identical just in case there is nothing which is a member of one and not of the other, whereas there are pairs of non-identical kinds such that there is nothing which is an example of one and not of the other.

Let us consider the latter point first. The standard criterion for the identity of classes or sets is the one cited; namely, that class *a* and class *b* are identical if and only if there is nothing which is a member of *a* and not of *b*, nor of *b* and not of *a*. That this is not the criterion for the identity of kinds, however, is perhaps most clearly seen from the case of a kind which never has examples. Consider, for instance, the Unicorn and the Hippogriff. I take it that neither of these kinds of animals has ever had any examples. Yet the Unicorn is surely not the same kind of animal as the Hippogriff. However, the *class* of all unicorns is identical with the *class* of all hippogriffs—it is the null class. So also, even if it were the case that all and only pro soccer players were stonecutters, still the Pro Soccer Player would not be the same kind as the Stonecutter.

The other point of difference between classes and kinds is that a class cannot have had a different membership from that which it does have, whereas at least some kinds can well have had different "example-ships" from what they do have. The phrase "the class of the apostles of Christ" might have stood for a different class from that for which it does in fact stand (if, for instance, fewer or more or other men had followed Christ than did). And the class of men which the phrase "the class of the apostles of Christ" does in fact stand for might have existed even though none of the men who did in fact follow Christ had followed him, or if no one had followed him (though in either of these cases we could not, of course, *refer to* the actual class of the apostles of Christ with the phrase "the class of the apostles of Christ"). But the class which this phrase does in fact stand for could not have had different or more or fewer members than it does have.

Kinds are not so. The null *class* could not have had members.[1] But the Unicorn, though it never had any examples, could have had some. There could have been some unicorn at some time or other. And there could very well have been fewer or more or different examples of Man from what there are. If Napoleon had not existed, it would not then be the case that our word "Man" would designate a different kind from that which it does in fact designate. Rather, Man would then lack one of the examples which in fact it has.

In conclusion to these brief remarks concerning the difference between kinds and classes, it should be said that it is probably true of ordinary parlance that often what is there called a *class* is what I here have been calling a *kind*. I have been using "class" to signify the same entities that logicians and mathematicians call sets.

The feature of kinds which, in the philosophical literature, has produced most puzzlement is the relationship between predications true of some kind and predications true of examples of the kind. Let us next, then, give some consideration to this matter.

The Grizzly is a kind. And the Grizzly is hairy. Does it follow that a certain kind is hairy? Can kinds be hairy?

It is true, is it not, that the Lion has four feet, that it roars, and that it is found largely in tropical countries? But how are we to understand such a proposition? Is it equivalent to this: There is something such that it is identical with the kind: Lion, and it has four feet and it roars and it is found largely in tropical countries? And if it is equivalent to this, does it follow that if we were making a list of all the things capable of roaring, we would have to include the kind: Lion, on the list, that if we were making a list of all the four-footed entities, we would have to include the

---

[1] Professor Peter deVos has pointed out to me that the null class must not be confused with the kind: the Null Class. This *kind* has an example, namely, the null class.

kind: Lion, and that if we but searched long enough in tropical countries we would find the kind: Lion? Can kinds roar? Can kinds have four legs? Can kinds dwell in tropical countries? Or is it that the kind: Lion, can indeed roar, but not roar in the usual sense of the word "roar"; have four legs, but not have four legs in the usual sense of the words "have four legs"; live in tropical countries, but not in the usual sense of the words "live in tropical countries"? Do our dictionary makers manifest a serious blind spot in not systematically distinguishing these non-usual senses of predicates for us? But suppose they tried to correct the blind spot, how would they define the non-usual sense of, say, "roar"? Evidently something in all this needs clarification.

What seems clear in the whole situation is this: One can indeed assertively utter, and thereby speak truly, the sentence "The Lion roars." And this also seems clear: Either it is not true of the kind: Lion, that it roars; or if it is true of it, what one asserts about the kind: Lion, in truly asserting of it that it roars, is different from what one asserts of some example of the kind: Lion, in truly asserting of *it* that it roars. And so it seems that in assertively uttering "The Lion roars," either one is not referring to the kind: Lion, in using the words "the Lion," or one is not using the word "roars" in its more usual sense. How are we to choose between these two possibilities?

One feels, intuitively, that there is some connection between the truth or falsehood of "The Lion roars" and the roaring or not roaring of examples of the kind: Lion. Schematically, one feels some connection between the K being f, and at least some K's being f. Perhaps if we can discover what this connection is, the situation will clarify itself.

It seems that the Lion has four legs just in case lions have four legs, and that the Grizzly roars just in case grizzlies roar. In fact, I see no reason to doubt that the proposition "The Lion has four legs" is not only equivalent to but identical with the proposition "Lions have four legs"; and that "The Grizzly roars" is identical with "Grizzlies roar."

Time of October 28, 1966, contained an essay entitled "What the Negro has—and has not—gained." Sprinkled throughout the essay is the phrase "the Negro," often with adjectival modifiers. So far as I can see, one could, throughout, change "the Negro" to "Negroes," and the very same proposition would be asserted. The only other change necessary would be a change in the grammatical number of the verbs for the sake of grammatical propriety. Here are just a few examples from the article:

> (1) The attitude of many white Americans is influenced by the belief that the Negro has made great gains in a relatively short time. . . .
> (2) . . . These two opposing views pose a root question about the state of the Negro in the U.S. today.
> (3) The Negro has enthusiastically participated in the U.S.'s steadily increasing material prosperity.
> (4) The middle-class Negro, on the other hand, is troubled by the riots and the chants of black power. . . .

Thus in many cases it seems to be no more than a matter of diction as to whether one shall use "the Negro" or "Negroes," "the Lion" or "lions," "the Grizzly" or "grizzlies." Whichever one uses, the very same proposition is asserted.

If this sort of choice were never anything more than a matter of diction, then one could conclude that the concept of the Negro was the same as the concept of Negroes, that the concept of the Lion was the same as the concept of lions; schematically, that the concept of the K was the same as the concept of K's. But I think that this quite clearly is not the case. Following is a list of examples in which it is far from clear that we can replace ⌐the K⌐ with ⌐K's⌐ and save the proposition. For in each case, though the proposition of the form *The K is f* is true, still it may well be that the corresponding one of the form *No K is f* is also true:

(1) The Lion is a symbol of strength.
(2) The Lion is king of the beasts.
(3) The apple blossom is the state flower of Michigan.
(4) The sheep-liver fluke will be our subject of investigation in this course.
(5) The Lion is a species of animal.
(6) In the Cleveland Zoo is an example of the Dodo.
(7) Audubon painted a picture of the Robin.
(8) The Grizzly is widely distributed across North America.
(9) The Wren's Song is to be heard in all the settled areas of Michigan.

So I think that the admittedly inviting temptation to regard the concept of the K as the same concept as the concept of K's will have to be resisted; there seems no reason to doubt that in each of the above nine cases one is referring to a distinct entity, a kind, and saying something about it. Yet, on the other hand, we have seen that in many other cases it is no more than a matter of diction as to whether one shall use ⌜the K⌝ or ⌜K's⌝.

We were inquiring into the connection between the truth of "The Lion has four feet" and the four-footedness of lions; between the truth of "The Grizzly roars" and the roaring of grizzlies. What we have seen is that "The lion has four feet" is the same proposition as "Lions have four feet," that "The Grizzly roars" is the same proposition as "Grizzlies roar." But we have still not really discovered the connection we wanted to discover. For just what is it that one is saying, in assertively uttering "Lions have four feet"? Is one saying that *all* lions have four feet? Is one saying that *some* lions have four feet? Is one saying that *most* lions have four feet? Upon reflection, it is clear that unquantified plurals—"lions," "grizzlies," "Negroes"—are themselves puzzling.

Wilfrid Sellars suggests that the following equivalence schema is the acceptable one:

The K is f ≡ All K's are f (necessarily).[2]

[2] "Abstract Entities" in *Review of Metaphysics* (June 1963), p. 632.

This suggestion, however, does not seem correct—neither in the case in which ⌜the K⌝ is replaceable by ⌜K's⌝, nor in the case in which it is *not* so replaceable. What is immediately to the point here is the former sort of case. It may be true that Negroes have (the Negro has) made great gains, even though it is not true, and certainly not *necessarily* true, that *every* Negro has made great gains. Some Negroes may have made no gains whatsoever, and it still be true that Negroes have (the Negro has) made great gains. So also, it is true that lions have (the Lion has) four feet, but it is probably not true that every lion has four feet. Here or there, in all likelihood, there is a maimed or defective lion which has only three feet. And certainly it is not *necessarily* true that all lions have four feet.

The situation is rather, I think, that locutions of the form "the K" and "K's," when interchangeable *salva propositione,* are ambiguous, depending a great deal for their sense on the particular sentence and the particular context in which they occur.

In assertively uttering "The Negro has made great gains," or "Negroes have made great gains," one is simply claiming, I should think, that *most* (if not all) Negroes have made great gains. And so also, in assertively uttering "Negroes have enthusiastically participated in the U.S.'s steadily increasing material prosperity," one is simply claiming, I should think, that *most* Negroes have enthusiastically participated in the U.S.'s steadily increasing material prosperity. Often, then, ⌜K's⌝, when interchangeable with ⌜the K⌝, has the force of ⌜most K's⌝.

In other cases, however, a sentence of the form *K's are f,* when interchangeable with one of the form *The K is f,* seems not to bear a reference to what is true of the majority of K's, but rather, to what is true of *normal, properly formed* K's. The whole sentence has a normative rather than a statistical force. In assertively uttering, for example, "Lions have four feet" (or, "The Lion has four feet") one is simply claiming, I should think, that every properly formed lion has four feet. It might be the case that most lions did not have four feet, that most of them were maimed, and still be true that lions have four feet. So also, in assertively uttering "Grizzlies roar" (or, "The Grizzly roars") one is claiming that every normal, properly formed grizzly roars. And this may be true even though some are mute; indeed, it may be true even though most are, for some reason or other, muted.

Similarly, suppose it is true that the Wren's Song has an interval of a sixth between the first and second notes—that is, that wren's songs have an interval of a sixth between the first and second notes. It certainly does not follow from this that it is true of *every* wren's song that there is an interval of a sixth between the first and second notes. For it may happen, in a given case, that something prevents the normal progress of the song; the wren "chokes up." But it does follow that it is true of *every properly executed* wren's song that there is an interval of a sixth between the first and second notes.

If we turn from the objects and occurrences of nature to the products and performances of men, the same phenomena confront us. For example, in assertively uttering "In draw plays (in the Draw Play) the quarterback hands off the ball to his fullback and then . . .", one is not asserting that in *every* draw play the quarterback hands off the ball to his fullback and then . . . For it may be that, in certain executions of the Draw Play, the quarterback does not succeed in handing off, but instead, rather luckily *fumbles off,* the ball to his fullback. That would then be a defective draw play, but a draw play nonetheless. But in assertively uttering such a sentence, one is also not merely claiming that in *most* draw plays, the quarterback hands off the ball to his fullback and then . . . Rather, what we are claiming is that in *every properly executed* draw play the quarterback hands off the ball to his fullback and then . . . Similarly, in assertively uttering "Barcelona chairs are some (the Barcelona chair is one) of the strongest ever constructed," we are not claiming that *every* Barcelona chair is one of the strongest ever constructed. For it may be that one of them has a flaw, and is defective, so that the first time anyone ever sits on it, it collapses. Rather, we are claiming that *every properly formed* Barcelona chair is one of the strongest ever constructed.

We have seen, then, that "The Lion has four feet" is the same proposition as "Every well-formed lion has four feet"; and that "The Negro has made great gains" is the same proposition as "Most Negroes have made great gains." So then, in assertively uttering "The Lion has four feet," are we referring to the kind: Lion, with "the Lion"; and are we predicating something of the kind: Lion, namely, that it has four feet; and is it true of the kind: Lion, that it has four feet just in case every normal lion has four feet; and are we asserting something which entails that there is something such that it is identical with the kind: Lion, and it has four feet? Or does "the Lion" stand for nothing at all in "The Lion has four feet"? Is this really not a subject-predicate sentence at all, is "the Lion" here just an alternative locution for "every normal lion"; and does what we assert not entail that there is something such that it is identical with the kind: Lion, and that it has four feet? Shall we say that the predicate in "The Lion has four feet" has a somewhat unusual sense, a sense which can be explained, nonetheless, by pointing out that it holds of the kind just in case it holds in the more usual sense of every normal example of the kind? Or shall we say that "the Lion" here has a peculiar function, not the function of a definite description, not the function of the name of a kind, but the same function as "every normal lion"?

So far as I can see, there is no good reason for preferring either of these alternative analyses to the other. There are, we have seen, important differences between the sentence "The Lion has four feet" and "Leo has four feet."[3] But so far as I can see, there is no good reason for preferring the view that "the Lion" in "The Lion has four feet" is standing for the kind: Lion, on which analysis the predicate "has four feet" does not have the same sense as that which it has in "Leo has four feet"; nor for preferring the alternative view that "the Lion" is just a dummy for "lions" or "every normal lion," in which case the sentence is not a subject-predicate sentence, though "has four feet" has the same sense as that which it has in the subject-predicate sentence "Leo has four feet." That is, there is no

[3] "Leo" here being used to name some *particular* lion.

good reason for holding the view that the analogy to "Leo has four feet" breaks down because of the different function of "the Lion," instead of holding the view that the analogy breaks down because of the different sense of "has four feet."

Further, whether "The Lion has four feet" entails "There is something such that it is identical with the kind: Lion, and that it has four feet" depends on what this second proposition is understood to be. If it is understood as the claim that the kind: Lion, has four feet in the same sense of "has four feet" as that in which it is true of some individual lions that they have four feet, then I think that "The Lion has four feet" does not entail this proposition. But if "There is something such that it is identical with the kind: Lion, and it has four feet" is understood as identical with the proposition "Lions have four feet" and with "Every normal lion has four feet," then I think that "The Lion has four feet" does entail this. And thus it also entails "There is something such that it has four feet." It is also, though, the case that "Leo has four feet" entails "There is something such that it has four feet." But these, then, are two different propositions which are entailed.

3. What I now wish to suggest is that the entities cited at the beginning of this discussion as examples of non-predicable universals—literary works, musical works, films, words, prints, dances, sculptures, car models, house models, furniture models, flags, games, newspapers, journals, books, plays, exercises, arguments, stamps, coins, diseases, biological species and genera—are, all of them, kinds. Perhaps this seems as dubious in the case of literary works and musical works as in any; so let us make out the case for them.

It seems clear that there is such a kind as: Copy of *Tom Jones*. This is a certain kind of copy. Copies, like other things, come in kinds; and the kind: Copy of *Tom Jones*, is one of them. Similarly, there is such a kind as: Performance of Bartók's Fifth Quartet. This is a certain kind of performance. Performances, too, come in kinds; and this is one of them.

The question I wish to raise is this: Is there any reason

for not identifying the kind: Copy of "Sailing to Byzantium," with the poem "Sailing to Byzantium"? And is there any reason for not identifying the kind: Performance of Bartok's Fifth Quartet, with Bartok's Fifth Quartet?

It must be admitted that we do not *say* that a copy of the poem "Sailing to Byzantium" is an example of it, nor do we *say* that it belongs to, or is a member of, it. And we do not *say* that a performance of Bartok's Fifth Quartet is an example of the Quartet; nor do we *say* that it belongs to, or is a member of, it. It is not clear, however, that these are anything more than facts about our language. It is not clear that they mark differences in the properties of non-linguistic entities.

It is also the case that we do not customarily form names of literary works and musical works in the fashion usual for familiarly recognized kinds. We do not, that is, take some common noun true of examples of the kind and preface it with "the." The name is simply "Sailing to Byzantium" and Bartok's Fifth Quartet. But not only is *this* linguistic fact also not ontologically decisive; the linguistic pattern itself breaks down in some cases in which we are dealing with familiarly recognized kinds. As we have seen before, "Man" is the common English name for the kind: Man. Further, it is worth noting that we do in fact have "the Bible" and "the Koran" corresponding to "a Bible" and "a Koran."

In short, I think it must be admitted that some features of the language standardly used in our speech about familiarly recognized kinds find almost no echo in the language standardly used in our speech about literary and musical works. But this phenomenon does not constitute a good reason for not regarding a literary work as a kind whose examples are its copies, and a musical work as a kind whose examples are its performances. Nor do I see any other phenomenon which constitutes such a good reason.

But is there anything *in favor* of making the identification? Or must the case rest on the fact—if it is one—that there is nothing against it?

Two sorts of considerations, I think, can be given in favor of the identification. These considerations are weak; they scarcely deserve the title of "arguments." Yet they do show that the view fits in with certain other relevant phenomena.

One consideration is this: The relation between what is true of a literary work and what is true of its copies, and what is true of a musical work and what is true of its performances, follows the pattern which we have discovered for the relation between what is true of a kind and what is true of its examples.

Sometimes, what is true of a musical work is true of it without being true of any performance of it; and sometimes what is true of a literary work is true of it without being true of any copy of it. For example, it is true of the *Missa Solemnis* that it was composed by Beethoven; but it is not true of any performance of it that it was composed by Beethoven. And if A. E. Housman's own testimony can be believed, some of his poems were composed while he was shaving; but it is in all likelihood not true that any copy was composed while he was shaving.

In other cases, what is true of a musical work seems to be true of it just in case the same thing is true of most if not all performances of it; and what is true of a literary work is true of it just in case the same thing is true of most if not all copies of it. For example, it would seem to be true of Bartok's Fifth Quartet that it sets people's nerves on edge just in case it is true of most if not all *performances* of Bartok's Fifth Quartet that they set people's nerves on edge. And it would seem to be true of "Sailing to Byzantium" that it is about a page long just in case it is true of most if not all *copies* of "Sailing to Byzantium" that they are about a page long.

But in yet other cases—and these are certainly the most interesting ones—something is true of a literary work just in case it is true of every correct copy of the work; and something is true of a musical work just in case it is true of every correct performance of the work. Suppose, for example, that someone claims that the third word of "Sailing to Byzantium" is "no." That could certainly be true even though not every copy of "Sailing to Byzantium" has "no" as its third word; for there could very well be some defective copy somewhere which has, say, "on" as its third word—but which is a copy of "Sailing to Byzantium" nonetheless. In fact, "Sailing to Byzantium" could have "no" as its third word even though, because of some early printer's error, *most* copies do not have "no" as their third word. The situation would then be that most copies were defective, incorrect copies. What does seem to be the case is this: It is true of "Sailing to Byzantium" that it has "no" as its third word just in case every *correct* copy of "Sailing to Byzantium" has "no" as its third word.

Similarly, suppose someone claims that a G flat occurs at the end of the fourth measure of Bartok's Fifth. That could certainly be true even though not every performance has a G flat at the end of the fourth measure; there might be a faulty performance of it—though a performance of it nonetheless—in which a G natural rather than a G flat gets played. Indeed, it may be that the difficulty of performance is such that *in most* performances it is a G natural rather than a G flat that gets played, even though the *work* has a G flat. Again, the situation seems to be this: It is true of Bartok's Fifth that it has a G flat at the end of the fourth measure just in case it is true of every *correct* performance of Bartok's Fifth that it has a G flat at the end of the fourth measure.

So there we have one consideration in favor of the view that a musical work is a kind of performance, and that a literary work is a kind of copy: The relation between what is true of a musical work and what is true of its performances, and the relation between what is true of a literary work and what is true of its copies, follow the same three-fold pattern that we uncovered when we discussed, for familiarly recognized kinds, the relation between what is true of the kind and what is true of its examples.

A second consideration, in support of the view we are propounding, is the fact that a literary work is a word-sequence which can be repeatedly copied out or uttered, along with the fact that such word-sequences, in general, are kinds; and the fact that a musical work is a sound-sequence which can be repeatedly sounded out, along with the fact that such sound-sequences, in general, are kinds.

That a literary work is a word-sequence, definite words in a definite sequence, the whole sequence capable of being repeatedly uttered and repeatedly copied out, seems clear enough. But the claim that all such words and word-sequences as can be repeatedly uttered or inscribed are kinds, needs perhaps a bit of explanation.

It has often been noted by philosophers that such a question as "How many different words are there on this page?" is ambiguous. For example, if "the" occurs three times, it may be that each distinct occurrence is to be counted as a distinct word, or it may be that each occurrence is to be counted as nothing more than another occurrence of the *same* word. Or, to take another example, suppose it is asked how many different words are contained in this box:

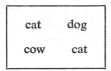

This too is an ambiguous question. The correct answer could be either "four" or "three," depending on what is to be counted as *a* word.

It will be evident, at a glance, that such questions as "How many different phrases are there on this page?" and "How many different sentences are there in this book?" are ambiguous in exactly the same way.

Now, though I know of no decisive argument in favor of the view, it seems plausible to regard words qua repeatable and word-sequences qua repeatable as *kinds*—kinds of word-occurrences, and kinds of word-sequence-occurrences, respectively. Word-occurrences, and word-sequence-occurrences, do after all come in kinds; and there seems to be nothing against identifying certain of such kinds with words qua repeatable and with word-sequences qua repeatable. Further, that words qua repeatable are not to be identified with the *class* of their occurrences, nor word-sequences qua repeatable with the *class* of their occurrences, seems clear enough. For these classes cannot have had different members from those they do have; whereas words qua repeatable and word-sequences qua repeatable can very well have had different occurrences from those they do have.

Of course, we do not customarily form the name of a specific word qua repeatable by prefacing a common noun true of word-occurrences with "the." One can, perhaps, without gravely offending usage, speak of each of the occurrences of the word "the" as *a* "the." And one can ask how many "the's" there are on a page. But the name of the word qua repeatable is not "the 'the,'" but rather just "the." So names of words qua repeatable are not formed in the fashion which we have found to be typical of familiarly recognized kinds. But this—as already remarked on another occasion—is no good reason for doubting that words qua repeatable and word-sequences qua repeatable are kinds. So if it is indeed true that literary works are word-sequences capable of repeated utterances and repeated inscriptions, and if it is indeed true that such word-sequences are kinds, then of course we have our conclusion: A literary work is a kind—a kind whose examples are certain word-sequence-occurrences, those, namely, which are copies and utterances of the work.

That a musical work is a sound-sequence, definite sounds in a definite sequence, the whole sequence capable of being repeatedly sounded, is also clear enough. But again, what perhaps needs a bit of explanation is the claim that sound sequences, understood as entities capable of being repeatedly sounded, are kinds. The point can be made in the same way that we used to make the parallel point for words; namely, by first pointing out the ambiguity in such a question as "How many different sounds did you hear?" This may be either a request to count the different *kinds* of sounds heard, or a request to count the different soundings. It may be, for example, that middle C as played by the oboe is to count as one sound, no matter how often it occurs; or it may be that each occurrence of middle C as played by the oboe is to count as one sound. Now sound-occurrences certainly come in various kinds; and there seems no reason whatsoever not to identify certain of these with sounds qua repeatable. And, if it is indeed the case that musical works are repeatable sound-sequences, then we have our conclusion: Musical works are kinds, kinds whose examples are certain sound-occurrences, those, namely, which are performances of the work.

The thesis we are maintaining here—that literary works and musical works, and their components, words and sounds, are kinds—is not, of course, wholly novel. C. S. Peirce is famous for having distinguished between a word understood as what he called a *type* and a word understood as what he called a *token*. Perhaps it is worth quoting what he says: "There will ordinarily be about twenty *the's* on a page, and of course they count as twenty words. In another sense of the word 'word,' however, there is but one word 'the' in the English language; and it is impossible that this word should lie visibly on a page or be heard in any voice, for the reason that it is not a Single thing or Single event. It does not exist; it only determines things that do exist. Such a definitely significant Form, I propose to term a Type." "A Single event which happens once and whose identity is limited to that one happening or a Single object or thing which is in some single place at any one instant of time, such event or thing being significant only as occurring just when and where it does, such as this or that word on a single line of a single page or a single copy of a book, I will venture to call a *Token*." "In order that a Type may be used, it has to be embodied in a Token which shall be a sign of the Type, and thereby of the object the Type signifies. I propose to call such a Token of a Type an *Instance* of the Type. Thus there may be 20 Instances of the Type 'the' on a page."[4]

Peirce in these passages is pointing to a distinction to which we also have been pointing—that between a word which is capable of many occurrences, and a word which is a word-occurrence. And though, so far as I know, he does not, he might well have pointed to the parallel distinction in the case of word-sequences. What is not clear, though,

[4] Collected works of C. S. Peirce (Cambridge, 1935), Vol. IV, p. 537.

from the words we have quoted from Peirce, nor, so far as I know, from any other words of Peirce, is how he understands the ontological nature of what he calls a type. Is a type a kind? Or is it a class? Or is it yet some third sort of thing?

C. L. Stevenson, in a discussion of the nature of the poem, applies Peirce's distinction and terminology to poems. He says: "A poem is a sequence of words, understanding this either as a token sequence or a type sequence, the latter being a *class*. Copies, then, are *of* the kind (class)."[5] Here Stevenson explicitly says that types are kinds; but he also explicitly indicates that he regards a kind as the same sort of thing as a class. Our contention is that kinds and classes are not the same sort of thing; and that literary works are kinds, not classes. That they are not classes can be seen by noting that they are not identical just in case they have exactly the same copies. For consider a literary work which has no copies; its copies have all vanished, or it never had any, being one of those poems which occurred to Housman as he was shaving, but which he neglected ever to inscribe. Such a literary work, if it were a class, would be identical with the null class; and since there are no prime numbers between five and seven, it would be identical with the class of prime numbers between five and seven. But this conclusion is absurd.

Another point, raised by both Peirce and Stevenson, should be considered. We heard Peirce saying that a type-word cannot be seen or heard. And in his essay Stevenson says that a type-poem, as contrasted with a token-poem, cannot be written down, cannot be recited, cannot be on the top shelf of my bookcase, etc. However, neither Peirce nor Stevenson gives any reason for holding these paradoxical views. And is it not much more plausible to hold that *in* seeing or hearing the token-word, one sees or hears the type-word? *In* writing or reciting or laying down a token-poem, one writes or recites or lays down a type-poem? *In* hearing a performance of Bartok's Fifth, one hears Bartok's Fifth? In general, we often do one thing *by* or

[5] *Phil. Rev.*, July 1957, p. 330.

in doing another. Why should that not also be the case here?

4. The question which remains to be considered is our principal question in this discussion, namely, is there any significant analogy between predicable universals and non-predicable universals? What we have seen thus far is that non-predicable universals are kinds. Accordingly, we can put our question thus: Is there any basis for our vague feeling that those predicables which can be truly predicated of many, and those non-predicable kinds which can have many examples, have some significant analogy to each other, an analogy which justifies us in calling entities of both sorts, *universals?*

The answer I wish to suggest is this: Predicables are themselves kinds, kinds of cases.

To make clear what this suggestion comes to, I must explain what sorts of things I shall call *cases.* I shall do so by giving examples.

Suppose that De Gaulle is courageous. Then there are the following three entities to be distinguished: the property of being courageous, De Gaulle, and De Gaulle's being courageous. I shall call De Gaulle an *instance* of the property of being courageous; and De Gaulle's being courageous, I shall call a *case* of the property of being courageous. Next, suppose that Mary is coughing. Then there are the following three entities to be distinguished: the action of coughing, Mary, and Mary's coughing. I shall call Mary an *instance* of the action of coughing, and I shall call Mary's coughing a *case* of the action of coughing.

Cases are what Aristotle called "entities present in something," what the medievals called "qualities," what Strawson calls "particularized qualities," what D. C. Williams calls "abstract particulars." Names of cases are conveniently formed in English by taking the name of some property, *f-ness,* or some action, *f-ing,* plus a term, *S,* which stands for an instance of the property or action, and combining the two in the following fashion: *S's f-ness* (*S's f-ing*), or alternatively, *the f-ness of S* (*the f-ing of S*).

My suggestion then is this: Every predicable is identical with the *kind* whose examples are the *cases* of the predica-

ble in question. For instance, the property of being coura-
geous is identical with the kind: Case of being courageous.
And the action of coughing is identical with the kind:
Case of coughing.

If there are kinds and cases at all, then there will presumably be many different kinds of cases. One such kind
will be this: Case of being courageous. And this kind corresponds in an obvious way to the property of being
courageous. Likewise, corresponding to the action of
coughing there will be the kind: Case of coughing. And in
general, corresponding to every predicable there will be the
kind whose examples are the cases of the predicable in
question. Now my suggestion is that these kinds of cases do
not only *correspond* to predicables, but that they are
identical with them.

It is worth noting, in the first place, that the sorts of
arguments which can be marshalled against the identification
of predicables, for example, properties and actions, with
classes, cannot be brought against their identification with
kinds. For one thing, two distinct properties or actions,
a and *b,* may both lack cases; but in such a circumstance,
the class of the cases of *a* will be identical with the class
of the cases of *b*—it will be the null class. Secondly, some
properties and actions can have had more or fewer or different cases than they do in fact have; but no class can have
had more or fewer or different members from those it does
have. Now in these two respects, properties and actions are
like kinds rather than like classes; for, as we have already
seen, two distinct kinds can both lack examples, and at
least some kinds can well have had different or more or
fewer examples than they do have.

Further, I think that it cannot be shown that there is any
divergence between the criteria for the existence of predicables, for example, properties and actions, and the
criteria for the existence of the corresponding kinds of
cases—in other words, between the conditions under which
there is a certain property or action, and the conditions
under which *there is* the kind whose examples are the
cases of that property or action.

Under what conditions is there such and such a kind?

For example, is there such a kind as the Dodo just in case there is a dodo—schematically, is there such a kind as *the K* if and only if there is *a k?* If so, there would of course be no such kind of bird as the Dodo, since there are now no dodoes. Or is the situation rather that there is such a kind as the Dodo just in case there is or was a dodo—schematically, is there such a kind as *the K* if and only if there is or was *a k?* On this view it would be true that there is such a kind of bird as the Dodo, since there once were dodoes; but it would be false that there is such a kind of animal as the Unicorn, since there never were unicorns. Or is the situation rather that there is such a kind as the Unicorn just in case there *could* at some time be a unicorn—schematically, is there such a kind as *the K* if and only if there could be *a k?* On this view, there is such a kind as the Unicorn, since there certainly could have been a unicorn; but there is no such kind of shape as the Square Circle, since there could not be a square circle. Or is the situation rather that there is such a kind of shape as the Square Circle even though there could not be any square circle? Is it not even requisite for the existence of a kind that there *could* have been examples?

These various possibilities—and I have not exhausted the possibilities—as to the existence-criteria for kinds, obviously have their parallels in the various possibilities as to the existence-criteria for properties and actions. One possible view on this matter is that there is such and such a property or action just in case *there is* a case or instance of it. Another is that there is such and such a property or action just in case *there is or was* a case or instance of it. Yet another is that there is such and such a property or action just in case *there could be* a case or instance of it. And yet another is that not even the *possibility* of cases and instances is requisite to the existence of properties and actions.

Now if one could show some divergence between the existence-criteria for properties or actions, and the existence-criteria for the corresponding case-kinds, one would have given an argument against their identification—e.g., if one could show that there can be such and such a property even though there is no case of it, whereas there

cannot be the corresponding case-kind unless there actually
is a case, one would have shown that these are not to be
identified. But I myself see no way of showing such a divergence. I see no way of showing one of the proposed criteria
concerning kinds to be correct, and the corresponding one
concerning properties and actions to be incorrect. Nor do I
see any way of showing, in a specific case, that a certain
property or action exists whereas the corresponding case-
kind does not; nor vice versa.

So far, then, we have turned up no reasons for thinking
that our suggestion, that predicables are to be identified
with their case-kinds, is incorrect.

I think it is apropos here to consider, for a moment, the
view that though predicables are identical with kinds, it is
not with their case-kinds but rather with their *instance-
kinds* that they are to be identified. For example, should
not the property of being a horse be identified with the
kind: Horse (i.e., instance of being a horse), rather than
with the kind: Case of being a Horse? And should not the
property of being white be identified with the kind: White
Thing (instance of being a white thing), rather than with
the kind: Case of being White?

It might seem that this alternative view is, on its face,
absurd. After all, is it not true that the Horse has four
legs? But can it with any plausibility whatsoever be held
that the *property* of being a horse has four legs? And the
White Thing is colored. But can it with any plausibility
whatsoever be held that the property of being white is
colored?

We saw earlier, however, that when someone assertively
utters "The Horse has four legs," we need not view him as
referring to a kind, viz., the Horse, and saying something of
it; but we can instead view him as saying what could also
be said with the sentence "Every properly formed horse
has four legs." So it is not at all clear that having four legs
is a property which the kind: Horse, has, but which the
property of being a horse lacks.

Yet I think that there are good reasons for rejecting the
view that predicables are, in general, identical with their
instance-kinds. Perhaps the most decisive reason is that

non-identical properties and actions can have identical
instance-kinds. Consider, for example, the property of
being a member of the genus *Metasequoia,* the property of
being a member of the redwood family and growing
natively only in an isolated valley of western China, and
the property of being a member of a genus unknown to
Western botanists before it was brought out of China in
1948. These seem clearly to be distinct properties. Yet the
kind: *Metasequoia,* is identical with the kind: Member of
the redwood family and growing natively only in an isolated
valley of western China. And it is also identical with the
kind: Member of a genus unknown to Western botanists
before it was brought out of China in 1948. But of course
it cannot be true that three non-identical properties are,
each of them, identical with one and the same instance-
kind.

Such considerations of identity and non-identity are not
the only reasons for resisting the view that predicables are
identical with their instance-kinds. There are also such
considerations as these: The Apple Blossom is the state
flower of Michigan, but certainly it is not the case that
the property of being an apple blossom is the state flower of
Michigan. And the Lion is a symbol of strength, whereas
it is not the case that the property of being a lion is a
symbol of strength.

So, having failed to uncover any arguments to the
contrary, I conclude that predicables are just kinds, of a
certain sort. They are certain kinds of cases. And, if this is
correct, then of course we have found a basis for our feeling that there is a close analogy between predicable universals on the one hand, and non-predicable universals on the
other. For these latter, we have seen, are also kinds. Perhaps
not everything which has ever been called a universal is a
kind. But universals of the sorts we have been considering
are, all of them, kinds.

PARTICULARS

PARTICULARS AND THEIR INDIVIDUATION

Michael J. Loux

Philosophers frequently speak of the problem of individuation. To judge from their remarks, there is simply one
problem here; but, as a matter of fact, two quite different
problems have traditionally gone by this name. One of these
is a problem parochial to realism; it arises when the realist
attempts to explicate the nature of particulars. The other
is a question about the basis for our ability to identify subjects of discourse and it arises quite independently of the
problem of universals. By way of introducing the readings
in this section, I shall try to outline the major issues connected with both questions. In the first section of the introduction, I shall discuss the problem of individuation as it
arises within the context of a realistic interpretation of
particulars; in the second, I shall examine questions about
our ability to identify material bodies and persons as distinct objects of reference.

I

CLUSTERS AND BUNDLES

Although the realist wants to distinguish between universals and particulars, between characteristics and the
things which possess them, he frequently finds it difficult to
make these distinctions clear within the context of a
thoroughgoing realism. According to the realist, there are a
large number of characteristics associated with any substance (material body or person). The desk on which I am

writing, for example, has a certain color, shape, texture, and so on; but as I list these things, I find that everything I can say about the desk is exhausted by a specification of its characteristics. Indeed, the desk seems to be nothing more than the characteristics associated with it.

Impressed by this line of reasoning, realists have sometimes denied that the distinction between universals and particulars is really ultimate.[1] Particular substances, they claim, are nothing more than collections of characteristics, complexes of universals. Frequently, this view is expressed metaphorically. We are told that material bodies and persons are just "clusters" or "bundles" of characteristics. Thus, my desk is just a cluster of characteristics related to each other both causally and spatiotemporally. Consequently, to speak of the desk as having any one of these characteristics is not to refer to any entity distinct from those characteristics. It is merely to say that a certain characteristic is related in various ways to other characteristics.[2]

A consequence of this account is that it is logically impossible for two or more substances to possess exactly the same characteristics. Substances possessing the same characteristics throughout would be composed of exactly the same entities; but this would make them numerically identical. The cluster theorist argues that while a characteristic can have several different instances, each complete set of characteristics comprising a material body or person is uniquely instantiated. This consequence of the cluster theory has been formalized in a principle known as the Identity of Indiscernibles. It is expressed as follows:

> If an entity, a, possesses exactly the same characteristics as an entity, b, then a is numerically identical with b.

[1] Cluster theorists have sometimes been nominalists. Although my account bears mainly on realistic versions of the theory, some of the things I say are relevant to nominalistic interpretations of the view.

[2] A. J. Ayer defends one version of the cluster theory in his paper "The Identity of Indiscernibles," reprinted in this anthology.

Despite its intuitive appeal, the claim that substances are just bundles of characteristics has frequently come under attack. Very generally, critics have claimed that this view fails to do justice to certain basic notions of our conceptual scheme. It is a commonplace, for example, that a material body can change with respect to one or more of its characteristics, while remaining numerically the same; however, on the cluster theory, identity through change is *prima facie* unintelligible. If a material body or person just is a set of characteristics, then any alteration in these will simply result in a different entity.

Likewise, we frequently speak of substances as possessing characteristics. The cluster theorist claims that he can make sense out of this notion; but this is not as clear as it might seem. The cluster theorist suggests that when I speak of a substance (e.g., my desk) as possessing a certain characteristic (e.g., a certain shade of green), I am saying that one of the characteristics (the shade of green) is co-present with certain other characteristics (a certain shape, texture, etc.). Unfortunately, a consequence of this suggestion is that I must be construed as doing what I am obviously not doing, namely, talking about something other than my desk. My desk is all of the characteristics in a certain place at a certain time, the relevant shade of green included, so that if the thing I refer to does not embody the relevant shade of green, it is simply not my desk.

An alternative account might be suggested. In claiming that my desk is such and such a shade of green, I am claiming that the color in question is one of a collection of characteristics. But which collection? If it does not include the color green, then we are once again faced with the absurd consequence of the first account. If it does, then it is not clear that what I say can be anything but tautological. My claim could hardly be taken as informative, since a person could know what I am talking about only if he knew in advance that one of the characteristics comprising the desk is the relevant shade of green; but, then, the predicate-term, "is such and such a shade of green" adds nothing to what he must know if he is to grasp the object I am referring to.

BARE PARTICULARS

The cluster theorist argued that it is logically impossible for two or more entities to have all of their characteristics in common. Since, on his view, substances just are the characteristics they exemplify, two substances with exactly the same characteristics are necessarily the same thing. Now, some philosophers have argued that there is nothing unintelligible in the suggestion that several material bodies or persons might have precisely the same characteristics. Admittedly, this sort of thing may never happen; it seems, nevertheless, logically possible. Since they have found the repetition of a complete set of characteristics conceivable, these philosophers have gone on to argue that substances cannot simply be the characteristics which we associate with them. They must contain something in addition to these characteristics. This "additional something" is called a bare particular. The view here is that underlying the characteristics of a substance is a characteristicless entity; and although ordinary language may suggest the contrary, this entity, and not the substance, is the literal bearer of the characteristics co-present with it. Bare particulars, while possessing the characteristics associated with a substance, confer individuality or uniqueness upon it; for whereas all of the characteristics of a substance might be present in some other substance, the bare particular underlying them is peculiar to just that substance. On this view, then, my desk is composed of several universals and a single bare particular; and while I may be tempted to speak of the desk as possessing the characteristics associated with it, the literal truth is that the bare particular co-present with them does the actual possessing.[8]

Philosophers appeal to the notion of a bare particular, then, because they feel that this is the only way of accounting for the logical possibility of two or more substances having all of their characteristics in common. Recent critics have argued, however, that the appeal to bare particu-

[8] For a continuing debate on bare particulars, see the papers by Allaire, Chappell, and Meiland which have been reprinted in this anthology.

lars is unnecessary in this context since the distinct spatio-temporal locations of two or more substances (whether exactly similar or not) is sufficient to guarantee their numerical diversity. In response, defenders of bare particulars argue that spatiotemporal differences presuppose rather than explain numerical difference. They claim that two things can occupy different regions of space at any one time only because they are numerically distinct; and, on their view, it is bare particulars which bring the required numerical diversity into the picture.

Without making any judgment on the response, it is worthwhile examining the basis of this objection. Critics are less anxious to defend some other theory than to show that the intelligibility of speaking about exactly similar substances does not commit one to the existence of bare particulars. Undoubtedly, the reason for this is that they find the notion of a bare particular epistemologically suspect. Bare particulars, philosophers have frequently urged, are essentially unknowable. Since they are lacking in all characteristics, they cannot be experienced, nor can they even be conceived. Proponents of the view argue that bare particulars are the bearers of characteristics; but critics have rejected this suggestion on the grounds that we are able to identify the things which possess characteristics. By the very fact that they are bare, however, bare particulars possess no marks by which they can be identified. If we are to identify a bare particular at all, it can only be by reference to the characteristics which it possesses; but then bare particulars simply cancel out in favor of clusters of characteristics; and it was precisely this notion that the defenders of bare particulars found incoherent.

CHARACTERIZED PARTICULARS

While maintaining the distinction between universals and particulars, some philosophers have sought to avoid the epistemological snares of bare particulars by claiming that the possessors of characteristics are themselves characterized. These philosophers frequently distinguish between essential and accidental characteristics. Essential characteristics are those which determine a particular as a thing of a certain kind. Consequently, such characteristics are said to be inseparable from a particular throughout the period of time in which it remains numerically the same thing. Because they are inseparable, essential characteristics are not, properly speaking, possessed at all. On the contrary, by constituting a particular as the kind of thing that it is, essential characteristics enable it to function as the possessor of other characteristics. Those characteristics which an essentially characterized particular can be said to possess are called accidental characteristics. It is in virtue of these that a particular is in a certain state or condition. Accidental characteristics are said to be separable from an essentially characterized particular, since a particular can undergo changes in its states or conditions while remaining numerically the same particular.[4]

Proponents of characterized particulars maintain that our ordinary way of talking about particulars and their characteristics is correct as it stands; for they generally identify the possessors of characteristics with what I have called substances—material bodies and persons. The characteristics which are essential to substances are those which constitute them as men, dogs, trees, etc; whereas their accidental characteristics are things like colors, shapes, etc. Thus, it is my desk, an essentially characterized particular, which possesses a certain color, shape, and texture; and not some characteristicless substrate. Nevertheless, while we can list a large number of possessed characteristics, we must remember that none of those characteristics which determine the desk as a desk can be said to be possessed by it. Of course, in ordinary language we would never say that they are. We would never speak, for example, of the desk as possessing deskness; nor do defenders of this view construe this an accident of surface

[4] D. C. Long's "Particulars and Their Qualities" (reprinted in this anthology) represents an attempt to defend the notion of a characterized particular. Long does not explicitly make use of the distinction between accidental and essential characteristics, although one might argue that a defense of his view would entail an appeal to that distinction. Irving Copi and H. S. Chandler, in papers entitled "Essence and Accident" (both of which are reprinted here), defend the distinction in question.

grammar. The grammatical fact, they would argue, has its basis in the metaphysical truth that an uncharacterized particular cannot function as the subject of predication.

It should be clear that the appeal to characterized particulars represents an attempt to avoid, on the one hand, the epistemological difficulties of bare particulars and, on the other, the supposed absurdities of the cluster theory. Since they are essentially characterized, the possessors of characteristics can be identified as things of such and such a kind. Further, it makes sense to speak of these things as remaining numerically identical through at least some changes—those involving their accidental characteristics. Finally, the commonplace that much of our talk about substances and their characteristics provides fresh information is preserved on this account. Since not all of a substance's characteristics are essential to it, it is possible to know what substance another person is referring to without knowing in advance all of that substance's characteristics.

Now, while the appeal to characterized particulars appears successful in resolving the difficulties inherent in other accounts of particulars, it has not been without its critics. Recent critics, for example, allege that the distinction between essential and accidental characteristics leads to contradictions. Suppose, for example, that a certain bachelor happens to be a trapeze artist. Being unmarried is an essential characteristic of bachelors, while being two-handed, let us say, is a characteristic essential to trapeze artists. Thus, we seem forced to construe each of these as essential characteristics of the man in question. Yet it is surely not essential to a bachelor that he have two hands; he may have lost one in an industrial accident. Nor is it essential to a trapeze artist that he be unmarried; it is quite conceivable that trapeze artists as a general rule marry two or three times. The absurd consequence of all this seems to be that both the characteristics of being unmarried and of having two hands are, at once, essential and accidental to a given individual.

Essentialists (as defenders of this distinction are called) frequently urge that this sort of criticism is based on a confusion. They argue that absolutely speaking, only those characteristics which determine a substance as the kind of thing that it is are essential to it. Characteristics like being unmarried and having two hands do not do this; they appear essential only because of the way in which we describe an individual, here as a bachelor and a trapeze artist; but surely it is merely a contingent fact that any particular man be a bachelor or a trapeze artist. Thus, the only characteristics which are, absolutely speaking (i.e., independently of the description we provide), essential to our unmarried trapeze artist are those which determine him as a man.

If the defender of characterized particulars is successful in meeting this objection, he has greater difficulty in responding to another criticism. As I have shown, the appeal to characterized particulars is motivated, at least in part, by the epistemological difficulties associated with bare particulars. At one level, characterized particulars certainly do not present such difficulties. The relationship between an essentially characterized particular and its accidental characteristics is readily intelligible on this view. At a deeper level, however, the old epistemological difficulties seem to re-emerge. A particular bears a certain relationship to its essential characteristics. The relevant relationship, we are told, is not one of possession; but then what sort of relationship is it? Similarly, what sort of thing is the particular which is determined by essential characteristics? Lacking all characteristics, it seems to be cloaked in the same mysterious hiddenness as the bare particular.

II

In discussing the view that substances are just clusters of characteristics, I referred to a principle known as the Identity of Indiscernibles; and although this principle was pivotal in the controversy between the cluster theorist and the defender of bare particulars, I never examined it very closely. I wish to examine that principle in some detail now. However, before I do, I would like to broaden the base of discussion. As I have presented it, the Identity of Indiscernibles reads, "If an entity, a, possesses exactly the same characteristics as an entity, b, then a is numerically identical with *b*." Now, we could alter this principle to read, "If all of the predicates holding true of an entity, *a*, are exactly the same as those holding true of an entity, *b*, then *a* is numerically identical with *b*"; and, in this way, we could make it possible for even the extreme nominalist, the philosopher who does not countenance characteristics, to hold the principle.[5]

Now, one might well question the point of reformulating the principle in this way. Within the context of the realist's appeal to the cluster theory, the reasons for holding the Identity of Indiscernibles were clear enough; but it becomes dubious what philosophical significance, if any, attaches to the principle once we remove it from that context. Admittedly, an extreme nominalist could consistently hold our second version of the principle; but what would he gain by so doing? What philosophical issues are at stake here?

Answers to these questions are to be found in the recognition of a philosophical problem quite different from those we have been considering up to now. The Identity of Indiscernibles provided the realist of the cluster theory variety with a principle of numerical diversity. According to that principle, substances are distinct because each possesses a unique set of characteristics; but, of course, numerical diversity was problematical there only because we had assumed the doctrine of realism. If we had approached problems about particulars from the standpoint of nominalism or extreme nominalism, no such questions would have arisen. Another kind of question, however, might have presented itself. We might have been struck by our ability to identify very similar things as distinct. We might have been amazed, that is, at our ability to distinguish where no differences are apparent; and we might have asked how we are able to do this. Now, one way of accounting for this ability is to claim that, despite appearances to the contrary, there always is a difference, expressible in terms of predicates, between two substances, a

[5] My use of the term "predicate" is meant to be theoretically neutral. The realist can interpret it as referring to characteristics, and his opponent, as referring to linguistic terms.

difference which we must necessarily grasp if we are, in fact, to distinguish them. This sort of answer would certainly involve an appeal to our second formulation of the Identity of Indiscernibles. That is to say, even the extreme nominalist is faced with questions about our ability to pick out or identify things in the world; and the Identity of Indiscernibles provides one account of how that is done. According to that principle, our ability to identify, both in thought and talk, the material bodies and persons around us presupposes that each of these things can be described by a unique set of predicates.

Since this version of the Identity of Indiscernibles addresses a broader philosophical audience, I shall examine it rather than the first version of the principle. A few preliminary remarks, however, are necessary. First, philosophers have frequently asked whether the Identity of Indiscernibles holds true of all things, including, besides material bodies and persons, characteristics and concepts. To avoid complications, I shall limit my treatment of the principle to the domain of substances.

Second, when philosophers have asked, "Is the Identity of Indiscernibles true?" they have not been asking whether it is, as a matter of fact, true that no two individuals can be described by the same set of predicates. Opponents of the principle have been willing to admit that this might be the case. The philosophical question is whether or not the principle holds necessarily; that is, whether or not it is logically or conceptually possible for two numerically distinct substances to be described by just one set of predicates.

Finally, the principle, as I have formulated it, might appear to be self-defeating. In the protasis of the conditional, reference is made to two different individuals, and in the apodosis it is claimed that they are numerically identical. One might want to claim that there is something unintelligible in this; for if they are two things, then they are numerically distinct; they cannot be one. This way with the principle, however, is too short; for it is certainly possible for one substance to have two names; and in the light of this possibility, we can amend our principle as follows:

> If all of the predicates holding true of a substance bearing the name "a" are the same as those holding true of a substance bearing the name "b," then the substance bearing the name "a" is numerically identical with the substance bearing the name "b."

Now, it has sometimes been claimed that we can establish this principle by showing that, for each substance, there is a predicate which holds true of it and only it. It has been argued that the concept of self-identity provides us with predicates of this sort. Each thing is identical with itself and with no other thing. Consequently, some philosophers have contended that it must be possible to construct, for each substance, a predicate of the form "is identical with x" (where "x" is a proper name of the substance).[6]

There are several difficulties with this suggestion. First of all, only a relatively small number of substances have proper names; and in the absence of the required proper names, it is not clear that the defender of the Identity of Indiscernibles can phrase his suggestion without begging the question. Second, predicates have generality of application. Indeed, if it is not, in principle, possible to apply an expression to several different things, the expression in question cannot function as a predicate. However, identity-expressions of the sort proposed necessarily apply to but one substance; therefore, they cannot function as predicates and so must be irrelevant to any discussion of our second version of the Identity of Indiscernibles.

If this objection is correct, then the Identity of Indiscernibles can be shown true in only one way. One must show that for each substance, there is a set of predicates, such that, although each of the members of the set has generality of application, the set taken as a whole necessarily applies to just one thing. One must show, that is,

---

[6] This, together with many of the other points I raise in connection with the Identity of Indiscernibles, is discussed by Black, Ayer, and O'Connor in papers entitled "The Identity of Indiscernibles" (all reprinted in this anthology).

that each substance is correlated with a set of expressions, all of them genuine predicates, which together imply uniqueness of application.

Unfortunately, proponents of the Identity of Indiscernibles have disagreed about the kind of predicate that is relevant here. They distinguish between "pure" predicates, expressions like "blue" and "man," which contain no reference to particulars, and "impure" predicates, expressions like "owned by John" and "four feet above the Eiffel Tower," which contain, either explicitly or implicitly, a reference to one or more particulars. Now, some philosophers have maintained that it is possible to specify a unique set of "pure" predicates for each substance. This is a daring claim, one which has seldom been supported by any sort of genuine argument. Indeed, no one has, to my knowledge, ever tried to specify even one set of purely general predicates which together imply uniqueness of application. This is not to say that we never identify substances solely in virtue of their "pure" predicates; certainly we do. The point is that when we attempt an identification of this sort, there is no guarantee that our description will pick out just one thing.

The appeal to predicates, at least some of which are "impure," has been more promising. By allowing "impure" predicates into the analysis, one is able to specify the spatiotemporal location of a thing; and many philosophers have held that this is something peculiar to each substance. The view here is that only one substance can occupy one region of space at any one time; and since we can specify spatiotemporal location by predicates, the Identity of Indiscernibles must be true.

Some philosophers have challenged the view that spatiotemporal location uniquely identifies substances. They have suggested that there is no reason why several, indeed an infinity of, exactly similar substances could not occupy one space at one time. On this view, there is nothing contradictory in the assumption that indefinitely many different hands, all following the same life history, might be occupying the same region of space which just one hand, my right hand, appears to occupy. It might seem that some version of the principle of parsimony is relevant here; but the present critic denies this. He argues that this principle can only tell us which of a number of possible hypotheses to adopt, not which hypotheses are possible.

The proponent of the Identity of Indiscernibles, however, can respond that it makes no sense to speak of plurality of hands here. We speak of a plurality of things only with reference to some possible procedure of enumeration; however, we can enumerate individuals only where it is, in principle, possible to discriminate between them; and, in the present case, no question of discrimination can arise.

However, even if we accept the view that each substance has a unique spatiotemporal location, it is not clear that the Identity of Indiscernibles follows as a necessary principle. Max Black, for example, sketches out an imaginary universe, the only existents of which are two exactly similar spheres. His claim seems to be that although the two spheres do occupy different regions of space at any one time, it is impossible to formulate a predicate (whether "pure" or "impure") which applies to one while not applying to the other.

Proponents of the Identity of Indiscernibles seldom find counterexamples like Black's very convincing. Thus, A. J. Ayer says, ". . . such examples seem intelligible to us only because we tacitly introduce into them some further feature by reference to which we do in fact discern between the objects we are supposing to be indiscernible." One might be baffled by all of this. Critics reject the Identity of Indiscernibles because they find the notion of indiscernible substances intelligible; whereas defenders of the principle argue that since the principle is necessarily true, such a notion cannot be intelligible. We seem to have reached an impasse. What the one side affirms, the other simply denies.

Actually, the situation is not altogether hopeless; for in this context, the burden of proof rests with the defender of the principle. His critic claims to have presented a logically possible universe in which the Identity of Indiscernibles fails. Now, the defender of the Identity of Indiscernibles simply begs the question when he counters these claims by reverting to the very principle that is at issue. He must provide independent reasons for thinking that supposedly indiscernible substances actually do differ with respect to their predicates; and this, of course, is what he never does.

As a consequence, most metaphysicians (at least nowadays) would deny that the Identity of Indiscernibles is a matter of necessary truth. Nevertheless, many of these same philosophers would want to claim that, as things actually stand, we are always able to distinguish the substances of our experience by reference to their predicates. These philosophers agree that no two substances can occupy exactly the same region of space at any one time. They claim, however, that our own universe differs from merely possible universals like Black's in that the spatiotemporal location of each substance *can* be specified by a unique set of "impure" predicates. Thus, although we can imagine universes where the set of predicates specifying spatiotemporal location is invariant over all substances, such is not the case in our universe.

The influence of this view is, in large part, traceable to the work of P. F. Strawson. In his book *Individuals,* Strawson presents a detailed exposition and defense of the view that space and time lie at the basis of all identification. According to Strawson, the speaker of a language communicates and thinks in terms of a conceptual scheme that is essentially spatiotemporal. Although the speaker of a language may sometimes succeed in identifying substances in other ways, Strawson argues that he is always able to locate them uniquely by relating them in terms of space and time to his own position within the conceptual scheme.

Despite its influence, the Strawsonian view is heir to a number of difficulties. Most interesting is the possibility that the account is circular. According to Strawson, we can always identify a substance by specifying its spatiotemporal location. However, if we grant, as many philosophers would, that our spatiotemporal framework is essentially relational, we seem forced to hold that our ability to identify spaces and times presupposes, in turn, the ability to identify independently material bodies and persons.

But then, the former ability could hardly explain the latter since, as it turns out, it presupposes that ability.[7]

Various ways out of this circle suggest themselves. One might, of course, simply deny that space and time are relational; or one could argue that some fairly strong version of the Identity of Indiscernibles (one making reference to only "pure" predicates) must be true after all. Alternatively, one might suggest that since a speaker of a language is capable of identifying himself without any reference to space or time, he can go on to establish a spatiotemporal system by relating other substances to himself. Finally, one might argue that the notion of circularity is inappropriate here. The identification of substances, on the one hand, and spaces and times, on the other, are so intimately related that it is simply impossible to examine one in isolation from the other.

[7] This point is developed by David Wiggins in his paper "The Individuation of Things and Places" (included in this anthology).

THE IDENTITY OF INDISCERNIBLES

Max Black

A. The principle of the Identity of Indiscernibles seems to me obviously true. And I don't see how we are going to define identity or establish the connexion between mathematics and logic without using it.

B. It seems to me obviously false. And your troubles as a mathematical logician are beside the point. If the principle is false you have no right to use it.

A. You simply *say* it's false—and even if you said so three times that wouldn't make it so.

B. Well, you haven't done anything more yourself than assert the principle to be true. As Bradley once said, "assertion can demand no more than counter-assertion; and what is affirmed on the one side, we on the other can simply deny".

A. How will this do for an argument? If two things, *a* and *b,* are given, the first has the property of being identical with *a.* Now *b* cannot have this property, for else *b* would be *a,* and we should have only one thing, not two as assumed. Hence *a* has at least one property, which *b* does not have, that is to say the property of being identical with *a.*

B. This is a roundabout way of saying nothing, for "*a* has the property of being identical with *a*" means no more than "*a* is *a*". When you begin to say "*a* is . . ." I am supposed to know what thing you are referring to as "*a*"

Reprinted from Max Black, *Problems of Analysis.* Copyright © 1954 by Cornell University. Used by permission of the Cornell University Press, Routledge and Kegan Paul, Ltd., and *Mind.* This paper was originally published in *Mind,* LXI (1952).

and I expect to be told something about that thing. But when you end the sentence with the words ". . . is *a*" I am left still waiting. The sentence "*a* is *a*" is a useless tautology.

A. Are you as scornful about difference as about identity? For *a* also has, and *b* does not have, the property of being different from *b*. This is a second property that the one thing has but not the other.

B. All you are saying is that *b* is different from *a*. I think the form of words "*a* is different from *b*" does have the advantage over "*a* is *a*" that it might be used to give information. I might learn from hearing it used that "*a*" and "*b*" were applied to different things. But this is not what you want to say, since you are trying to use the names, not mention them. When I already know what "*a*" and "*b*" stand for, "*a* is different from *b*" tells me nothing. It, too, is a useless tautology.

A. I wouldn't have expected you to treat "tautology" as a term of abuse. Tautology or not, the sentence has a philosophical use. It expresses the necessary truth that different things have at least one property not in common. Thus different things must be discernible; and hence, by contraposition, indiscernible things must be identical. Q.E.D.

B. Why obscure matters by this old-fashioned language? By "indiscernible" I suppose you mean the same as "having all properties in common". Do you claim to have proved that two things having all their properties in common are identical?

A. Exactly.

B. Then this is a poor way of stating your conclusion. If *a* and *b* are identical, there is just one thing having the two names "*a*" and "*b*"; and in that case it is absurd to say that *a* and *b* are two. Conversely, once you have supposed there are *two* things having all their properties in common, you can't without contradicting yourself say that *they* are "identical".

A. I can't believe you were really misled. I simply meant to say it is logically impossible for two things to have all their properties in common. I showed that *a* must have at

least two properties—the property of being identical with
a, and the property of being different from *b*—neither of
which can be a property of *b.* Doesn't this prove the principle of Identity of Indiscernibles?

B. Perhaps you have proved something. If so, the nature
of your proof should show us exactly what you have
proved. If you want to call "being identical with *a*" a
"property" I suppose I can't prevent you. But you must
then accept the consequences of this way of talking. All
you mean when you say "*a* has the property of being
identical with *a*" is that *a* is *a.* And all you mean when you
say "*b* does not have the property of being identical with
a" is that *b* is not *a.* So what you have "proved" is that
a is *a* and *b* is not *a,* that is to say, *b* and *a* are different.
Similarly, when you said that *a,* but not *b,* had the property
of being different from *b,* you were simply saying that *a*
and *b* were different. In fact you are merely redescribing
the hypothesis that *a* and *b* are different by calling it a case
of "difference of properties". Drop the misleading description and your famous principle reduces to the truism that
different things are different. How true! And how uninteresting!

A. Well, the properties of identity and difference may be
uninteresting, but they *are* properties. If I had shown that
grass was green, I suppose you would say I hadn't shown
that grass was coloured.

B. You certainly would not have shown that grass had
any colour *other than* green.

A. What it comes to is that you object to the conclusion of my argument *following* from the premise that *a*
and *b* are different.

B. No, I object to the triviality of the conclusion. If you
want to have an interesting principle to defend, you must
interpret "property" more narrowly—enough so, at any
rate, for "identity" and "difference" not to count as
properties.

A. Your notion of an interesting principle seems to be
one which I shall have difficulty in establishing. Will you
at least allow me to include among "properties" what are
sometimes called "relational characteristics"—like *being*

married to Caesar or *being at a distance from London?*

B. Why not? If you are going to defend the principle, it is for you to decide what version you wish to defend.

A. In that case, I don't need to count identity and difference as properties. Here is a different argument that seems to me quite conclusive. The only way we can discover that two different things exist is by finding out that one has a quality not possessed by the other or else that one has a relational characteristic that the other hasn't.

If *both* are blue and hard and sweet and so on, and have the same shape and dimensions and are in the same relations to everything in the universe, it is logically impossible to tell them apart. The supposition that in such a case there might really be two things would be unverifiable *in principle*. Hence it would be meaningless.

B. You are going too fast for me.

A. Think of it this way. If the principle were false, the fact that I can see only two of your hands would be no proof that you had just two. And even if every conceivable test agreed with the supposition that you had two hands, you might all the time have three, four, or any number. You might have nine hands, different from one another and all indistinguishable from your left hand, and nine more all different from each other but indistinguishable from your right hand. And even if you really did have just two hands, and no more, neither you nor I nor anybody else could ever know that fact. This is too much for me to swallow. This is the kind of absurdity you get into, as soon as you abandon verifiability as a test of meaning.

B. Far be it from me to abandon your sacred cow. Before I give you a direct answer, let me try to describe a counter-example.

Isn't it logically possible that the universe should have contained nothing but two exactly similar spheres? We might suppose that each was made of chemically pure iron, had a diameter of one mile, that they had the same temperature, colour, and so on, and that nothing else existed. Then every quality and relational characteristic of the one would also be a property of the other. Now if what I am describing is logically possible, it is not impossible for

two things to have all their properties in common. This
seems to me to *refute* the Principle.

A. Your supposition, I repeat, isn't verifiable and therefore can't be regarded as meaningful. But supposing you
have described a possible world, I still don't see that you
have refuted the principle. Consider one of the spheres,
a, . . .

B. How can I, since there is no way of telling them
apart? *Which* one do you want me to consider?

A. This is very foolish. I mean either of the two spheres,
leaving you to decide which one you wished to consider.
If I were to say to you "Take any book off the shelf" it
would be foolish on your part to reply "Which?"

B. It's a poor analogy. I know how to take a book off a
shelf, but I don't know how to identify one of two spheres
supposed to be alone in space and so symmetrically placed
with respect to each other that neither has any quality
or character the other does not also have.

A. All of which goes to show as I said before, the un-
verifiability of your supposition. Can't you imagine that
one sphere has been designated as *"a"*?

B. I can imagine only what is logically possible. Now it
is logically possible that somebody should enter the universe I have described, see one of the spheres on his left
hand and proceed to call it *"a"*. I can imagine that all right,
if that's enough to satisfy you.

A. Very well, now let me try to finish what I began to
say about *a* . . .

B. I still can't let you, because you, in your present situation, have no right to talk about *a*. All I have conceded is
that if something were to happen to introduce a change
into my universe, so that an observer entered and could
see the two spheres, one of them could then have a name.
But this would be a different supposition from the one I
wanted to consider. My spheres don't yet have names.
If an observer were to enter the scene, he could perhaps
put a red mark on one of the spheres. You might just as
well say "By '*a*' I mean the sphere which would be the
first to be marked by a red mark if anyone were to arrive
and were to proceed to make a red mark!" You might just

as well ask me to consider the first daisy in my lawn that
would be picked by a child, if a child were to come along
and do the picking. This doesn't now distinguish any daisy
from the others. You are just pretending to use a name.

A. And I think you are just pretending not to understand me. All I am asking you to do is to think of one of
your spheres, no matter which, so that I may go on to say
something about it when you give me a chance.

B. You talk as if naming an object and then thinking
about it were the easiest thing in the world. But it isn't so
easy. Suppose I tell you to name any spider in my garden:
if you can catch one first or describe one uniquely you can
name it easily enough. But you can't pick one out, let
alone "name" it, by just thinking. You remind me of
the mathematicians who thought that talking about an
Axiom of Choice would really allow them to choose a single member of a collection when they had no criterion of
choice.

A. At this rate you will never give me a chance to say
anything. Let me try to make my point without using
names. Each of the spheres will surely differ from the other
in being at some distance from that other one, but at no
distance from itself—that is to say, it will bear at least one
relation to itself—*being at no distance from,* or *being in
the same place as*—that it does not bear to the other. And
this will serve to distinguish it from the other.

B. Not at all. *Each* will have the relational characteristic *being at a distance of two miles,* say, *from the
centre of a sphere one mile in diameter,* etc. And each
will have the relational characteristic (if you want to call
it that) of *being in the same place as itself.* The two are
alike in this respect as in all others.

A. But look here. Each sphere occupies a different
place; and this at least will distinguish them from one another.

B. This sounds as if you thought the places had some
independent existence, though I don't suppose you really
think so. To say the spheres are in "different places" is
just to say that there is a distance between the two spheres;
and we have already seen that will not serve to distinguish

them. Each is at a distance—indeed the same distance—from the other.

A. When I said they were at different places I didn't mean simply that they were at a distance from one another. That one sphere is in a certain place does not entail the existence of any *other* sphere. So to say that one sphere is in its place, and the other in its place, and then to add that these places are different seems to me different from saying the spheres are at a distance from one another.

B. What does it mean to say "a sphere is in its place"? Nothing at all, so far as I can see. Where else could it be? *All* you are saying is that the spheres are in different places.

A. Then my retort is, What does it mean to say "Two spheres are in different places"? Or, as you so neatly put it, "Where else could they be?"

B. You have a point. What I should have said was that your assertion that the spheres occupied different places said nothing at all, unless you were drawing attention to the necessary truth that different physical objects must be in different places. Now if two spheres must be in different places, as indeed they must, to say that the spheres occupy different places is to say no more than they are two spheres.

A. This is like a point you made before. You won't allow me to deduce anything from the supposition that there are two spheres.

B. Let me put it another way. In the two-sphere universe, the only reason for saying that the places occupied were different would be that different things occupied them. So in order to show the places were different you would first have to show, in some other way, that the spheres were different. You will never be able to distinguish the spheres by means of the places they occupy.

A. A minute ago, you were willing to allow that somebody might give your spheres different names. Will you let me suppose that some traveller has visited your monotonous "universe" and has named one sphere "Castor" and the other "Pollux"?

B. All right—provided you don't try to use those names yourself.

A. Wouldn't the traveller, at least, have to recognise that *being at a distance of two miles from Castor* was not the same property as being at a distance of two miles *from Pollux?*

B. I don't see why. If he were to see that Castor and Pollux had exactly the same properties, he would see that "being at a distance of two miles from Castor" meant exactly the same as "being at a distance of two miles from Pollux".

A. They couldn't mean the same. If they did, *"being at a distance of two miles from Castor and at the same time not being at a distance of two miles from Pollux"* would be a self-contradictory description. But plenty of bodies could answer to this description. Again if the two expressions meant the same, anything which was two miles from Castor would have to be two miles from Pollux— which is clearly false. So the two expressions don't mean the same and the two spheres have at least two properties not in common.

B. Which?

A. *Being at a distance of two miles from Castor* and *being at a distance of two miles from Pollux.*

B. But now you are *using* the words "Castor" and "Pollux" as if they really stood for something. They are just our old friends *"a"* and *"b"* in disguise.

A. You surely don't want to say that the arrival of the name-giving traveller creates spatial properties? Perhaps we can't name your spheres and therefore can't name the corresponding properties; but the properties must be there.

B. What can this mean? The traveller has not visited the spheres, and the spheres have no names—neither "Castor", nor "Pollux", nor *"a"*, nor *"b"*, nor any others. Yet you still want to say they have certain properties which cannot be referred to without using names for the spheres. You want to say "the property of being at a distance from Castor" though it is logically impossible for you to talk in this way. You can't speak, but you won't be silent.

A. How eloquent, and how unconvincing! But since you

seem to have convinced yourself, at least, perhaps you can
explain another thing that bothers me: I don't see that you
have a right to talk as you do about places or spatial relations in connexion with your so-called "universe". So long
as we are talking about our own universe—*the* universe—I
know what you mean by "distance", "diameter", "place"
and so on. But in what you want to call a universe, even
though it contains only two objects, I don't see what such
words could mean. So far as I can see, you are applying
these spatial terms in their present usage to a hypothetical
situation which contradicts the presuppositions of that
usage.

B. What do you mean by "presupposition"?

A. Well, you spoke of measured distances, for one
thing. Now this presupposes some means of measurement.
Hence your "universe" must contain at least a third thing—
a ruler or some other measuring device.

B. Are you claiming that a universe must have at least
three things in it? What is the least number of things required to make a world?

A. No, all I am saying is that you cannot describe a configuration as *spatial* unless it includes at least three objects.
This is part of the meaning of "spatial"—and it is no more
mysterious than saying you can't have a game of chess without there existing at least thirty-five things (thirty-two
pieces, a chessboard, and two players).

B. If this is all that bothers you, I can easily provide for
three or any number of things without changing the force
of my counter-example. The important thing, for my
purpose, was that the configuration of two spheres was symmetrical. So long as we preserve this feature of the imaginary universe, we can now allow any number of objects to
be found in it.

A. You mean any *even* number of objects.

B. Quite right. Why not imagine a plane running clear
through space, with everything that happens on one side of
it always exactly duplicated at an equal distance in the
other side.

A. A kind of cosmic mirror producing real images.

B. Yes, except that there wouldn't be any mirror! The

point is that in *this* world we can imagine any degree of complexity and change to occur. No reason to exclude rulers, compasses, and weighing machines. No reason, for that matter, why the Battle of Waterloo shouldn't happen.

A. Twice over, you mean—with Napoleon surrendering later in two different places simultaneously!

B. Provided you wanted to call both of them "Napoleon".

A. So your point is that everything could be duplicated on the other side of the non-existent Looking Glass. I suppose whenever a man got married, his identical twin would be marrying the identical twin of the first man's fiancée?

B. Exactly.

A. Except that "identical twins" wouldn't be *numerically* identical?

B. You seem to be agreeing with me.

A. Far from it. This is just a piece of gratuitous metaphysics. If the inhabitants of your world had enough sense to know what was sense and what wasn't, they would never suppose all the events in their world were duplicated. It would be much more sensible for them to regard the "second" Napoleon as a mere mirror image—and similarly for all the other supposed "duplicates".

B. But they could walk through the "mirror" and find water just as wet, sugar just as sweet, and grass just as green on the other side.

A. You don't understand me. They would not postulate "another side". A man looking at the "mirror" would be seeing *himself,* not a duplicate. If he walked in a straight line toward the "mirror" he would eventually find himself back at his starting point, not at a duplicate of his starting point. This would involve their having a different geometry from ours—but that would be preferable to the logician's nightmare of the reduplicated universe.

B. They might think so—until the twins really began to behave differently for the first time!

A. Now it's you who are tinkering with your supposition. You can't have your universe and change it too.

B. All right, I retract.

A. The more I think about your "universe" the queerer it seems. What would happen when a man crossed your invisible "mirror"? While he was actually crossing, his body would have to change shape, in order to preserve the symmetry. Would it gradually shrink to nothing and then expand again?

B. I confess I hadn't thought of that.

A. And here is something that explodes the whole notion. Would you say that one of the two Napoleons in your universe had his heart in the right place—literally, I mean?

B. Why, of course.

A. In that case his "mirror-image" twin would have the heart on the opposite side of the body. One Napoleon would have his heart on the left of his body, and the other would have it on the right of his body.

B. It's a good point, though it would still make objects like spheres indistinguishable. But let me try again. Let me abandon the original idea of a *plane* of symmetry and to suppose instead that we have only a *centre* of symmetry. I mean that everything that happened at any place would be exactly duplicated at a place an equal distance on the opposite side of the centre of symmetry. In short, the universe would be what the mathematicians call "radially symmetrical". And to avoid complications we could suppose that the centre of symmetry itself was physically inaccessible, so that it would be impossible for any material body to pass through it. Now in *this* universe, identical twins would have to be either both right-handed or both left-handed.

A. Your universes are beginning to be as plentiful as blackberries. You are too ingenuous to see the force of my argument about verifiability. Can't you see that your supposed description of a universe in which everything has its "identical twin" doesn't describe anything verifiably different from a corresponding universe without such duplication? This must be so, no matter what kind of symmetry your universe manifested.

B. You are assuming that in order to verify that there are two things of a certain kind, it must be possible to show that one has a property not possessed by the other. But this is not so. A pair of very close but similar magnetic poles produce a characteristic field of force which assures me that there are two poles, even if I have no way of examining them separately. The presence of two exactly similar stars at a great distance might be detected by some resultant gravitational effect or by optical interference—or in some such similar way—even though we had no way of inspecting one in isolation from the other. Don't physicists say something like this about the electrons inside an atom? We can verify *that* there are two, that is to say a certain property of the whole configuration, even though there is no way of detecting any character that uniquely characterises any element of the configuration.

A. But if you were to approach your two stars one would have to be on your left and one on the right. And this would distinguish them.

B. I agree. Why shouldn't we say that the two stars are distinguishable—meaning that it would be possible for an observer to see one on his left and the other on his right, or more generally, that it would be *possible* for one star to come to have a relation to a third object that the second star would not have to that third object.

A. So you agree with me after all.

B. Not if you mean that the two stars do not have all their properties in common. All I said was that it was logically possible for them to enter into different relationships with a third object. But this would be a change in the universe.

A. If you are right, nothing unobserved would be observable. For the presence of an observer would always change it, and the observation would always be an observation of something else.

B. I don't say that every observation changes what is observed. My point is that there isn't any *being to the right* or *being to the left* in the two-sphere universe until an observer is introduced, that is to say until a real change is made.

A. But the spheres themselves wouldn't have changed.

B. Indeed they would: they would have acquired new relational characteristics. In the absence of any asymmetric observer, I repeat, the spheres would have all their properties in common (including, if you like, the power to enter into different relations with other objects). Hence the principle of Identity of Indiscernibles is false.

A. So perhaps you really do have twenty hands after all?

B. Not a bit of it. Nothing that I have said prevents me from holding that we can verify *that* there are exactly two. But we could know *that* two things existed without there being any way to distinguish one from the other. The Principle is false.

A. I am not surprised that you ended in this way, since you assumed it in the description of your fantastic "universe". Of course, if you began by assuming that the spheres were numerically different though qualitatively alike, you could end by "proving" what you first assumed.

B. But I wasn't "proving" anything. I tried to support my contention that it is logically possible for two things to have all their properties in common by giving an illustrative description. (Similarly, if I had to show it is logically possible for nothing at all to be seen I would ask you to imagine a universe in which everybody was blind.) It was for you to show that my description concealed some hidden contradiction. And you haven't done so.

A. All the same I am not convinced.

B. Well, then, you ought to be.

THE IDENTITY OF INDISCERNIBLES

A. J. Ayer

The principle of the identity of indiscernibles would
seem, in the forms in which it is usually stated, to be at
best contingently true. It does not appear that even Leibniz
held it to be logically inconceivable that different things
should have all their properties in common. That 'no substances are completely similar, or differ *solo numero*'[1] was
established, in his view, by the principle of sufficient reason, but he conceded that 'the supposition of two indiscernibles seems to be possible in abstract terms'.[2] Indeed,
it may plausibly be argued that even to ask whether things
can be different without being discernible from one another is to admit that it is logically possible. For what sense
could there be either in affirming or in denying that two
things could have all their properties in common unless
they were already distinguished? As Russell put it, 'it is a
sheer logical error to suppose that, if there were an ultimate distinction between subjects and predicates, subjects
could be distinguished by differences of predicates. For
before two subjects can differ as to predicates, they must
already be two; and thus the immediate diversity is prior
to that obtained from diversity of predicates. Again, two
terms cannot be distinguished in the first instance by dif-

From A. J. Ayer, *Philosophical Essays* (1954). Reprinted by permission of the author, St. Martin's Press, Macmillan and Co., Ltd.,
and Macmillan and Co., Canada, Ltd.

[1] C. J. Gerhardt, *Die philosopischen Schriften von G. W. Leibniz*,
vol. iv, p. 433.
[2] Leibniz, fifth letter to Clarke, quoted by Bertrand Russell, *The
Philosophy of Leibniz*, p. 55.

ference of relation to other terms; for difference of relation presupposes two distinct terms, and cannot therefore be the ground of their distinctness.'[3] It is true that Russell himself is prepared to disregard this argument, no doubt because he does not assume that there is any ultimate distinction between subjects and predicates; for his own definition of identity is that x and y are identical if and only if x satisfies just those predicative functions that are satisfied by y.[4] But for this he is taken to task by Wittgenstein. 'Russell's definition of "=" won't do; because according to it one cannot say that two objects have all their properties in common. (Even if this proposition is never true, it is nevertheless significant)';[5] and in saying that this proposition is at least significant Wittgenstein means also to imply that it is not self-contradictory.

But if it is to be admitted from the outset that the principle of the identity of indiscernibles can be denied without self-contradiction, then surely it is divested of any philosophical interest. No doubt the discovery, if it could be made, that there actually were different objects which were mutually indiscernible, would come as a surprise; but so long as the bounds of logical possibility are respected, it is not for the philosopher to set any limit to the marvels of nature. Philosophically, the grounds for a denial of existence are always *a priori*. The proof that nothing does answer to a given description is that nothing could, and the proof of this is that the description in question is meaningless or self-contradictory. I propose, therefore, regardless of what Leibniz may originally have meant in affirming the identity of indiscernibles, to treat the principle as a candidate only for necessary truth. What we have to consider is not whether there actually are 'in nature two indiscernible real absolute beings'[6] but whether it makes sense to say that there are. And for this purpose we need to reformulate the principle, in such a way that it does not itself appear to make the purely numerical

---

[3] Bertrand Russell, *The Principles of Mathematics*, p. 452.
[4] Russell and Whitehead, *Principia Mathematica*, vol. i, p. 168.
[5] L. Wittgenstein, *Tractatus Logico-Philosophicus*, s. 4302.
[6] Gerhardt, *op. cit.* vol. vii, p. 393.

distinction between objects which it declares to be impossible.

The defect of the usual formulations is, as Russell saw, that they already imply the distinction between subjects and predicates. The question whether indiscernibles are necessarily identical is made to look as if it were a question about the capacities of substances. Is it, or is it not, within the power of different things to achieve an entire community of properties? But this way of putting it makes there appear to be no problem. The philosopher who wishes to maintain that things which are not discernible from one another must be identical is represented as saying that he is unable to distinguish what he has already recognized to be distinct. It is easy enough, however, to see what his difficulty is. He doubts whether there can be any sense in talking of a plurality of objects unless it is a way of talking about differences of properties. Accordingly, if justice is to be done to his position, the question must be rephrased as a question about predicates. *What are the conditions which a set of predicates must satisfy for it to count as descriptive of a single individual?* Since the criteria for the identity of different individuals are of various sorts, there is no simple answer to this question; but it is not here required that we should examine it in detail. It is enough that we propound a rule which has the principle of the identity of indiscernibles as a logical consequence. Thus, it may be suggested that it is a necessary, though not indeed a sufficient, condition for any two sets of predicates to apply to different things either that one set should contain at least one member which is not a member of the other, or that there should be at least one further predicate which is co-instantiated with one set but not with the other. If this rule is valid, the principle of the identity of indiscernibles becomes analytic; for it will then be necessarily true that there is no difference between things that cannot be represented as a difference between properties.

At this point, however, some indication must be given as to what is, or at any rate what is not, to be counted as a predicate. For if no restriction is placed upon the type of predicate to be admitted, our rule very easily becomes trivial. Thus if A is allowed to have the property of being identical with itself, it is clear that there will be at least one predicate which will not be included in any set of predicates applying to something other than A, namely the predicate of being identical with A. Under these conditions, if A and B are different there can be no doubt that they are discernible; for even if they share all their other properties, A alone of the two will be different from B and identical with A, while B alone will be different from A and identical with B. To avoid such trivialities it is not sufficient, and indeed not even necessary, to make the ruling that 'identity' and 'difference' are not genuine predicates. Neither is it necessary to exclude such relational predicates as 'being spatially co-extensive with' or 'being at no distance from'. Any qualitative or relational predicate may be admitted, provided that it has a descriptive meaning. It is, however, essential that its meaning be purely descriptive. The objection, in this context, to such an expression as 'being identical with A' is not that it mentions the dubious relation of identity but that it contains the name 'A'. If 'A' were replaced by an indefinite description the objection would fall. The principle which here comes into play is that descriptions are essentially general; to describe anything is to attribute to it a property of a certain sort, a property which is capable, in theory, of being manifested in any number of different contexts, whether or not it is so manifested in fact. And the corollary of this is that a description may contain no reference to any object which is not itself described in this indefinite way. Consequently, an expression is, for our present purposes, to be accounted fully predicative only if all the demonstrative or individuating elements that it may contain are replaced by indefinite descriptions. And when it is claimed that objects can be differentiated only through their properties, or rather, that to speak of different objects can only be a way of speaking of different sets of properties, the only expressions that are to be regarded as designating properties are those that are fully predicative in this sense.

When it is interpreted in this way, the principle of the identity of indiscernibles is still necessarily true, if

it is true at all; but this is not to say that its truth is by any
means obvious. The motives for holding it to be true are
the same as those that have led philosophers to adopt, in
one form or another, the view that things are only 'bundles of qualities'. It is thought that to describe the character of any thing is to list the functions which it satisfies;
these functions may themselves contain references to other
things, but these things in their turn can be described only
by listing the functions which they satisfy. The demand
that all such descriptions be made fully explicit leads, as
we have seen, to their being rendered wholly general. It
may in fact be the case that a given function is satisfied
by only one individual, or indeed that it is satisfied by none,
but provided that it is logically capable of being satisfied
at all, there can be nothing in the nature of the function
to limit the number of individuals, or sets of individuals,
which satisfy it. That a predicate is uniquely instantiated
is always a contingent, never a necessary, fact. In our
ordinary way of speaking, we do indeed appear to distinguish between functions and the individuals which satisfy
them, between properties and the things which they characterize. But this appearance, so it is argued, is fallacious.
For if we are asked what the thing is that has the properties in question, the only informative answer that we
can give is to enumerate further properties. What remains
undescribed is the thing itself, the substance, the 'unknown
somewhat' in which the properties adhere. But this, it is
maintained, is a metaphysical invention. And if it is a metaphysical invention, then it seems to follow that things can
be differentiated only through their properties. And this,
on the interpretation that we have given, is just another
way of saying that things are different only to the extent
that they are discernible from one another.

I confess that I am sympathetic to this argument, and
therefore I am inclined to accept the principle of the
identity of indiscernibles, not merely in some trivial sense
but in the controversial form in which we have stated it.
My difficulty is that it seems possible to devise counterexamples to it. Thus, Professor Max Black, in an interesting
paper which he has devoted to this problem, invites us to

imagine a 'radially symmetrical' universe in which 'everything that happened at any place would be exactly duplicated at a place an equal distance on the opposite side of
the centre of symmetry'.[7] In such a universe every object
would have its exact counterpart 'through the looking-glass'
and every function that was satisfied by either would be
satisfied by the other. They would be numerically different,
but also, in our sense, indiscernible. In terms of indefinite
descriptions there would be no way of differentiating them.
Consequently, if such a universe is even imaginable, the
principle of the identity of indiscernibles is false. A simpler example is that of an infinite series of sounds . . .
$A \ B \ C \ D \ A \ B \ C \ D \ A$ . . . , succeeding one another at
equal intervals, with no first or last term. It is assumed that
there is no qualitative difference between any two As;
neither do they differ in their relational properties, for each
is preceded and succeeded by the same number of $B \ C \ D$s,
at the same intervals and in the same order. If there is any
sense at all in speaking of a plurality of As in such a
case, it would seem to follow that there is also sense in
saying that they differ only numerically. It is, indeed, hard
to conceive of a universe consisting only of such a series
of sounds; some might say that it was impossible. But it
does at least appear that we can describe such a series
without referring to, or in any way implying, the existence
of anything outside it; and this is all that the argument
requires.

A possible way to meet it would be to maintain that
such examples seem intelligible to us only because we
tacitly introduce into them some further feature by reference to which we do in fact discern between the objects
which we are supposing to be indiscernible. Thus, it
might be argued that if we are able to imagine Professor
Black's radially symmetrical universe, it is because we
surreptitiously bring into the picture a point of observation
with respect to which the two halves of the universe are
differently situated. In the case of the uniform succession
of sounds, it might be held that we are able to think of

[7] Max Black, 'The Identity of Indiscernibles', *Mind*, vol. lxi, no.
242, p. 161 [p. 208 in this anthology].

them, in default of any other distinction, as being separated in time, only because we envisage some other sequence of events as being correlated with them. But then it is required that this second series of events should not itself be cyclical. Suppose, for example, that the sounds were correlated with a stop-watch, marking only intervals of seconds, and that they succeeded one another at fifteen-second intervals, as defined by the movements of the hand around the dial of the watch. In that case, provided that the events consisting in the coincidences of the hand with figures on the dial themselves formed an infinite series with no first or last term, the sounds whose quality was the same would still be indiscernible from one another. Every *A* would be simultaneous with the hand's coinciding with the figure 60, and each of them would be preceded by a *D* which was simultaneous with the hand's coinciding with the figure 45, and succeeded by a *B* which was simultaneous with the hand's coinciding with the figure 15. It is only by bringing in some event, or pattern of events, which is not uniformly repeated that we can secure the discernibility that we are seeking. And I suppose it can be argued that this is what one always does when one constructs such examples, even though one may not be aware of it. On the other hand, it is certainly not obvious that the conception of a completely cyclical universe, however constituted, with no beginning or end in time, must be self-contradictory or meaningless. There would, of course, be no way of describing any one turn of the cycle so as to distinguish it from any other, but this, it may well be said, is no objection to their actually being, or even to their being thought to be, distinct.

It is, however, to be noticed that in framing such examples a use is freely made of the distinction between subjects and predicates. It is assumed, for instance, that one is entitled to refer to a plurality of sounds in order then to raise the question whether they are all discernible from one another. And this being so it is not surprising that these examples should appear to refute the principle of the identity of indiscernibles; for thereby, as we saw at the outset, they simply take for granted what it is intended to deny. But it is just here, it may be argued, that the mistake arises. Being accustomed to speak of objects in the plural without further qualification, we come to think that this alone is enough to differentiate them. We are led to treat numerical difference as a relation among others, which may obtain independently of anything else. But this, the argument continues, is an illegitimate extension of the concept of number. It is only where there is discernibility that it makes any sense to talk of a plurality of objects. In a wholly predicative language these fanciful universes, in which things are supposed to differ only numerically, could not even be described.

Although I attach some weight to this argument, I admit that I do not find it altogether convincing. At the same time I am somewhat disturbed by what appear to me to be the consequences of rejecting it. It may be that I am unduly suspicious of the category of substance, but I still cannot see how asserting that an individual exists can be to assert anything more than that some predicate, or set of predicates, is instantiated. No doubt there are many philosophers for whom this question presents no difficulty; but I am not of their number. And the proof of this is that, in spite of all that can be urged against it, I am still inclined to hold that the principle of the identity of indiscernibles is necessarily true.

THE IDENTITY OF INDISCERNIBLES

D. J. O'Connor

I shall assume in this paper that the principle of the Identity of Indiscernibles is a necessary proposition to the effect that it is impossible for two or more distinct individuals to possess all their properties in common. By an individual, I shall mean any entity that possesses qualities (including relational properties) and is not itself an instance of either a quality or a relation. (This is substantially McTaggart's definition of a substance.[1]) As I have stated it, the principle is, as we shall see, pretty vague. But it may avoid needless ambiguity if we postulate that it is a necessary principle. Leibniz, for example, does not make it quite clear whether the principle is a necessary one or not. He offers proofs that seem appropriate to a necessary statement but, on the other hand, he cites empirical evidence in its favour.

However, I wish for the present to leave open the question whether the necessary character of the Identity of Indiscernibles entails that it is merely analytic. One reason for this is that we have now to ask what we are to understand by the term "property" and its synonyms "quality", "attribute" and so on. There are some senses of these words in which the principle is manifestly true but equally manifestly trivial. If it is to be worth discussing at all, we have to construe it in a sense that is not patently tautologous. Unfortunately, there is no obvious

From *Analysis*, Vol. XVI (1954). Reprinted by permission of the author, the editor of *Analysis*, and Basil Blackwell and Mott, Ltd.
[1] *The Nature of Existence*, p. 67.

way of guaranteeing such a non-trivial construction by a simple qualification of the statement I have given above. For example, it is very difficult, as we shall see, to find a definition of "property" that will not beg the question one way or the other before we start to discuss the principle at all. There are indeed some obvious examples of "properties" that will trivialise the Identity of Indiscernibles at once. Let us suppose, for instance, that there are two individuals, A and B, and postulate that they possess all their properties in common. That is to say, let us suppose that if any property P is a property of A, it is also a property of B. Then if we interpret the word "property" in a very wide sense, it is plain that our supposition is self-refuting. For A must have at least the property of not being B and conversely B has the property of not being A. But this consequence follows from the mere fact that we are talking about two distinct individuals. In other words, it is an analytic statement that if A is other than B, then it is other-than-B. Thus we must restrict our interpretation of the term "property" to exclude identity and difference if we are to make the Identity of Indiscernibles interesting and philosophically significant. We may state this restriction more generally by adopting McTaggart's rejection of any interpretation of the principle that makes its truth follow analytically from the fact that it applies only to sets of two or more individuals.

But this does not remove the difficulty. For we can still ask: what sort of properties do we have to exclude from the purview of the principle in order to make sure of this? Some of them are obvious enough; but some of them are more elusive and others are borderline cases. And we may find that in putting these doubtful cases on one or other side of the borderline, we are not *proving* or *disproving* the maxim at all but are merely making it analytic or self-contradictory by edict. If we do this, we frustrate our purpose by depriving the Identity of Indiscernibles of any philosophical interest.

Let us start with an argument that looks plausible enough. If we list the properties belonging to a given individual A, we shall have a set of properties, $P_1, P_1 \ldots$.

P_{n}, which must be mutually compatible or *compossible*, to use Leibniz's word. *If they were not, they clearly could* not all be predicated truly of A. Now if we take these properties one by one, it seems plain that not only *may* each of them qualify more than one individual but it is essential to their nature as properties that they should be capable of doing this. There might, for example, be only one red thing in the whole universe. Nevertheless, we commonly suppose that it would still be inherent in the nature of the quality "red" that it should be *capable of* qualifying an indefinite number of individuals.

Thus we can say two things:

(i) if we suppose that every member of a given set of properties S is compatible with every other member, taken singly or collectively, we may conclude that if any individual A can have any property P_n in S, it can also have P_{n+1}.

(ii) if a property P_n can characterise any individual A, then it can also characterise any other individual B.

And from these two statements it would seem to follow recursively that if any individual A can have *any* set of compossible properties then any other individual B can have *the same set* of properties. And this is contrary to the maxim of the Identity of Indiscernibles. For this maxim asserts that to give a complete description of an entity is to *individuate* that entity.

This will perhaps make it clear how extraordinary a claim is made by the principle under consideration. The supporters of the principle do not openly deny that any simple property must be of such a nature as to be capable of qualifying an indefinite number of individuals. But they assert nevertheless that there is always one property that is unique in every individual in the sense that the compound property consisting of *the conjunction of all the attributes* that qualify a given individual must be uniquely instantiated. The point of such a claim must either be that the totality of properties that qualify an individual has some emergent characteristic of uniqueness or that in any given totality of properties, all of which are co-instantiated, there must always be one special property of this unique kind. However, the first alternative seems to be a quite ungrounded assumption which amounts to no more than a reassertion in a disguised form of the maxim under dispute. But the second alternative has some plausibility because there do seem to be some characteristics that possess such an individuating function.

Suppose that I have on the table before me two spheres of pure silver that are identical in size, colour and every other empirical attribute (other than relational properties). I can, of course, still tell them apart because they occupy different places at the same instant and can only occupy the same place at different instants. I can identify the places that they occupy by assigning coordinates in an arbitrarily selected system of axes. For example, sphere A is at x_1, y_1, z_1 at t_1 while sphere B is at, say, x_1, y_2, z_3 at t_1. Now are we to say that "having the coordinate set (x_1, y_1, z_1, t_1)" is a *property* of A? If we do so, then clearly the principle of the Identity of Indiscernibles is true for any individuals that can be identified by their spatio-temporal characteristics. It will still remain an open question if it applies to *all* individuals, since not all individuals are obviously spatio-temporal existents.

What will be the consequence of saying that "having the coordinate set (x_1, y_1, z_1, t_1)" is a property? There is one very important and striking consequence, namely, that some properties are intrinsically incapable of being shared by more than one individual. But if this is so, why do we call them "properties" at all? Might we not more appropriately call them by some such title as "principles of individuation"? For it is commonly taken to be a defining characteristic of a property that it is capable of qualifying an indefinite number of individuals and to be indifferent to the spatio-temporal occasions of its instantiation. Do we not need convincing reasons for extending the range of application of a term in this way? And must we not enquire carefully into the consequences of such an extension? In this position, there are various expedients open to us. If *we wish to maintain the truth of the Identity of Indiscernibles*, we can look for other examples of compound properties that cannot be shared by more than one entity even though the simple attributes of which such compounds are made up *are* thus multiply predicable. Or we might even look for simple properties that are capable only of unique instantiation. Thus it looks as though we cannot answer the question of the truth of the Identity of Indiscernibles until we have first answered the much wider question: what is it to be a property? Thus the justification of the Identity of Indiscernibles is really a matter of justifying linguistic categories.

Let us look at these allegedly unique spatio-temporal attributes. It is clear that they are compounds of four simpler properties, three spatial and one temporal, each of which can qualify an indefinite number of individuals. By saying that they are *compounds* of four such properties, I mean merely that an instance of such an allegedly unique property is a co-instantiation of four simpler properties. Such simpler properties can of course, be co-instantiated in more than one individual provided that they are taken in groups of less than four. It is only if we assign all four coordinates to a single object that we individuate it, or, to put it the other way round, it is only in a unique individual that we find compound properties of the type "possessing the coordinates (x_r, y_n, z_n, t_n)" instantiated. Now what sort of a statement is this? It is important how we answer this question because the plausibility of the maxim that we are considering depends largely upon examples of this kind.

If we say that it is a necessary proposition that two or more material objects cannot have the same coordinate description, then we rest the necessary truth of the Identity of Indiscernibles on the alleged necessity of the proposition embodying the definition of the phrase "one and the same material object". But to do this is to do the very thing that we have already ruled out of consideration, on the ground that it trivialises the principle. That is to say, we make the truth of the Identity of Indiscernibles follow analytically from the definition of "one and the same material object". But might we not say that the principle was necessary, for all that, because it was entailed by a necessary proposition, namely, the proposition that expresses the truth conveyed by this definition? For it might be asserted that the definition is not merely arbitrary but is based on a necessary truth about the world. We could say this for what it is worth. But in any case it can be argued that the proposition that two physical objects cannot exist in the same place at the same time is *not* a necessary proposition but a definition that is convenient only because it is based on empirical facts.

Let us suppose a world in which certain types of material objects, say, billiard balls, did not repel each other upon impact but first merged and then separated to continue on their original paths. Looking at such a material body, we could never be sure whether it was indeed one body or two or perhaps many more.[2] Or again suppose a world in which certain sorts of material bodies had the power of dividing like paramecia and then merging again. We should never know without prolonged observation of such a set of bodies how many of them there were and even then our estimate would be merely a statistical one. In such circumstances, we should probably never ask the question "how many"? unless it was suitably qualified to "how many at this instant?" or "how many on the average over a period of an hour?" In any case, we should never, in such worlds as these, apply the allegedly necessary rules "two or more bodies cannot occupy the same place at the same time" or "a single body cannot occupy different places at the same time". Let us call these propositions P and Q for short. The wording of P and Q is unfortunate in that it suggests that we have tests for sameness and difference of times and places that we do not have for bodies. But to say, for example, "one and the same body cannot have incompatible coordinate measurements" raises the same problem. (What would be the force of 'incompatible' here?) In so far as we did admit such tests for sameness and difference of times and places, our willingness to do so would be a sign that we had shifted the locus of our problem from the nature of material bodies to the nature of space and time. The point I wish to make is this: we should never, in the imaginary worlds postulated above, come to apply

[2] Cf. Max Black, *Mind*, 1952, pp. 155–56 [pp. 212–14 in this anthology].

rules like P and Q because the facts would not support them. (Perhaps it was something like this that J. S. Mill had vaguely in mind when he suggested that the truths of arithmetic were merely very well founded empirical generalisations). Thus it might well be argued that the supposedly necessary propositions P and Q from which the Identity of Indiscernibles might be deduced are after all empirical, though canonised by long usage and convenience into definitions.

It was suggested by Professor Broad[3] that many people have believed in the Identity of Indiscernibles because they have also believed that there is only one spatio-temporal system in which every particular must have its own place and date. And he adds that this is not necessarily true even if it is true at all. But the supporter of the principle could very well admit Broad's contention and still hold that the principle was true. For suppose that A had the property of possessing coordinate measurements x_1, y_1, z_1, t_1 in system S_1 and B had the same coordinate measurements in system S_2. A and B would now be dissimilar in that one belonged to S_1 and the other to S_2. But if they did so, they could not strictly be compared in respect of spatio-temporal position. (This is, presumably, part of what is meant by saying that they belong to different spatio-temporal systems). Moreover, what could it mean to say that A had the *same* coordinate measurements in one system that B had in another?

It will be obvious from this very brief discussion of spatio-temporal predicates that the philosophical puzzles about space and time are another of the hidden sources of our difficulty in accepting or rejecting the Identity of Indiscernibles. My conclusions so far are very tentative and amount to the following suggestions:

(i) that the supporter of the Identity of Indiscernibles has to extend unwarrantably the denotation of words like "property", "attribute", "quality" and their synonyms by weakening their connotation in a crucial respect.

(ii) that the result of this extension is, after all, only to

[3] *Examination of McTaggart's Philosophy,* Vol. I, p. 176–77.

make the principle an analytic consequence of the allegedly necessary propositions P and Q.

(iii) that even if we waive objection (ii), it is arguable that P and Q are not necessary but merely well-grounded empirical generalisations that have hardened into definitions. In a world where objects behaved very differently, we would be prepared to abandon them. And no necessary conclusions can follow from premises that are not themselves necessary, unless such conclusions are mere analytic trivialities.

So far then, I have tried to suggest, though very tentatively, that the Principle of the Identity of Indiscernibles is not a necessary proposition with any philosophical importance. If it is necessary it is also trivial. And if it is more than trivial, there is good reason to believe that it is false. In this, it shows the characteristic behaviour of many metaphysical propositions. They work very often at two levels. At a superficial level, they are uninteresting and harmless because trivial. But at a deeper level, though interesting and full of consequences, they are usually also demonstrably untrue.

But there is something to be said on the other side as well. In order to bring this out, I shall conclude by summarising the basic differences between the supporters of the principle and its opponents. Its supporters want to interpret the term "property" widely enough to include relational properties. And its opponents want to exclude at least some relational properties from the denotation of the word. For once we admit them, even if we reject such obviously question-begging properties as identity and difference, we are committed to properties that by their nature can be instantiated only uniquely. Admittedly, it is in part a question of language whether or not we exclude these contentious cases. But like most linguistic questions, it can be supported on both sides by empirical considerations.

There are three main reasons for wishing to reject the claim of relational properties to rank as properties. First, many such properties can, by their nature, qualify one object only. And this settles the question at once in favour of the Identity of Indiscernibles if we can show that every individual must possess at least one such property. Secondly, relational properties (unlike relations) involve a reference to individuals that is felt to prejudice the issue in favour of the principle. "To the left of" or "larger than" are relations. But the corresponding relational properties are *not* "being to the left of x" or "being larger than x" where "x" is an unspecified variable. They are, for example, "being to the left of this tree" or "being larger than the sun". And such properties obviously have a very strong individuating force. Lastly, it is felt that to stretch the denotation of "property" in this way is to drop from the connotation of the word the notion of a capacity for being possessed in common by several individuals. And this is felt to be an "essential" feature of the concept.

On the other hand, the supporters of the maxim also have good reasons for their semantic recommendations. In support of their proposal to extend the meaning of the word to include relational attributes, they can point out, first, that some relational properties, at least, cannot be distinguished from ordinary qualities. Adjectives like "large", "small", "quick", "loud", "useful" and so on stand for attributes that are essentially relational in character. They are elliptical ways of referring to certain relational properties of individuals. Yet it would clearly be absurd to deny them the status of properties. What other status could we accord them? Moreover, even if we take such prima facie non-relational qualities as "red", "sweet", "fragrant" and so on, we are at once talking of relational properties if we use these adjectives in their comparative and superlative forms. "A is sweeter than B" or "X is the most fragrant" are instances of the predication of relational attributes. (These superlatives might indeed be supposed to stand for *simple* qualities which can be instantiated uniquely, if at all.) Thus it might be alleged that the opponents of the principle of the Identity of Indiscernibles cannot solve their difficulty by excluding from the category of "property" *all* relational attributes. But if they exclude merely those that admit only unique instantiation, they are begging the question in their own favour.

Thus there seems to be no way of settling this issue

decisively so long as we refuse to discuss the much wider questions that arise from it. I have tried to indicate what some of these questions are—the nature of space and time, the nature of properties and relations, the principle of individuation, the antithesis between necessary and factual propositions and several others. We can settle the truth of the principle of the Identity of Indiscernibles, considered by itself as an isolated problem, only by taking somewhat arbitrary decisions on these difficult matters. That is to say, as is common in philosophical discussions, we can clarify the situation in our immediate vicinity by sweeping the difficulties out to the periphery. But sooner or later, these peripheral problems will become central in another context and we shall then find that our piecemeal methods of philosophising have shifted our difficulties from one place to another instead of solving them. And that is, I suppose, one justification of the philosophical system-building that is at present so unfashionable.

BARE PARTICULARS

Edwin B. Allaire

Consider "this is red," asserted truly of a colored disc. Some philosophers claim that the sentence refers to a fact consisting of two (kinds of) entities, an individual (bare particular) and a character (universal), referred to by "this" and "red," respectively. They claim further that the two entities stand in the exemplification relation, represented by "is." Currently, that claim is widely rejected. Underlying the many arguments supporting that rejection is a rather simple idea which Russell once expressed: "One is tempted to regard 'This is red' as a subject-predicate proposition, but if one does so, one finds that 'this' becomes a substance, an unknowable something in which predicates inhere. . . ."[1]

Though awkwardly expressed, Russell's point is clear: The individual-character analysis is at odds with the empirical tradition. That is, if one claims that "this is red" is a subject-predicate proposition *in the sense that "this" and "red" refer to unanalyzable entities of different ontological kinds,* then one has violated the Principle of Acquaintance (PA),[2] a basic tenet of empiricism. One is not acquainted with "a something" which could be construed as an entity of a kind different from red, except in

From *Philosophical Studies,* Vol. XVI (1963). Reprinted by permission of the author and the editor of *Philosophical Studies.*
[1] Bertrand Russell, *An Inquiry into Meaning and Truth* (London: Allen and Unwin, 1948), p. 97.
[2] The PA states that the indefinable terms of any "ontological" description must refer to entities with which one is directly acquainted. Furthermore, "an unanalyzable entity" is explicated to mean an entity represented by an indefinable term.

the sense that *this* is a "collection" of the same kind of things as red, e.g., square and bright. The heart of Russell's point is thus that the individuals of the individual-character analysis are unknowable in the sense that one is not directly acquainted with them.

I propose to explore whether or not one can propound the individual-character analysis without abandoning the PA. In particular, I want to discuss Bergmann's assertion that "being acquainted with a red spot, and nothing else, one is presented not with just one thing but two, a particular . . . and a character. . . ." If I understand Bergmann, he is maintaining precisely what Russell denies, namely, that one is on such occasions acquainted with an individual or, as he prefers to call it, a particular. His motivation is clear. He attempts to reconcile the individual-character analysis with the PA.

Before discussing his attempt it will be helpful to examine the dialectics which give rise to the problem. I will do that by commenting briefly on two other analyses of the disc: (I) The disc is a collection of what has sometimes been called "perfect particulars." "This is red," asserted truly of our disc, is analyzed as follows: "This" refers to a collection of entities, one of which is referred to by "red." This latter entity is such that if there were two red discs, there would be two such entities (perfect particulars), each unanalyzable and numerically different from the other. (II) The disc is a collection of characters (universals). "This is red" is analyzed as in (I), except that the entities are such that if there were two red discs, the two collections would have one member in common, i.e., one member which is literally the same.

Each of these analyses encounters an immediate and, I believe, insurmountable objection. Consider two discs of the same (shade of) color, size, shape, and so on. The objection to (I) is that it *cannot account for the sameness* of the discs since the members of the two collections are all unanalyzable and different from each other. In other words, though both collections contain a member referred to by "red," (I) provides nothing they have in common since the members are unanalyzable as well as different.

The objection to (II) is that it *cannot account for the difference,* since each collection has literally the same members.[3]

The individual-character analysis encounters neither objection. That is its strength. The difference of the discs is accounted for by each containing a different individual; the sameness, by each containing literally the same characters (as in (II)). The individual-character analysis thus allows one to solve the problems of sameness and difference, at least as they arise in connection with "things." Speaking more traditionally, it provides a solution to the nominalism-realism issue.

Notice that a proponent of the individual-character analysis, or, as I shall henceforth call him, a realist, explicitly *grounds* (by means of entities) the sameness as well as the difference of the two discs. There must be entities to account for the discs being called the same or, less accurately, there must be a shared something in order to account for the same word ("red") being truly predicated of "this" and "that." The objection to (I) is in fact sometimes expressed as follows. Since the two red entities of the two collections are different and unanalyzable, there is no way of accounting for their being referred to by the same word ("red"). So expressed the objection is misleading. Moreover, it tempts a defender of (I) to appeal mistakenly to a variant of the meaning-is-use doctrine.

The demand for grounding sameness is at present suspect. The suspicion makes (I) seem attractive. Consider two discs of *different shades* of red. In ordinary language, "red" may be correctly used to refer to either. It appears that a realist, to be consistent, must also ground the sameness of the different shades. For, if he objects to (I) because it does not explain why the same word is used to refer to two "perfect particulars," he must take seriously the same objection in the case of "red" when applied to different shades. Moreover, since each shade is simple and unanalyzable, the ground (i.e., the shared entity) must be

[3] Cf. Gustav Bergmann, "Russell on Particulars," *Philosophical Review,* 56:59–72 (1947). Reprinted in *The Metaphysics of Logical Positivism* (London: Longmans, Green, 1954), pp. 197–214.

of a different kind. Thus, a third kind makes its appearance. For those of a Platonic stripe, this third is a "transcendent universal or concept."[4] Each shade is red by virtue of *participating* in the same transcendent universal, which is the proper referent of "red." Hence, either the PA cannot be maintained or we must be acquainted with ("intuit") concepts. The second alternative has been unacceptable to those who embrace the PA.

The realist thus seems doomed to Platonism. The proponent of (I) who denies the need for grounding sameness does not. This seeming advantage has had its effects. Recently, it has been argued that the root of Platonism is the mistaken way in which we sometimes look at language. In particular, the very attempt to ground sameness reveals the mistaken belief that there must be a referent to justify the use of a word. Not even the "referring use" of a word requires a referent, or so it is argued. What holds in general holds for "red." Hence, its use in referring to different shades need not be grounded. Thus, we are told, "the sameness of the shades" merely means that they are referred to by the same word. Moreover, it is claimed, even in the case of things of the same shade each exemplification of it is really different and unanalyzable. In other words, their sameness also consists merely in their being referred to by the same word.[5]

A defender of (I) may thus attempt to dispose of the objection that he cannot account for the sameness of "things" by arguing that the very attempt to account for it is mistaken. The attempt, he holds, inevitably leads to Platonism with all its horrors of transcendent entities. That shows why the use doctrine may be attractive to a defender of (I).

Consider again two discs of the same (shade of) color, size, shape, and so on. Suppose they are shown to you, one to the left of the other. If after a while you are shown them again, you will not be able to tell which is which. In

---

[4] For a discussion of concepts, see Reinhardt Grossman, "Conceptualism," *Review of Metaphysics*, 14:243–54 (December 1960).
[5] This explication of sameness may well explicate the *flatus vocis* doctrine of some medievals.

fact, you will not be able to tell whether the two you now see are the two you saw earlier. You can only tell that the two you now see have all the properties that the two you saw earlier had. In other words, taken as such and in themselves, two perfect particulars of the same shade cannot be told apart. That means that in this case at least the sameness is grounded. We know how the realist grounds it. It remains to be shown that he need not therefore ground the sameness of different shades in order to justify the use of "red" for any of them.

My realist takes advantage of what the use doctrine has taught us, namely, (a) that from the fact that the same word is used to refer to two things it does not *always* follow that the two share an entity. (Indeed, we cannot decide to use just one word to refer to green and red.) On the other hand, it does not follow (b) that they never do. The proponents of (I) rashly infer (b) from (a). Their rashness, I have argued, may be due to their mistaken belief that even (b) commits one to Platonism. Some things, our two discs for example, are the same shade of color. This is not a linguistic fact; i.e., not merely the fact that they are referred to by the same word. They are the same in that they are indistinguishable as such, or, more precisely, one cannot differentiate them by their color alone.

Let us take stock. The problem of analyzing such things as colored discs arises in the context of the realism-nominalism issue. That issue, we saw, cannot really be handled by accounting for the sameness in the discs in terms of the sameness of words. At some point sameness must be grounded in entities. To believe otherwise is to put upon the meaning-is-use doctrine a burden greater than it can bear. Thus, in our case, it remains the first task of analysis to single out the unanalyzable entities which account for the difference and the sameness of the two discs. The second task or step, as in all cases, is to employ the result obtained in the first step to explicate certain philosophical uses of words, thereby dissolving the traditional dialectics. The realistic analysis provides the required grounding. Yet it is tainted. Like Russell, many philosophers claim that they are not acquainted with individuals. The heart of the matter is whether or not Bergmann's claim that one is in fact acquainted with individuals (bare particulars) is defensible or, even, whether it can be made intelligible.

An obvious objection is that the claim merely springs from the dialectical needs it satisfies and is not borne out by careful inspection of what is in fact presented. Indeed, Bergmann himself invites this objection. "I, of course, have convinced myself that I am actually presented with two things. Yet I am loath to rest the case on this conviction; for I am also convinced that a very major part of it is dialectical."[6]

One cannot but wonder how one does convince oneself of such matters. In the light of what he himself says, one is indeed tempted to conclude that his conviction is dialectical rather than phenomenological, if I may so express myself. If so, then he has abandoned the PA. Whether or not under the pressure of the dialectic he has actually done that is not my concern. The point is rather whether or not the "description" he proposes can be defended independently of the dialectics.

Phenomenological description is prompted by philosophical puzzles. One turns to the former as a prelude to the dissolution of the latter. The dangers are obvious. One may think that one still describes when in fact one already argues. That makes all alleged descriptions suspect. The best one can do is elaborate them in several ways, always on guard against the various biases that might creep in. Once a description has been accepted, the puzzles must be solved by speaking commonsensically about it. In the course of thus speaking about it, one may well be led to reconsider it. After all, it was prompted by the puzzles. Nevertheless, one must not and cannot give away the game by maintaining that the description is forced upon one by the dialectics. Bergmann in the quoted passage comes dangerously close to doing just that. The most one could say is that the dialectics directs our attention toward what

[6] Bergmann, "Strawson's Ontology," p. 616.

is presented. But it does not and cannot tell us what actually is presented.

A comparison may help to make the point clear. The later Wittgenstein, believing that the philosophical puzzles arise from the misuse of words, undertook to describe their correct use. The misuses are engendered by what he calls misleading grammatical analogies. Once these latter are recognized as such, the philosophical puzzles disappear. This is his basic idea. To speak as before, Wittgenstein's description of correct (and) incorrect use is the prelude to his solution of the philosophical puzzles. Are then his descriptions unbiased? There is no guarantee. Nor is it reasonable to demand one beforehand. Wittgenstein's description proceeds directly from what he considers a puzzle and thus indirectly from what he considers an illicit use. Thus, the dialectics may have influenced the description. But once more, the best one can do is guard against the biases that may have been introduced. So, too, with phenomenological description. In this regard all philosophers are in the same boat. They all start from what they consider unproblematical or, as it is sometimes put, from what they hold to be commonsensical. With respect to their starting point they must always be vigilant. One cannot do more; one must not do less.

I return to the issue: Can the realistic analysis be defended on phenomenological grounds? It will be well to distinguish between two uses of "know." First, there is the use of "know" in which to know something means to be acquainted with it. Second, there is the use in which to know means to be able to recognize it. In the second sense individuals as such or in themselves are unknowable. Consider again the two discs and the situation in which you are shown them twice. Since you can only tell that the two you now see have all the properties that the two you saw earlier had, it follows that if each consists of an individual and the several characters it exemplifies, the individuals as such or in themselves are not recognizable or, as I prefer to say, not reidentifiable. The characters are. To express the point differently, two individuals are merely numerically different, whereas two characters are intrinsically different as well.

Russell held that individuals are unknowable. A defender of the realistic analysis may take him to have held merely that they are not recognizable, i.e., that they cannot be known in the second sense of "know." This, though, is not at all what Russell meant. Rather, in saying that individuals are unknowable, he used "know" in the first sense. In turn, I hold with Bergmann that while they are indeed unknowable in the second sense, they are known in the first. Accordingly, I cannot get away with just maintaining that they are merely numerically different. I must show in what sense one is acquainted with them. Not to recognize this obligation would be to confuse again the two uses of "know." Nevertheless, in pointing out that individuals are not recognizable, i.e., are merely numerically different, one has arrived at the heart of the matter. *Individuals are just those entities which do ground the numerical difference of two things which are the same in all (nonrelational) respects.*

Consider once more the two discs. When presented together, they are presented as numerically different. That *difference* is presented as is their sameness with respect to shape, (shade of) color, and so on. What accounts for the difference is the numerically different individuals. No character or group of characters can do that. Thus, to say that there are individuals is to say that things may be merely numerically different. No matter what description one proposes, the numerical difference of two things which are alike in all (nonrelational) respects must be accounted for. Consider (II). To claim that both discs are but collections of literally the same universals does not account for the *thisness* and *thatness* which are implicitly referred to in speaking of them as *two* collections. That is, the two collections of characters—if one persists in speaking that way—are, as presented, numerically different. Clearly, therefore, something other than a character must also be presented. That something is what proponents of the realistic analysis call a bare particular. Or, perhaps better, that is their explication of "bare particular."

One difficulty remains. Bergmann claims that in being presented with one red spot one is presented with two things. That may be misleading. The most prevalent use of "two" carries a spatial connotation. That is, if there are two things then they are spatially related. Yet exemplification, the "relation" obtaining between a character and an individual, is obviously not spatial. Thus, the sense in which there are two things is merely the sense in which there are two characters (red and square) in the presentation of a red square. For red and square are not spatially related. Nor are an individual and the character or characters it exemplifies. If one should insist that the two characters are in fact spatially related, arguing that they are *at the same place,* I merely ask him what he means by "place." There is only one answer I can think of which would help. A place as such is itself an entity. But, then, this answer makes places into bare particulars. This piece of dialectics is well known. Consider again "this is red," asserted truly of a colored disc. To what does "this" refer? That it does refer to something is obvious. It does not always refer to the entity referred to by "red." That is, "is" in this utterance does not always stand for identity. Hence, "this" can only refer to one of two things: an individual or a collection of characters, one of which is red.[7] We know already that the latter alternative fails, for in the case of *two* collections of characters the members of which are the same, the numerical difference between the two collections is left unaccounted for. The realistic analysis does account for it. Moreover, two individuals are presented in the sense that the two collections are presented as numerically different. That is not to deny, though, that individuals are *merely* numerically different from each other and thus not reidentifiable as such. That they are explains why they have been overlooked so often.

I have argued that one can propound a realistic analysis without abandoning the PA. Moreover, one can single out the bare particulars without using "exist" philosophically, thus avoiding the dialectics of the nominalism-

[7] As I have shown, the "perfect-particular" analysis (i.e., (I)) is unacceptable because it does not account for sameness.

realism issue. In trying to do this, I described, or tried to describe, the sort of entity an individual is. Positively, individuals are the carriers of numerical difference as directly presented to us. Negatively, individuals are not rudimentary Aristotelian substances. Thus, they are not the sort of things Russell probably had in mind when he denied that they can be known. To the sort of thing he had in mind Locke's phrase "a something I know not what" does indeed apply. To what I mean by an individual, it does not. To one who accepts the PA, Locke's phrase provides sufficient ground for rejecting the entities he speaks of. The individuals I want to keep from being overlooked are not such entities. That is why one need not abandon the PA in order to maintain that we are presented with bare particulars.

PARTICULARS RE-CLOTHED

V. C. Chappell

In his paper "Bare Particulars" Allaire seeks to reconcile
what he calls the "individual-character analysis," or later
the "realistic analysis," of things like colored discs
with the Russellian "principle of acquaintance."[1] He
wants to show that these are not incompatible, presumably,
because he thinks that both are correct or true and ought
to be accepted by philosophers. It seems to me, however,
that both the individual-character analysis and the principle of acquaintance are mistaken at best. If so, the task
of reconciling them is no real problem for philosophers,
however interesting it might be as an academic exercise.

The individual-character analysis is evidently founded
on certain views about reference, or rather about what
Allaire calls reference, which is to say, broadly, about how
linguistic expressions apply or are applied to things. True
sentences refer (or are used to refer) to facts, demonstratives refer to characterless ("bare") particulars, adjectives
in the predicate position refer to universals. Allaire does
not defend these views in his paper, so I do not know just
how to take them. Taken literally, however, they seem to
me to be wrong, wrong about reference and wrong in
what they imply about facts, particulars, and universals.
Taken in some other way, they may be true but true by
definition, and not only can I see no reason for accepting the consequent definitions, I think there is good reason

From *Philosophical Studies*, Vol. XV (1964). Reprinted by permission of the author and the editor of *Philosophical Studies*.
[1] *Philosophical Studies*, 14:1–8 (1963) [pp. 235–44 in this an-
thology].

not to accept them, namely that they produce or invite confusion. An instance of such confusion shows, I think, in the considerations concerning sameness and difference which Allaire cites to support the individual-character analysis. It is a strength of this analysis, he claims, that it can "account" for the sameness and difference of things. In fact it is no strength but a foregone conclusion, for Allaire's conception of what is required to account for the sameness and difference of things is surely determined by this analysis, or by the views about "reference" which determine it. In any case, Allaire's conception of sameness and difference is very curious, to say the least. Among the views he seems to hold are that two things cannot be similar unless they have some numerically identical element in common, and that two things cannot be numerically different unless each has some unique element which it does not share with the other, both of which seem to me to be false. Allaire also holds that sameness, by which I think he here means similarity, must be "grounded in entities," i.e., cannot just be a matter of linguistic convention, except that it is just or mainly that in some cases. This is muddled if not plainly wrong: numerical sameness is always and qualitative sameness or similarity is sometimes a matter of linguistic convention, but neither is ever *just* that, but is also in part a matter of "entities" or of facts. In any case, Allaire's allusions to sameness and difference confound the individual-character analysis; they certainly do not support it. Nor can I think of any sound argument which would support it, or which would justify the "bare particulars" which it requires.

As for the principle of acquaintance, Allaire says one thing that I think is plainly false, namely that there is a sense of "know" in which "to know" means "to be acquainted with." Of course I may know Jones by being acquainted with him, but this is not the sense of "acquainted with" that Allaire has in mind, or anyhow that Russell had in mind; for in that sense I cannot be acquainted with Jones or with anybody or anything other than my own sense data. Secondly, Allaire implies that when one has experience or is experiencing something one is acquainted with something (in the requisite sense), and this too I think is false, unless again made a matter of definition. Thirdly, I think it is doubtful that anyone is ever acquainted with anything in the Allairian, Russellian sense. Finally, the principle of acquaintance is certainly not, as Allaire says, "a basic tenet of empiricism," if by that he means either that all empiricists do or that any empiricist must hold it to be true.

In sum, I think there are serious and indeed vitiating difficulties in the views and assumptions from which Allaire's problem, or supposed problem, arises. I do not see that his problem is a genuine one at all—though of course there are great and important problems about the topics with which these views and assumptions are concerned.

But this is not all. It also seems to me that Allaire's proposed solution to his problem is defective, quite apart from the fact that the problem is, from the outset, spurious. I shall mention three ways in which it is defective.

1. Allaire's solution fails to meet his own condition for such a solution, that it be a result of "phenomenological description" and not a mere response to "dialectical needs." I think it is doubtful that there is any such thing as phenomenological description in the sense Allaire intends, or that if there is it has any place in philosophy. But that aside, I think it is clear that Allaire's solution is not the report of a discovery, and not a description of something found at all. His very language gives him away. He says we are acquainted with bare particulars upon occasion (hence the principle of acquaintance is not violated), namely when we are presented with two things that are exactly similar in all non-relational respects, i.e., that differ *solo numero,* at one and the same time. But we are acquainted with them because we *must* be, Allaire says; "something other than a character must also be presented" (p. 7). We are presented with two things as two things, which by hypothesis differ only numerically; hence we must be presented with their difference also, or rather with "what accounts for it," namely the two "numerically different individuals" (bare particulars). The two individuals

are not presented; they must be acknowledged to *account for* what is presented: two different but exactly similar things. This certainly sounds like argument and not discovery, like "dialectics" and not "phenomenology."

2. The conclusion which constitutes Allaire's solution to his problem is a *non sequitur*. I have suggested that this solution does spring from an argument; the argument is that since when we are presented with two things differing *solo numero* we are presented with two things, we must be presented with their difference, or that which accounts for their difference; and this can only be the different bare particulars which the two respectively embody, since by hypothesis they do not differ in respect of any character or property. But the hypothesis is that they do not differ in respect of any *non-relational* property. Not only may they differ in respect of relational properties, but if the two are presented to a perceiver they *must* differ in respect of some such properties at least—one must appear at some distance and in some direction from the other, for example, and though the other appears at the same distance from it, it does not appear in the same direction from it. That A is north of B is then sufficient to differentiate the two, since B cannot be north of A; the differentiation is established by this difference in the relational properties of A and B, and since this difference is sufficient to differentiate them, i.e., to enable a perceiver to perceive them as two, there is no need to call in the supposed bare particulars which each embodies or contains. It is just the absence of this difference in relational properties (at least in those properties resulting from their relation to one another) that makes the two things indistinguishable when they are not "presented together." Hence Allaire's conclusion, that the two things owe their appearance as two, when they are presented together, to their perceiver's capacity to discern or "be acquainted with" their respective bare particulars, does not follow.

3. Allaire's solution seems to me to be inconsistent with the doctrines that form the dialectical conditions from which the solution emerges. Allaire concludes that the numerical difference, or the ground of the numerical

difference, of two exactly similar things, which is to say the bare particulars which they respectively embody, is presented when they are presented together. But if so, how can it be maintained that this numerical difference is not itself a character, albeit not a non-relational character? Or better, how can it be maintained that the bare particularity of a thing is not a character, one which makes its appearance only when the thing is presented to a perceiver with another, contrasting thing? The ground of the distinction between characters and individuals or bare particulars would seem to disappear (if it ever did exist) if the bare particularity of a thing be allowed to appear in perception, even under special conditions. Or to put it the other way around, if a difference between two things can appear in perception, as Allaire alleges the numerical difference of two exactly similar things can do, how can it be maintained that the difference is one of number solely? If the difference were solely one of number it ought to be incapable of appearing or being presented in perception; two things differing *solo numero* must be absolutely indiscernible, not merely indistinguishable under some conditions.

I suspect that what is at the bottom of a good deal of what I take to be defective in Allaire's position is a confusion over the relation between numerical and qualitative difference—and, correspondingly, over the relation between numerical and qualitative sameness or similarity—a confusion which has given rise, *inter alia*, to the doctrine of the identity of indiscernibles. In this Allaire appears to follow Leibniz, and Leibniz, I think, was wrong.

ANOTHER LOOK AT BARE PARTICULARS

Edwin B. Allaire

Chappell's basic criticism of "Bare Particulars"[1] is that it engages a *spurious* problem; namely, to show that one is presented with bare particulars. The criticism rests on these claims: (1) The realistic analysis is itself a response to a spurious problem—the individuation problem, as I shall call it. (II) The "correct" solution to the "spurious" individuation problem does not require bare particulars.

I shall ignore (I). Chappell does not support it (perhaps because he believes that he can, if necessary, solve the individuation problem without bare particulars). He merely alludes to the current dogma that ontological problems arise from mistaken views about reference. I shall not ignore (II). Chappell does support it, but unsuccessfully, as I shall show. He argues that relations individuate.

I shall not ignore two other criticisms made by Chappell. (1) A proponent of the realistic analysis cannot exhibit the difference *in kind* between bare particulars and characters. (2) My defense of the realistic analysis against the acquaintance objection is dialectical and not, as I allege, descriptive.

Assume that there are *two* things both of which have the same nonrelational characters. What accounts for their being (numerically) *different*? That is the problem of in-

From *Philosophical Studies*, Vol. XVI (1965). Reprinted by permission of the author and the editor of *Philosophical Studies*.

[1] *Philosophical Studies*, 14:1–8 (January–February 1963) [pp. 235–44 in this anthology].

dividuation. To grasp it as well as to solve it, one must attend to the uses of 'same' and 'different.' I begin with 'same' in 'same characters.'

For convenience, assume that our two things have but one nonrelational character, say, a color. Let 'R' be the name given to that color. In saying that the things have the *same* color I mean, first, that 'R' is (truly) applicable to each thing and, second, that the entity *in* the one thing that grounds or justifies the application of 'R' is *indistinguishable* from the entity *in* the other. R is an entity; in particular, a character. Moreover, in the case at hand, it is *in* both things—that is the implication of saying that the color of the one is indistinguishable from the color of the other.

At this point I must try to put down a nominalistic uprising. Many, though not apparently Chappell, would object to the claim that R is *in two* things; that is, that *one and the same* character is a constituent of both things.[2] The uprising has four main roots.

i. *Since 'R' applies to two things, its ground must be different.* This root grows out of confusing the character of a thing with the thing having it; or, analogously, out of confusing that which grounds the application of 'R' with what 'R' is applied to.[3] By speaking of 'R' both as the name

[2] Implicit in this objection is the nominalistic doctrine that characters are as unique as the things they characterize. For an explicit statement and defense of the doctrine see A. K. Stout, "The Nature of Universals and Propositions," *Proceedings of the British Academy,* Vol. 10 (1921–23), pp. 157–72. For two excellent criticisms of the doctrine see G. E. Moore, "Are the Characteristics of Particular Things Universal or Particular?" *Proceedings of the Aristotelian Society,* Supplementary Vol. III (1923), pp. 95–113, and Gustav Bergmann, "Synthetic *A Priori,*" *Logic and Reality* (Madison: University of Wisconsin Press, 1964), pp. 272–301.

[3] The confusion (along with some others) is handsomely exemplified in the following remark by Austin (*Philosophical Papers* (Oxford: Clarendon Press, 1961), p. 90n2): ". . . for a statement to be true one state of affairs must be *like* certain others, which is a natural relation, but also *sufficiently* like to merit the same 'description,' which is no longer a purely natural relation. . . . That things are *similar,* or even 'exactly' similar, I may literally see, but that they are the *same* I cannot literally see—in calling them the same colour a convention is involved additional to the conventional choice of the name to be given to the colour which they are said to be." The slide from things to their characters is patent. For

of a color and as applying to (being a name of) a thing, we create the illusion that R cannot be a constituent of two things. The common-proper name terminology misleads us into believing that since 'R' applies to two things it must name two characters.

ii. *Since the things are in different places, R must also be in different places. That is absurd: a "thing" cannot be in two places at once.* This root also grows out of confusing a thing with its characters. Here, however, the confusion is spawned by the ambiguity of 'in.' Things, but not their characters, are in places, for things, but not their characters, exemplify spatial relations. By speaking of characters as *in* things we tempt ourselves to think of characters as *parts* of things and thus as *spatial* parts of things. But characters are *in* things only in the sense that they are elements or constituents of the analysis of things. Of course, one might try—indeed some have tried—to deny that things have constituents. The denial is absurd. 'R' applies to a thing because the thing is R. Plainly, the thing is not R because 'R' applies to it.

iii. *One character cannot be a constituent of two things, for each thing has "a" character. There is "the color of the one" and "the color of the other." Hence, even if two things have the same shade of color, each must have a (numerically) different character.* This root grows out of misunderstanding such phrases as 'the color of this' and 'the color of that.' Those phrases do not single out characters which are particular in the sense of being peculiar to the things having them. Rather, they single out characters which are particular in the sense of being distinguishable from other characters. 'The color of this,' 'the white in Socrates,' and so on are names of specific shades of colors. The names are specific because the things having the colors named are unique. Two things may nevertheless have the same specific shade of color.

iv. *To say that two things have the same color is merely to say that their "colors" are exactly similar.* 'Similar' and

---

an excellent criticism of the proper-common name doctrine see Reinhardt Grossmann, "Common Names," in Edwin B. Allaire *et al.,* *Essays in Ontology* (The Hague: Nijhoff, 1963), pp. 64–75.

'exactly similar' are forever ensnaring us. 'A is similar to B' and 'A is exactly similar to B,' where 'A' and 'B' refer to things, are analyzable into statements containing 'same'; e.g., 'A and B have the same color' and 'A and B have the same characters.' ('Same' may not mean "one and the same." Two things having different shades of red are sometimes said to have the same color: they are called by the same color word. 'Same' may mean "one and the same," though. Two things having the same shade of color are sometimes said to have the same color; the color of the one is indistinguishable from the color of the other.) Now two shades of red may also be said to be similar. (How this use of 'similar' is to be analyzed is a further issue.) It thus appears that we may also speak of two characters as exactly similar. That is, it appears that two characters may be merely numerically different. But we cannot give a sense to such difference without either putting characters in space or blurring the difference between characters and things. One could, of course, maintain that characters, like things, are complex. But that leads once more to the individuation problem, though now at the level of characters. 'A is exactly similar to B,' where 'A' and 'B' refer to characters, means, if anything, that 'A' and 'B' refer to one and the same character. Different words or phrases (e.g., 'the white in this paper' and 'the white in Socrates'), even though they have different "meanings," do not imply that the entities they name are different.

I turn again to our two things. They have the same nonrelational character. Each contains R. Faced with that fact, a proponent of the realistic analysis claims that each thing also contains a bare particular. The bare particulars, being different, account for the numerical difference of the things; account, in other words, for our referring to the things as "the one" and "the other." Bare particulars are, therefore, the entities *in* things accounting for the numerical difference *of* things.

Chappell, though apparently agreeing that two things may and sometimes do have the same nonrelational characters, rejects the realistic analysis. He argues that the admitted relational difference of the two things accounts for their being numerically different. Chappell tries to solve the individuation problem by making relations *individuate*. (He uses, revealingly, 'differentiates.') This solution will not do, as Russell once demonstrated.[4] Relations—I'll stick with spatial ones—*presuppose* numerical difference; they do not account for it. The *thisness* and the *thatness* of things is presupposed in saying that *the one* is to the left of *the other*. Were it not, then in at least some cases we would be forced to say what we all know to be false; namely, that the same *thing* is to the left of itself.

That relations presuppose the numerical difference of the things exemplifying the relations may be brought out in the following way. Let us represent things by means of the nonrelational characters in them, and let 'A,' 'B,' 'C,' and so on stand for different sets of characters. (The difference is with respect to one or more characters.) Further, let 'L' stand for to-the-left-of; and 'L(—,. . .)' be the form for representing the fact that L is exemplified. Given that there are things which have the same nonrelational characters, we may encounter this representation 'L(A,A).' Thus we would have to say that the same thing is to the left of itself. But we do not wish to say that, for, as we know, there is one thing to the left of the other. Hence, in representing that things are spatially related, something more than merely characters and relations must be *represented*. The question is: Is that something more *presented*?

One may object at this point, maintaining that L *cannot* be exemplified by one thing. I agree. But we know that only because we know that things exemplifying L are at least numerically different. And our knowledge of that is primary. It does not depend on our knowing that the things stand in different relations. That L is asymmetrical is factual, not logical.

The mistaken belief that relations individuate derives from confusing numerical difference—call it simply difference—with qualitative (relational or nonrelational) differ-

[4] Bertrand Russell, "On the Relations of Universals and Particulars," *Logic and Knowledge* (London: George Allen and Unwin, 1956), pp. 105–24.

ence—call it simply nonidentity. Difference is primary; nonidentity is not. That may be shown by considering a
representation, an improved language as some say, built in
accord with the rule that there is but one sign for one entity.
In such a representation, the difference of two entities, say,
a and *b,* shows itself in the difference of '*a*' and '*b*.' The
nonidentity of *a* and *b* shows itself in the occurrence of at
least two sentences, one true and the other false, which are
the same except for the one containing '*a*,' the other '*b*.'
One implication of distinguishing difference from nonidentity is that the former does not logically entail the
latter. More pointedly, the Russell-Leibniz definition of
'$\neq$' cannot be used to transcribe 'different,' only 'non-
identical.'[5]

The fundamental difference *in kind* between particulars
and characters is that the former are bare, the latter are
not. That is, particulars cannot be recognized ('re-recog-
nized' would be better perhaps), characters can be. This
is brought out by the fact that (at least some) characters
are reidentifiable without criteria, things are not. There
may, of course, be further differences between particulars
and characters. Whether or not there are depends, first,
on how particulars and characters are *tied* into things
(that is, on what *tie* ties particulars and characters into
things), and, second, on how spatial relations are tied to
things (that is, on whether things or the particulars *in* them
exemplify the spatial relations in which things are said
to stand). But whether or not there are further categorial
differences, there is at least this one: particulars are bare,
characters are not.

I turn finally to Chappell's criticism that I defend dialectically against the acquaintance objection. The point of
the criticism is that I claim, in effect, that one must be
presented with particulars because the individuation problem cannot be solved without them. The key passage is
this: ". . . the two collections of characters . . . are as
presented numerically different. Clearly, therefore, some-

[5] Cf. Gustav Bergmann, "Sameness, Meaning and Identity," *Meaning and Existence* (Madison: University of Wisconsin Press, 1960),
pp. 132–38.

thing other than a character must be presented. That something is what the proponents of the realistic analysis call a bare particular."

At issue is the use of 'must.' Unlike Chappell, I do not think that its use is dialectical. Whatever force it has in the quoted passage is founded on the requirement of completely describing the things. If one is to give a complete description of what is presented when presented with two things having the same nonrelational characters, then one must include their numerical difference. Further, since the description is in terms of entities, one must include bare particulars, the entities which carry the numerical difference, the entities which ground the numerical difference of the things.

Particulars are controversial. Hence, no description of things yielding particulars will be dialectically untainted. Consequently, I conclude by outlining one root of the claim that they are not presented.

Assume that 'this' refers to a thing; that a thing consists, at the *minimum,* of what we call its characters (properties); and that we can know, just by looking, all the characters of *this.* Suppose we are presented with *this.* What are we presented with? *This.* Of course. But we are also presented with the constituents of *this,* even though we may not immediately notice them. What are those constituents? To find out we must describe *this.* Suppose *this* is R, S, and C. The temptation is to claim that R, S, and C are the constituents of *this.* But here we have identified description with predication and so have excluded the possibility of including in our description that which accounts for the *thisness* of *this.* In describing a single thing, the omission does not disturb. But in describing two things having the same characters, the omission does disturb. One thus says that things plainly contain bare particulars, which are, like characters, presented. However, a particular is different in kind from a character and is thus squeezed out of the description. One cannot predicate a particular of a thing. For, particulars, being bare, cannot be named as characters can be. Particulars are in that sense ineffable.

Moreover, the only words we have for referring to them are 'this' and 'that,' and these are used to refer to things. Particulars are once more ineffable. They are not therefore unpresentable, though.

DO RELATIONS INDIVIDUATE?

J. W. Meiland

What is it that renders two exactly similar material objects
numerically different from one another? One possible answer to this question is that the two objects have different
relational properties or stand in different relations. They
stand in different spatial relations to some other material
objects and, perhaps, to one another. For example, one
object X may be to the left of the other, Y (this relation
hereafter being called "Relation L"), while Y is to the
right of X. E. B. Allaire rejects this answer on the grounds
that X and Y first must be numerically different before they
can stand in Relation L: "Relations—I'll stick with spatial
ones—*presuppose* numerical difference; they do not account for it. The *thisness* and the *thatness* of things is
presupposed in saying that *the one* is to the left of *the
other*."[1] Allaire's own answer to the question stated above
is that each of the two numerically different material objects contains a different "bare particular" (a particular of
this sort being called "bare" because it itself has no properties): "Bare particulars are, therefore, the entities *in*
things accounting for the numerical difference *of* things."[2]
I wish to show that the theory of bare particulars is highly
implausible and that relations do individuate material objects.

From *Philosophical Studies*, Vol. XVII (1966). Reprinted by permission of the author and the editor of *Philosophical Studies*.
[1] E. B. Allaire, "Another Look at Bare Particulars," *Philosophical
Studies*, 16:19 (1965) [p. 254 in this anthology].
[2] *Ibid.*, p. 18 [pp. 252–53 in this anthology].

I

What is Allaire's argument for the claim that "relations presuppose numerical difference?" He says that if this were not so, "then in at least some cases we would be forced to say what we all know to be false; namely, that the same *thing* is to the left of itself."[3] But perhaps saying that the same thing is to the left of itself is false just because Relation L does individuate—that is, just because if X and Y stand in Relation L to one another, then it is logically impossible for X and Y to be numerically identical. Perhaps that X and Y stand in Relation L is a logically sufficient condition of the numerical difference of X and Y. If so, then standing in that relation would *by itself* guarantee that the terms of the relation are numerically different; and thus bare particulars would not be required to account for this difference.

Allaire denies that standing in Relation L is a logically sufficient condition of numerical difference. He admits that Relation L *"cannot* be exemplified by one thing." But he says: "That L is asymmetrical is factual, not logical."[4] Since asymmetry implies irreflexivity, Allaire is claiming that it is a factual matter, not a logical truth, that Relation L is irreflexive. He does not give any argument for this claim. But this claim is crucial to the plausibility of this theory of bare particulars, as I now wish to show.

If it is merely a factual matter that Relation L cannot be exemplified by one thing, then it is logically possible that it be exemplified by one thing. Let us suppose that we are observing a case of what we would describe as "one material object X being to the left of another, Y." Since on the theory of bare particulars, objects *contain* bare particulars, Allaire would say that if this is in fact a case involving two different objects, then there is one bare particular in the location occupied by X and a different bare particular in the location occupied by Y. But, if Allaire is correct about Relation L, it is logically possible that this

[3] *Ibid.,* p. 19 [p. 254 in this anthology].
[4] *Ibid.*

case is not a case involving two different objects, X and Y, even though in every observable respect this case is just like a case involving two different objects. That is, it is logically possible that the *numerically same bare particular* occupies two different locations (those which, as we say, are occupied by X and Y). So in claiming that the irreflexivity of Relation L is factual, not logical, Allaire is claiming that the numerically same bare particular can occupy two different locations. But there is no way to determine, in a case of the sort described above, whether the two locations are occupied by different bare particulars or by the same bare particular, for what is observed is the same in either case. Hence, if Allaire is correct, there is no way to determine whether such a case is a case of numerical difference or of numerical identity. That X and Y occupy different locations does not settle the matter, if Allaire is correct, since those different locations may be occupied by the same bare particular.

But then what basis could anyone have for asserting that in a case of the sort described above, X and Y are numerically different or that they are numerically the same? One could not even have an inductive basis for such assertions. For to have an inductive basis for this, one would have to have found that in some previous cases of objects that occupy different locations, those objects were numerically different (or identical). But in order to acquire such inductive evidence, we would first have to possess a way of determining whether a given case is a case of numerical identity or of numerical difference.

Since there could be no basis for saying, with certainty or with probability, that two exactly similar material objects are numerically identical or numerically different, one could never know, in a given case, how many bare particulars are present. So the theory of bare particulars provides an account of the numerical differences of things at the price of making it impossible for us to determine whether or not a given case is a case of numerical difference. Thus, if the theory of bare particulars is correct, it can never be employed in a particular case. The only reason that Allaire gives for supposing that there are bare particulars is that they are required to "account for the numerical difference of things." But if the theory of bare particulars is correct, then no cases could be known to exist for which it was needed to account. For although bare particulars are supposed to explain numerical difference rather than provide a criterion for detecting numerical difference, the existence of bare particulars would seem to eliminate the possibility of having any criterion for detecting numerical difference in cases of two bodies that have exactly the same properties (other than spatial properties).

It is true that one could still say: "*If* this particular case is a case of numerical difference, then it is a case involving two different bare particulars." But is to say that two different bare particulars are present in such a case to say anything more than that it is a case of numerical difference? And if it is not to say anything more than this, then in what sense does saying that different bare particulars are present account for numerical difference?

Could Allaire say that the irreflexivity of Relation L is logical rather than factual? To do so would meet the objections above. But to do so would also allow relations to individuate. For then standing in Relation L would *by itself*, regardless of the existence or nonexistence of bare particulars, guarantee numerical difference. Objects would be numerically different solely in virtue of standing in Relation L. And then there would be no need to postulate the existence of bare particulars. Numerical difference could be accounted for by citing the relations in which the objects in question stand.

II

There are two sorts of situations which involve numerical identity or difference. The first concerns objects existing at a given moment; the second concerns objects existing at different moments. As a situation of the first sort, let us suppose that two exactly similar objects X and Y coexist but occupy different locations. If it is only factually the case, rather than logically necessary, that X and Y are numerically different, then it is logically possible that exactly similar objects which occupy different locations are numerically identical. But then what would it *mean* to say of such objects that they are numerically identical? If we do not employ a theory of substance as substratum or a theory of bare particulars, there seems to be nothing that could be meant by saying that they are numerically *identical;* if it is only factually the case that X and Y are numerically identical, then a situation that is exactly the same as the described situation in every observable respect could be a situation involving numerical *difference* of objects. So unless we say that ascriptions of numerical identity and difference in situations of this first sort are about something unobservable (a substratum or bare particulars), we must say either (i) that ascription of numerical identity or difference in situations of this first sort has no meaning, or else (ii) that what it *means* to say that two exactly similar objects are numerically different is that they occupy different locations. That is, in order to provide a meaning for such ascriptions without referring to something unobservable, we must deny that it is a merely factual matter that objects occupying different locations are numerically different. We must say that "occupying different locations" is what the expression 'numerically different' *means* in such a situation. Only in this way will it not be a merely factual matter that objects occupying different locations are numerically different. And hence only in this way will the expression 'numerically different' have a meaning in the first type of situation without invoking something unobservable.

In every situation of the first sort—that is, situations involving coexisting material bodies—two such bodies are numerically different if and only if (or when and only when) they occupy different locations. The meaning of the expression 'numerically different' is "occupying different locations." But the following objection might be raised to this position:

This position on the meaning of 'numerically different' is satisfactory only if we consider only the first sort of case. Let us now consider situations in which the two entities in question do not coexist. We often say that what I am now observing (call this "X") is numerically different from what I previously observed (call this "Y"). Yet what I now observe can be both exactly similar to and in the same location as what I previously observed, even though the two things are numerically different. Therefore the expression 'X is numerically different from Y' cannot *mean* "X and Y occupy different locations," unless the expression 'numerically different' is equivocal, that is, unless it has one meaning in the first sort of situation and a different meaning in the second sort of situation.

What this objection shows is that we must add to the expression which renders the meaning of 'numerically different': "Two objects are numerically different (a) if they coexist, then when and only when they occupy different locations, or (b) in case they in fact never coexist, if and only if they would have occupied different locations had they coexisted." But to make the addition represented by part (b) is only to add further specification concerning the locations of bodies. It is not to mention something unobservable which is said to be contained within material objects. It seems, then, that a substratum or bare particulars need not be postulated if the expression 'numerical difference' has the meaning suggested above. But if it has the suggested meaning, then relations do individuate. For then X and Y are numerically different when and only when they have or would have had different locations, that is, when and only when they have or would have had different spatial relations to other bodies.

PARTICULARS AND THEIR QUALITIES

Douglas C. Long

The traditional analysis of substances in terms of qualities which are supported by a "substratum" was rejected by conscientious empiricists like Berkeley, Hume and Russell on the grounds that only qualities, not the substratum, could be experienced. To these philosophers the proper alternative seemed obvious. One simply eliminates the "unknowable" element in which qualities are alleged to inhere. In Russell's words, "What would commonly be called a 'thing' is nothing but a bundle of coexisting qualities such as redness, hardness, etc."[1]

But this empiricist formula has difficulties of its own, and some philosophers have attempted to develop other views of particulars which avoid the errors of the Substratum Doctrine on the one hand and the Bundle-of-Qualities Theory on the other.[2] Discussions of what this third alternative might be have generally approached the question through an examination of the epistemologically suspect concepts of a substratum and its close relative, the concept of a "bare particular". The concept of a quality of something, because it seemingly presents no epistemological difficulties, has attracted much less critical at-

From *Philosophical Quarterly*, Vol. XVIII (1968). Reprinted by permission of the author and the editor of *Philosophical Quarterly*.
[1] Bertrand Russell, *An Inquiry into Meaning and Truth* (London, 1940), p. 97. This book will be cited hereafter as *Inquiry*.
[2] See, for example, Wilfrid Sellars, "Particulars", *Philosophy and Phenomenological Research*, Dec. 1952, pp. 184–99; Edwin B. Allaire, "Bare Particulars", *Philosophical Studies*, Jan.–Feb. 1963, pp. 1–8 [pp. 235–44 in this anthology]; Morris Lazerowitz, *The Structure of Metaphysics* (London, 1955), chap. 7, "Substratum".

tention. This imbalance in critical interest is unfortunate, however, for a close scrutiny of this latter concept, especially in its role as the key element in the "bundle" analysis of particulars, throws a great deal of light on the relation between particulars and their attributes.

In what follows I propose to examine representatives of two types of Bundle Theory (BT) with the intention of showing (1) that neither of the concepts of "a quality" employed by these versions of the BT can be used to state the theory coherently, and (2) that the fatal defects in these concepts point to easily overlooked but essential features of the correct alternative to both the Substratum Doctrine and the BT. This alternative, which I will call the Qualified Particulars Theory (QPT), is implicit in our pre-philosophical conception of things and their qualities. In fact it is so much a part of our thought that its details are not easily made explicit. However, this difficulty is greatly diminished when the QPT is contrasted not only with the Substratum Doctrine but also with examples of the unsuccessful BT. The two versions of the latter theory which I will discuss I have taken from the writings of Bertrand Russell[3] and G. F. Stout,[4] because these authors employ concepts of a quality, in their analyses of particulars, which differ in a very important respect. According to Russell, qualities can occur at more than one place at a time, while Stout maintains that the qualities of things are unique items, like particulars. In each case a different aspect of our ordinary view of qualified particulars is stressed while others are ignored. However, by properly blending the two versions of the BT with the Substratum Doctrine and making adjustments for their respective errors, the correct view of particulars may be obtained.

While the main portion of my discussion will be de-

[3] Russell presents his theory mainly in *Inquiry* and in *Human Knowledge: Its Scope and Limits* (New York, 1948), chaps. 3 and 8 (hereafter cited as *Human Knowledge*).

[4] See his Henriette Hertz Lecture, "The Nature of Universals and Propositions", *Proceedings of the British Academy*, 10 (1921). This essay is reprinted as the final paper in his *Studies in Philosophy and Psychology* (London, 1936), pp. 384–403, and my subsequent references to Stout's views will cite passages from this book.

voted to the controversy concerning "material" substances and particulars, in my final section I will point
out certain features of the present topic which have ana-
logues in another philosophical issue. I refer to Hume's
analysis of "minds" or persons as bundles of perceptions.
He himself remarks in the Appendix to his *Treatise* that

> philosophers begin to be reconcil'd to the prin-
> ciple, *that we have no idea of external sub-*
> *stance, distinct from the ideas of particular*
> *qualities.* This must pave the way for a like
> principle with regard to the mind, *that we have no*
> *notion of it, distinct from the particular per-*
> *ceptions.*[5]

Hume is quite right to point out this analogy, but it cuts
both ways. As I will explain, criticism of the Bundle Theory concerning objects paves the way for a like criticism
of Hume's own theory of mind.

I

The concept of a quality employed by the BT is generated in reaction to the type of view which was being defended by Locke when he wrote:

> we must take notice, that our complex ideas of
> substances, besides all those simple ideas they
> are made up of, have always the confused idea
> of something to which they belong, and in
> which they subsist: and therefore when we speak
> of any sort of substance, we say it is a thing
> having such or such qualities; as body is a thing
> that is extended, figured, and capable of mo-
> tion; spirit, a thing capable of thinking; and so
> hardness, friability, and power to draw iron, we
> say, are qualities to be found in a loadstone.[6]

[5] David Hume, *A Treatise of Human Nature*, ed. L. A. Selby-
Bigge (Oxford, 1888), p. 635.
[6] *An Essay Concerning Human Understanding*, ed. A. C. Fraser,
Bk. II, chap. XXIII, sec. 3.

But Locke then adds a candid remark about his analysis of substances which led later empiricists to reject his view. Referring to the ascription of attributes to body, spirit, and the loadstone, he says that "these and the like fashions of speaking, intimate that the substance is supposed always *something besides* the extension, figure, solidity, motion, thinking, or other observable ideas, though we know not what it is".[7] Locke's admission that it is not possible for us to know the nature of this substance or "substratum" or even that there is such a thing, opened the way for Berkeley, Hume, Russell, and others to reject the idea that qualities have something supporting them, a move which leaves us with precisely the conception of a complex of qualities.

A striking feature of these "qualities", however, is that they are basically not possessed by anything. Defenders of the BT will of course insist that they can express the fact that, for example, a certain ball has a red colour and a spherical shape. But what they really mean by these attributions is that redness and sphericity are grouped together with other appropriate qualities at a certain location. Thus the qualities in question are "nonpossessed" in the sense that the particular which is nominally said to have them is eliminated at the most basic level. Indeed the qualities of things are themselves regarded as particulars. That they are so regarded is of course a salient characteristic of Stout's view, but it is no less important to Russell's, even if it is less obvious. If we look closely at Russell's theory we see that syntactically what it does is to convert adjectives, which typically occur in the predicates of sentences, into nouns and noun phrases which are then placed in the subject position. For instance, 'The pencil is red' is replaced by such sentences as 'Redness is at such-and-such a place-time'. In the latter sentence 'redness' is intended to be a name, not a predicate. What it names is a "repeatable" particular which is "universal" in that it can occur at an indefinite number of places at a given time. It nevertheless resembles a particular since it does occur in space-time, and it is not predicable of anything else.[8]

---

[7] *Ibid.*
[8] In his reply to Morris Weitz in *The Philosophy of Bertrand*

For this reason it is misleading to claim that the BT eliminates *particulars* in favour of bundles of *qualities*. It is more
accurate to say that it attempts to eliminate both "bare
particulars" and what we ordinarily think of as the qualities of things, in favour of special particulars.

Because this peculiar concept of "a quality" differs from
that of the "substratum" in that it is apparently above
suspicion on epistemological grounds, Hume, Russell, Stout
and others have accepted it uncritically. They have
failed to see that merely erasing part of the Substratum
Doctrine and accepting what remains has carried the confusion which led to that doctrine over into their own view.
Their simple correction of the traditional analysis of particulars is in fact an over-correction which discards our
familiar concept of a quality and with it our conception of
qualified particulars. And because they have passed over
the QPT, they are compelled to provide special features
in their theories which are meant to account for the individuation of qualities and groups of qualities to form
particular objects. But, as I will explain in the next two
sections, their artificial attempts to make up for the loss
of particular subjects of qualities are completely unsuccessful. I will first show this in the case of Russell's formulation and then in the case of Stout's.

II

Because Russell's "qualities" are "repeatable particulars" which need not have a unique location, it would appear that, as he himself points out, an Eiffel Tower in New
York would be identical with the Eiffel Tower in Paris if
they consisted of the same qualities.[9] Russell seeks to avoid
this consequence of his theory by using different spatio-
temporal locations to individuate exactly similar groups
of qualities. Thus the universal-*cum*-location which constitutes each quality-instance in one of the towers would
contain a different location from the quality-instances of

Russell, ed. P. A. Schilpp (Evanston, Ill., 1944), p. 685, Russell
makes it clear that the "qualities" to which he refers are *particulars*
which can occur at many places at one time.

[9] Russell, *Inquiry*, p. 97.

the other tower. This point must not be misunderstood, however. Although the BT must "tie" qualities to an object's location in order to capture its particularity, this does not commit it to the meaninglessness of propositions such as 'This pencil which I have in my hand might have been in the drawer at this moment instead'. The qualities in the pencil-bundle are supposed to be tied to whatever locations the pencil in fact has. But the claim that the pencil might have had a different history can easily be interpreted on the BT in terms of alternative space-time "worms" which represent careers the pencil might have had.

Nevertheless, the need for spatio-temporal individuation of his "qualities" does raise a serious problem which Russell himself saw and attempted to meet. He must introduce a space-time grid in which to place those "qualities" without making use of any unique particulars. In an early paper Russell insisted that particulars occupying one place at a time were required by our conceptual scheme since "whatever may be the case with 'real' space, perceived space is certainly not absolute, i.e. absolute positions are not among the objects of perception".[10] However, by the time he came to write *Inquiry into Meaning and Truth* he had become convinced that position in the visual field is absolute and can be counted as a sensible quality.[11] This suggested to him that he could do without any particulars other than qualities if this latter class included locational qualities. Thus a red patch in his visual field is to be considered a complex consisting of redness at a certain place in that field or redness "compresent"[12] with certain locational

[10] Russell, "On the Relations of Universals and Particulars", *Proceedings of the Aristotelian Society*, 12 (1912), p. 15.

[11] *Inquiry*, p. 99. This view still seemed satisfactory to him when he wrote *My Philosophical Development* (London, 1959); see pp. 161–71.

[12] In *Human Knowledge*, p. 297, Russell explains that "compresence" is a relation which can be given an ostensive definition simply by calling attention to the relation "which holds between two or more qualities when one person experiences them simultaneously—for example, between high C and vermilion when you hear one and see the other". In the physical world outside the experiences of an individual the relation holds between the qualities which "overlap in space-time".

qualities, e.g., "centrality" or degrees of "leftness" or "rightness".[13]

However, Russell does not mean to apply his theory only to patterns in the visual field. That he means to extend it to objects in physical space is quite clear from his own explicit remarks and from his examples. In *Inquiry* he says, for instance: "I wish to suggest that, wherever there is, for common sense, a 'thing' having the quality C, we should say, instead, that C itself exists in that place, and that the 'thing' is to be replaced by the collection of qualities existing in the place in question".[14] In *Human Knowledge* he remarks: "It is only the assemblage of qualities that makes the instance unique. Every man, in fact, is defined by such an assemblage of qualities, of which humanity is one".[15] But once we leave the visual field and attempt to apply the theory to the sorts of objects to which we commonly give names, the relational character of space raises new problems for Russell. Admitting that his chief problem in this case is to account for the diversity of exactly similar quality-complexes, he suggests that it is possible to extend the space-time order beyond one person's experience to the physical world by taking as spatio-temporal points extremely complex bundles of "compresent" qualities. These bundles would be so complex in fact that it is "very probable" that they would be unique. Ordinary objects would then be regarded as complexes of qualities occupying limited but continuous regions of the space-time order thus defined.[16]

This is not a satisfactory solution to his problem, however. Since, on Russell's theory, position outside the visual field is not given by groups of qualities which can be guaranteed to be unique, his "bundles" have a *de facto* uniqueness which depends upon the world's being very

[13] For a criticism of Russell's attempt to describe the patterns occurring in the visual field with only names of universals and relations of order and coincidence, see Gustav Bergmann, "Russell on Particulars", *The Philosophical Review*, Jan. 1947, pp. 59–72.

[14] *Inquiry*, p. 98.

[15] *Human Knowledge*, p. 298.

[16] See Russell's *Human Knowledge*, pp. 304–7 for a summary of his views concerning the "construction" of objects.

complex. His concept of a bundle of qualities is not equivalent, therefore, to our concept of a qualified particular. In order to express our conception of objects as being unique individuals, even when they inhabit a universe with objects exactly like themselves, the BT requires an absolute spatiotemporal grid which would permit particular spatiotemporal locations to play the role which irreducible particulars would otherwise play. But this leaves the BT open to the obvious objection that it turns "places into bare particulars",[17] thus defeating its whole purpose. Moreover, mere places cannot be distinguished from one another and individual locations re-identified without reference to some unique item existing at some location or other.[18] But if particular individuals of which one can keep track are required to serve as points of reference for a system of locations, the BT cannot reproduce particular things with its limited means.

Apparently Russell was not enough impressed by these difficulties to give up his view, possibly because his "constructed" spatio-temporal locations were more acceptable than the recognition of "bare particulars" which he assumed was the only alternative to some sort of Bundle Theory. What he failed to see is that even if he is granted a spatio-temporal grid of locations his theory is unacceptable. It depends upon the supposition that it makes sense to assign locations to colours, shapes, sizes, and hardnesses, independently of the location of the particulars which are said to have these qualities.[19] But contrary to what philosophers have generally supposed, the assignment of a location directly to a quality of an object is not possible. It only appears to be possible because we are able to give the location of the object to which the quality is attributed.

[17] Edwin B. Allaire, *op. cit.,* p. 7 [p. 243 in this anthology].

[18] See P. F. Strawson, *Individuals* (London, 1959), pp. 36–37, for further discussion of this point.

[19] For instance, in *The Logical Syntax of Language* (London, 1937), pp. 12–13, Rudolph Carnap suggests that we may assign qualities to spatio-temporal positions in order to eliminate proper names. Thus we would say that "the position (x, y, z, t) is blue" instead of "The object *a* is blue". This suggestion is discussed by Russell in *Human Knowledge,* pp. 73–78.

To see that this is so we have only to consider a few illustrations. For example, suppose that we are asked to give the location of an instance of a particular shape, e.g., the shape of the red rubber ball which is on the table near the door. Presumably we are to say that sphericity is located tangentially above that table, along with redness. But does this make any sense? Is sphericity itself extended, for example, so that it occupies the same volume of space occupied by the ball? I think not, since saying this suggests that sphericity is a particular entity which is itself spherical and that its instances come in various sizes like the very objects which the BT is proposing to analyse. Then are we to say that sphericity occurs at each point within the volume of the ball? This makes sense only if we give it some sense. But what could justify our saying this about each of those *points?* Nothing other than the fact that *something* spherical occupies the volume containing those places.

Again, suppose that one is asked to locate an instance of a colour, say, the red colour of the ball in our example. We are to locate not the ball, however, but simply its colour. To suppose that this makes sense is to commit what some philosophers like to call a "category mistake". There is no way to give a location to the colour *per se.* If we try to pin it down we merely find ourselves attempting to locate the pigmented surface of the ball, just that very thinnest coating of material that is red. But even that is not the colour *per se.* The colour itself, the abstract aspect of the ball, can be given no spatial location. To say, for example, that redness is at s_1, t_1 can only make sense if we understand it to mean that something red occupies s_1, t_1. Likewise, to assert, for instance, that this greyness is five feet to the north of that blackness is merely a distorted way of expressing the fact that something grey (the filing cabinet) is just that distance from something black (my briefcase). To say that those *colours* themselves are at that distance from one another is unintelligible. To give still another illustration of my point, the claim that redness and being four inches in length are moving through space can only be understood as meaning that some object which is red and four inches long is moving through space.

Notice that I am not merely objecting that the direct location of qualities is equivalent to giving the position of a particular thing having those qualities. My point is that we do not understand the assignment of locations to qualities independently of the location of the things having those qualities. It is easy to think that we do understand this direct quality-location, however, because we have no difficulty in "reading" the Bundle Theory's assertions in terms of the location of particulars having the qualities in question. But the placing of qualities cannot serve the purposes of the Bundle Theory if assigning spatio-temporal position to them directly makes no sense. For if individual qualities cannot be said to have location directly, there is no reason to think that collections of qualities are any different in this respect. This is particularly obvious if the "bundling" relation is "compresence" in space-time, for that relation is inapplicable if the present objection is correct. And if places must be assigned to qualified particulars rather than to groups of their attributes, then the BT cannot individuate by location the "bundles" which it intends to put in place of ordinary particulars. Therefore, Russell's theory cannot be made to work even if he is permitted the use of a spatio-temporal grid.

III

But individuation of qualities by spatio-temporal location is not the only possibility we have to consider. Some philosophers have rejected the idea that qualities are literally shared by objects, and in view of the failure of a form of BT which employs universals or "repeatable" particulars, it does appear at this point that the only hope for a successful BT lies with this suggestion that individual qualities, which, unlike universals, require no further individuation, should form the basis of the analysis of particular substantial entities. This concept of a quality is generally associated with the name of G. F. Stout, who insisted that a character characterizing a concrete thing or individual is as particular as the thing or individual which it characterizes. Of two billiard balls, each has its own particular roundness separate and distinct from that of the other, just as the billiard balls themselves are distinct and separate. As Jones is separate and distinct from Robinson, so the particular happiness of Jones is separate and distinct from that of Robinson. What then do we mean when we say, for instance, that roundness is a character common to all billiard balls? I answer that the phrase "common character" is elliptical. It really signifies a certain general kind or class of characters. To say that particular things share in the common character is to say that each of them has a character which is a particular instance of this kind or class of characters. The particular instances are distributed amongst the particular things and so share by them.[20]

In fairness to Stout, however, I must point out that it is not entirely clear that he would describe his view as a "bundle" theory. He says that a thing or substance is a "complex unity of an altogether ultimate and peculiar type, including with it all characters truly predicable of it",[21] a remark which suggests that he would be reluctant to accept the idea that the qualities of a thing form an accidental unity. Yet he also says that a substance is "nothing apart from its qualities",[22] and this together with his view that qualities are particulars in their own right makes it difficult to see how the unity of the substance could be anything but a contingent grouping of such qualities. In any case his view supplies the essential ingredient of an alternative to Russell's bundle theory, namely the idea that a particular quality of something is as separate and distinct from the "same" quality of another thing as the two things are from

[20] Stout, *Studies in Philosophy and Psychology*, p. 386.
[21] *Ibid.*, p. 393.
[22] *Ibid.*, p. 391.

each other. It is this feature which appears to relieve us of the burden of individuating qualities in formulating a Bundle Theory.[23]

But this advantage of Stout's suggestion is only an illusion. One must still ask how particular quality-instances of the same kind are to be distinguished from one another. How are they to be individually identified? For instance, what distinguishes the red quality of this ball from the red quality of that fire engine? Of course, we cannot suppose that the distinction lies in a difference in the shade of red of each or in the other qualities which the two objects have, for, according to Stout's view, instances of exactly the same shade of red exhibited by exactly similar objects would be utterly distinct. When this point is acknowledged, there seem to be only three possible answers to our question.

(1) We might take the distinct identity of instances of qualities to be a fundamental fact which cannot be further accounted for.

(2) We might say that this instance of red is distinct from that exactly similar one because this instance includes essentially, and thus is identified by, a location which is different from the location included in that instance.

(3) We might say that this instance of red is distinct from that because the first is identified essentially as the colour-quality of one particular and the second is identified as the colour-quality of another particular, where the particulars referred to are not qualities but ordinary coloured objects.

This third alternative is clearly not one which Stout would accept, since it implies that the particularity of qualities of things derives from the particularity of the things themselves, and he wishes to maintain that the characters are

---

[23] D. C. Williams has developed in detail this type of "bundle" theory in his two-part article, "The Elements of Being", *Review of Metaphysics*, Sept. 1953, pp. 3–18, and Dec. 1953, pp. 171–92.

as particular as the substances they characterize. Which of the first two listed alternatives he would accept is not entirely clear from his writings. However, he does argue that one particular cannot be distinguished from another by its relations to other particulars, "for in order that one particular may be known as related in the required way to others, it is a logical precondition that it shall itself be known as one particular among others".[24] On a relational view of spatial location this would entail that unless instances are seen to be distinct they could not be seen to have different locations. Thus alternative (1) seems to be favoured by this "logical precondition". Moreover, if we adopted the suggestion that qualities contain a location within their "essence" we would have a view which is not interestingly different from the one considered in the previous section where quality-instances were individuated by their location. Therefore, I will suppose that the present version of the BT accepts alternative (1) as an explanation of the uniqueness of quality-instances.

This alternative invites us to regard such instances as being identifiable in their own right. By this I mean, for example, that it should be possible to understand the suggestion that the particular instance of red which characterizes the pencil which I hold in my hand right now might have characterized the fire engine across the street instead. For one would expect qualities which are numerically distinct to have the sort of identity which would permit such things to be said of them. But the suggestion turns out not to make any sense because there is no criterion for the identity of colour instances which renders intelligible the possibility that the very same colour-quality belonging to one particular might have belonged to another particular instead. The concept of numerical identity and difference, if it applies to qualities at all, surely does not apply to them in this way.

But if quality-instances are not distinct in the sense of being individually identifiable in their own right, this eliminates the first type of explanation concerning the

[24] Stout, *op. cit.*, p. 391.

individuation of quality-instances which we previously listed. And since we have already rejected individuation by location, it appears that we must seriously consider the third alternative once again in spite of Stout's protests. According to that alternative, unique quality-instances are identified by reference to the particulars to which they belong. But this means that a particular cannot be analysed in terms of quality-instances at all. In order to identify the elements of the proposed analysis one would have to identify them essentially as qualities of the particular to be analysed. For example, suppose one attempts to refer to a certain group of quality-instances, hoping thereby to be referring to elements constituting "this pencil". One of these instances is "this particular redness". But precisely what colour-instance is intended? The colour of a certain area of the object? The colour of the object itself? The colour of the various objects in the room which resemble each other in colour? To what does the phrase 'this redness' refer? Let us suppose that the instance in which we are interested is the colour which this pencil has and which no other thing has, not even the pencil which came just after it out of the factory. The instance in question then is "the-redness-of-this-pencil". But if the identification of the instance requires us to mention the object to which it belongs, we cannot provide an analysis of particular objects merely in terms of their quality-instances. Hence a coherent formulation of the BT cannot be given in terms of Stout's qualities any more than it can be if we begin with qualities that are "repeatable". Problems of individuation and identification of instances defeat the attempt at each turn.

IV

Having completed my criticism of the two principal types of bundle theory, I now propose to use what we have learned from their failures as a basis for developing a third alternative to replace both it and the Substratum Doctrine. This is the view which I call the Qualified Particulars Theory or QPT.

Let us return to the point in the controversy at which the BT is first introduced, namely the point at which the support for qualities is rejected. This deceptively simple excision of the substratum from Locke's analysis constitutes an unfortunate over-reaction to his view, in that it discards not only the substratum but also the idea that a quality must be ascribed to something. Locke rightly points out that "when we speak of any sort of substance, we say it is a thing having such or such qualities",[25] and doubtless he wanted his theory to preserve the connection between a quality and that to which it is ascribed. But because his critics accept his mistaken description of the subject of qualities as an unknowable item, they assume that the way to eliminate his epistemological problem is to eliminate the subject of qualities altogether. Thus his confusion is carried over into their own theory, although its nefarious influence is now represented by the acceptance of "non-possessed" qualities which belong to something only if they are "compresent" with certain other qualities which together constitute that thing. It is even possible on this view for individual attributes to occur in isolation from others and hence not be attributes of anything at all.

The proper reaction to Locke's view, however, is a refusal to accept his claim that the subject of qualities is itself "unknowable", if this means that "we experience qualities, but not the subject in which they are supposed to inhere".[26] Our conviction on this score is what gives rise to the suspicion that the BT denies that there are objects and then tries to placate us by substituting in their places groups of abstractions, i.e., mere qualities. In opposition to both views we must retain our familiar conception of a qualified particular, according to which there is no such thing as an instance of a "bare" or "non-possessed" quality any more than there is an instance of a "bare" particular. An observed quality-instance is always a quality of something, e.g., a material entity, a reflection, a shadow, an appearance, etc., although we may not be able to perceive at a given moment exactly what it is that has the quality.

[25] *Essay*, Bk. II, Chap. XXIII, sec. 3.
[26] Russell, *Inquiry*, p. 98.

For instance, we may see only "something" red down at the end of the hall, without being able to see whether it is a picture, a piece of cloth, or merely a reflection on the wall. But we do not see mere "redness", as though it could be an open question whether or not it is the redness of something. This conceptual point is reflected in the fact that when we describe what we perceive we employ adjectives which must be syntactically associated with nouns and noun phrases.

Moreover, the claim that there are no "bare" or "non-possessed" qualities applies even in complex cases of perception where we must consider the apparent qualities of objects. For instance, suppose that one sees something with an elliptical shape resting on a shelf across a large room. Initially it can be an open question whether one is perceiving the true shape of a material object or not. It might turn out to be a round, flat plate which is being viewed at an angle, so that there is no elliptical object "there" to be seen. But there is no question that whatever qualities one perceives belong to some particular or other. There are two alternative ways to describe the case, both of which support this claim. We might say either (1) it turned out to be an elliptical appearance which one saw, a move which provides a particular subject for the adjective 'elliptical', or (2) it turned out that the plate only appeared elliptical and was really circular. This last suggests that the "elliptical shape" is not really a quality of anything after all, although failing to be a quality of something is in this instance not a quality's failing to have a subject. We simply do not have a genuine quality. Hence, on either interpretation we do not have a "non-possessed" quality.

A quality-instance not only must belong to some particular or other; it must also belong to that particular which has it and no other. Contrary to what Stout supposed, a quality of a thing is not a particular in its own right, but must be picked out from among other instances as the one belonging to such and such a thing. Thus, while it is a contingent fact that this ball which I have in my hand is red, it is not contingent that the instance identified as "the-particular-redness-of-this-ball" belongs to this ball. In other words, when we say of the ball that it is red, we are not saying of an instance of that colour that it belongs to the ball as a matter of fact.[27] This is why it makes no sense to suppose that the colour-instance of a particular pencil might have belonged to a particular fire engine instead. I believe that this also explains why some critics have felt that the BT lacked a "principle of unity" which would account for the "substantial unity in things behind the multiplicity of their states and qualities".[28] There is indeed more than an accidental unity among the qualities of a thing where these qualities are thought of as instances belonging to that thing and no other. But this is because such instances are not independently identifiable particulars which may or may not belong to a certain substantial entity. There is no "disunity" possible among the qualities of a particular, and so no additional "principle of unity" is required to account for the grouping of those instances with a certain individual substance. Such a principle appears to be necessary to critics of the BT only because they have already accepted that theory's suggestion that qualities are distinct particulars.

I wish to make it clear, however, that rejection of the BT does not entail acceptance of "bare" particulars, the mere kernel of objects "which remains after a thing has been stripped bare of its qualities . . ."[29] The things which are characterized by qualities are objects like tables, persons, molecules, etc., hence the name 'Qualified Particulars Theory'. These objects are distinct from their qualities in that they cannot be reduced to them as the BT suggests. In this sense objects are something "over and above" their qualities. But this is not to say that they are distinct from their qualities in the sense that they contain a distinct element which somehow possesses no qualities itself yet which is, as a matter of fact, characterized by them. Of course there is a respect in which it is not neces-

[27] An interesting parallel to this point may be found in remarks by Sydney Shoemaker, concerning the "bundle" theory of the self, in *Self-Knowledge and Self-Identity* (Ithaca, N.Y., 1963), p. 110.

[28] A. E. Taylor, *Elements of Metaphysics* (New York, 1961), p. 133.

[29] Lazerowitz, *op. cit.*, p. 159.

sary that a particular thing have the quality-instances that it does have. Although a certain instance must belong to a certain particular given the occurrence of that instance, it is not necessary that the instance occur in the world. For example, it is not necessary that this pencil which I have in my hand be red, and so the redness-of-this-pencil might not have existed. Likewise the pencil need not have this colour or shape or size or other particular values of its various determinables. But this does not entail that the pencil could exist without having any qualities or that the concept of something remaining when all of its qualities are "stripped away" is intelligible.

Edwin Allaire has argued that what he calls "bare particulars" are required to "ground the numerical difference of two things which are the same in all (non-relational) respects".[30] Inviting us to consider two red discs that are exactly alike, he reasons as follows:

> To claim that both discs are but collections of literally the same universals does not account for the *thisness* and *thatness* which are implicitly referred to in speaking of them as *two* collections. That is, the two collections of characters . . . are, as presented, numerically different. Clearly, therefore, something other than a character must also be presented. That something is what proponents of the realistic analysis call a bare particular. Or, perhaps better, that is their explication of 'bare particular'.[31]

Allaire fails to explain, however, why he thinks that the element required in his account is a "bare" particular rather than an ordinary qualified object. Nor does he make it clear in what sense such a particular is "other than a character". He says that "in being presented with a red spot one is presented with two things", an individual and a character, and that "the sense in which there are two things is merely the sense in which there are two char-

[30] Allaire, *op. cit.*, p. 6 [p. 241 in this anthology].
[31] *Ibid.*, p. 7 [pp. 242–44 in this anthology].

acters (red and square) in the presentation of a red square".[32] But by this he means only that the individual and character are not spatially related, which does not tell us much.

We can agree that for distinguishable things to be exactly alike there must be something other than universal characteristics presented. But what is presented in fact are two similar qualified objects which are neither bundles of qualities nor bare particulars. No advantage is gained in principle by locating the particularity of those objects in some other element whose individuality must itself be accepted without further explanation. The idea that a bare particular must be brought into the account is simply a counterpart of the Bundle Theory. Allaire's own argument illustrates this point. When one finds that the BT does not satisfactorily explain the distinctness of similar objects there is a temptation not to reject the view as a whole, but to add to each bundle of qualities a distinct "quality-less" individual. The qualified object then becomes a complex of two types of independent items, an individual and its various characteristics. However, we should reject the Bundle Theory as a whole and with it the counter-thesis that qualities of things are associated with "bare" particulars. The correct alternative to these theories is to acknowledge that the particularity of "substances" is borne by the qualified particular itself.

Summarizing briefly, we have seen that if we try to analyse a "thing" in terms of qualities alone we find ourselves requiring particulars to provide the individuation which Russell expected locations to supply and which Stout thought was already built into qualities. On the other hand, the suggestion that the particulars which are required are both intrinsically without qualities and yet somehow characterized by them is not intelligible. In the sense that the concept of a qualified particular is not analysable in these terms, that concept must be regarded as being basic to the metaphysical framework in terms of which we speak of particulars and their qualities. This is the main tenet of the Qualified Particulars Theory.

[32] *Ibid.*

V

The points which I have been arguing in criticism of the BT and in defence of the QPT are analogous to ones which can be made against the Humean theory that a person is essentially a bundle of perceptions. It is illuminating to compare the BT and Hume's theory in this respect. (I will merely call attention to the analogies without attempting to argue over again in detail for each point.)

There is a sense in which a pain or an after-image experienced by Smith is distinct from an exactly similar pain or after-image experienced by Jones. This suggests that it is possible to analyse Smith and Jones in terms of their respective experiences. For instance, it seems that certain thoughts, memory-impressions, and mental images standing in some empirical relation to one another constitute one distinct group to which we give the name 'Smith', while we give the name 'Jones' to another group of distinct "perceptions". But what distinguishes one such "person" from another? There seems to be a perfectly good sense in which perceptions may be regarded as being universals, i.e., as being simultaneously repeatable like Russell's qualities. This is the sense in which Smith might complain of "that same throbbing, slightly nauseating headache" that Jones suffered from the week before, or the sense in which the two of them might have the same green spot before their eyes after looking into a red light. Nor is it inconceivable that all of the thoughts, sensations, and memory-impressions of two persons might be exactly similar, however unlikely this may be. For this reason reliance upon Russell's device, i.e., the suggestion that bundles of perceptions are sufficiently complex to guarantee a high probability that such collections are qualitatively distinct, will not suffice to reproduce our concept of a person. And as in the case of qualities, spatio-temporal locations cannot be used to individuate perceptions, since it is not possible to assign a spatial location to a thought, feeling, or memory-impression. The closest we can come to this is to assign a location to the person who has them, but this can be of no use to the "bundle" analysis of persons.

At this point the analogue to Stout's theory suggests itself. Perhaps we can regard perceptions as particulars in their own right. But if so, it should be possible to identify each perception independently of the person to whom it belongs. For instance, we should be able to make sense of the suggestion that the particular pain which Smith is suffering right now might have occurred to Jones instead of to Smith. This is not to suppose merely that Smith might not have had the pain he now feels and that Jones might have had an exactly similar pain. The claim is that Jones might have had Smith's pain instead of Smith. But our present criteria for the identity of pains do not permit us to say this, any more than we can say that the particular red quality-instance of this object might have belonged to that other object instead. It seems that we distinguish the perceptions and sensations of different persons by identifying them as the experiences of different individuals, not by identifying them as individuals in their own right.[33] Thus, although exactly similar after-images experienced by Smith and Jones may be regarded as *particular* experiences in that they belong to different persons, they are not *particulars* which are contingently related to the persons having them. Therefore, the attempts to express the particularity of persons in terms of their perceptions and the particularity of objects in terms of their qualities are equally unsuccessful and for similar reasons. In this respect the concept of a particular person or subject of psychological attributes is no more reducible to its alleged elements than is the general concept of a qualified particular.

[33] For further discussion of these points concerning the individuation of experiences see Strawson, *op. cit.*, p. 41, and Jerome Shaffer, "Persons and Their Bodies", *Philosophical Review*, Jan. 1966, p. 66.

ESSENCE AND ACCIDENT

Irving M. Copi

The notions of essence and accident play important and unobjectionable roles in pre-analytic or pre-philosophical thought and discourse. These roles are familiar, and need no elaboration here. Philosophers cannot ignore them, but must either explain them or (somehow) explain them away. My interest is in explaining them.

If they are taken seriously, the notions of essence and accident seem to me most appropriately discussed within the framework of a metaphysic of substance, which I shall accordingly assume. The account of essence and accident that I wish to set forth and argue for derives very largely from Aristotle, although it is not strictly Aristotelian. Where it differs from Aristotle's account it does so in order to accommodate some of the insights formulated by Locke in his discussion of "real" and "nominal" essences. My discussion is to be located, then, against the background of a substance metaphysic and a realist epistemology. The theory of essence and accident to be proposed seems to me not only to fit the demands of the general philosophical position mentioned, but also to be consistent with the apparent requirements of contemporary scientific development. I wish to begin my discussion with some historical remarks.

The earliest Western philosophers were much concerned with change and permanence, taking positions so sharply opposed that the issue appeared to be more paradox than

From *The Journal of Philosophy*, Vol. LI (1954). Reprinted by permission of the author and editor of *The Journal of Philosophy*.

problem. If an object which changes really changes, then it cannot literally be one and the same object which undergoes the change. But if the changing thing retains its identity, then it cannot really have changed. Small wonder that early cosmologists divided into warring factions, each embracing a separate horn of their common dilemma, the one denying permanence of any sort, the other denying the very possibility of change.

Aristotle discussed this problem in several of his treatises, bringing to bear on it not only his superb dialectical skill but an admirable, common-sense, dogged insistence that some things do maintain their identity while undergoing change. To explain the observed facts he was led to distinguish different kinds of change. A man does retain his identity though his complexion may change from ruddy to pale, or though he may move from one place to another. He is the same man though he become corpulent in middle life or his sinews shrink with age. In these types of change, called *alteration, locomotion, growth,* and *diminution,* the changing thing remains substantially or essentially what it was before changing.

Another type of change, however, was admitted to be more thoroughgoing. To take, for example, an artificial substance, we can say that if a wooden table is not just painted or moved, but destroyed by fire, we have neither alteration, locomotion, growth, nor diminution alone, but *substantial* change. The characteristic mark of substantial change is that the object undergoing the change does not survive that change or persist through it, but is destroyed in the process. The ashes (and gas and radiant energy) that appear in place of the burned table are not an altered, moved, or larger or smaller table, but no table at all. In substantial change its essential property of being a table disappears.

It seems clear that distinguishing these different kinds of change involves distinguishing different kinds of attributes. The basic dichotomy between substantial change and other kinds of change is parallel to that between essential attributes or *essences,* and other kinds of attributes, which may be lumped together as accidental attributes or *accidents.* (Here we diverge rather sharply from at least one moment of Aristotle's own terminology, in ignoring the intermediate category of "property" or "proprium.")

Of the various bases that have been proposed for distinguishing between essence and accident, two stand out as most reasonable. The first has already been implied. If we can distinguish the different kinds of change, then we can say that a given attribute is essential to an object if its loss would result in the destruction of that object, whereas an attribute is a mere accident if the object would remain identifiably and substantially the same without it. This basis for distinguishing between essence and accident, although helpful heuristically, is not adequate philosophically, for it seems to me that the distinctions among these kinds of change presuppose those among the different kinds of attributes.

The other, more satisfactory basis for distinguishing essence from accident is an epistemological or methodological one. Knowledge of the essence of a thing is said to be more important than knowledge of its other attributes. In the *Metaphysics* Aristotle wrote: ". . . we know each thing most fully, when we know what it is, e.g. what man is or what fire is, rather than when we know its quality, its quantity, or its place. . . ."[1] It is the essence that is intended here, for a subsequent passage explains that: ". . . the essence is precisely what something *is*. . . ."[2] It is perhaps an understatement to say that Aristotle held knowledge of essence to be "more important" than knowledge of accidents, for he later says explicitly that: ". . . to *know* each thing . . . is just to know its essence. . . ."[3] And if we confine our attention to scientific knowledge, Aristotle repeatedly assures us that there is no knowledge of accidents at all,[4] but only of essences.[5]

Aristotle was led to draw an ontological conclusion from the foregoing epistemological doctrine. If some attributes of objects are epistemologically significant and

[1] 1028a37–1028b2. Quotations are from the Oxford translation.
[2] 1030a1.
[3] 1031b20.
[4] 1026b4; 1027a20, 28; 1064b30; 1065a4. Cf. also *Posterior Analytics* 75a18–22.
[5] 75a28–30.

others are not, the implication is that the former constitute the real natures of those objects, whereas the latter can be relegated to some less ultimate category. I must confess that I am in sympathy with the realist position which underlies and justifies such an inference, but to expound it in detail would take us too far afield.

As a biologist Aristotle was led to classify things into genera and species, holding that things belong to the same species if and only if they share a common essence. In remarking this fact we need not commit ourselves to any position with respect to the systematic or genetic priority of either logic or biology in Aristotle's thought. He apparently believed these species to be fixed and limited, and tended to ignore whatever could not be conveniently classified within them, holding, for example, that "the production of a mule by a horse" was "contrary to nature,"[6] a curious phrase. Some modern writers have tended to regard this shortcoming as fatal to the Aristotelian system. Thus Susan Stebbing wrote: "Modern theories of organic evolution have combined with modern theories of mathematics to destroy the basis of the Aristotelian conception of essence. . . ."[7] It seems to me, however, that the fixity of species is a casual rather than an integral part of the Aristotelian system, which in its broad outlines as a metaphysical framework can be retained and rendered adequate to the most contemporary of scientific developments. A not dissimilar objection was made by Dewey, who wrote that: "In Aristotelian cosmology, ontology and logic . . . all quantitative determinations were relegated to the state of *accidents,* so that apprehension of them had no scientific standing. . . . Observe by contrast the place occupied by measuring in modern knowledge. Is it then credible that the logic of Greek knowledge has relevance to the logic of modern knowledge?"[8] But the Aristotelian notion of essence *can* admit of quantitative determination, as is suggested by Aristotle himself in admitting ratio as essence.[9]

[6] 1033b33. But cf. 770b9–13.
[7] *A Modern Introduction to Logic,* p. 433.
[8] *Logic: The Theory of Inquiry,* pp. 89–90.
[9] 993a17–20.

Hence I do not think that this criticism of Dewey's can be regarded as any more decisive than that of Miss Stebbing.

Having set forth in outline an Aristotelian philosophy of essence and accident, I propose next to examine what I consider to be the most serious objection that has been raised against it. According to this criticism, the distinction between essence and accident is not an objective or intrinsic one between genuinely different types of attributes. Attributes are really all of the same basic kind, it is said, and the alleged distinction between essence and accident is simply a projection of differences in human interests or a reflection of peculiarities of vocabulary. Let us try to understand this criticism in as sympathetic a fashion as we can.

The distinction between different kinds of change, on this view, is subjective rather than objective. We happen to be interested, usually, in some attributes of a thing more than in others. When the thing changes, we say that it persists through the change provided that it does not lose those attributes by whose possession it satisfies our interests. For example, our interest in tables is for the most part independent of their colors. Hence that interest remains satisfiable by a given table regardless of any alteration it may suffer with respect to color. Paint a brown table green, and it remains substantially or essentially the same; the change was only an accidental one. If our interests were different, the same objective fact would be classified quite differently. Were our interest to lie in *brown* tables exclusively, then the application of green paint would destroy the object of our interest, would change it substantially or essentially from something which satisfied our interest to something which did not. The implication is that attributes are neither essential nor accidental in themselves, but can be so classified only on the basis of our subjective interests in them. Dewey stated this point of view very succinctly, writing: "As far as present logical texts still continue to talk about essences, properties and accidents as something inherently different from one another, they are repeating distinctions that once had an ontological meaning and that no longer have it. Anything is 'essential' which is indispensable in a given inquiry and anything is 'accidental' which is superfluous."[10]

The present criticism lends itself easily to reformulation in more language-oriented terms. That we regard a table as essentially the same despite alteration in color or movement from place to place is a consequence of the peculiar nature and limitations of our vocabulary, which has a single word for tables, regardless of color, but lacks special words for tables of different colors. Suppose that our language contained no word for tables in general, but had instead—say—the word "towble" for brown table and the word "teeble" for green table. Then the application of green paint to a towble would be said to change it essentially, it might be argued, for no towble would remain; in its place would appear a teeble. Or if there were a single word which applied indiscriminately to tables and heaps of ashes, say "tashble," with no special substantive denoting either of them univocally, then perhaps the destruction of a table by fire would not be regarded as an essential change. That which appeared at the end of the process would admittedly be in a different state from what was there at the start, but it would still be identifiably the same tashble. C. I. Lewis regards the difference between essence and accident to be strictly relative to vocabulary, writing: "Traditionally any attribute required for application of a term is said to be of the essence of the thing named. It is, of course, meaningless to speak of the essence of a thing except relative to its being named by a particular term."[11]

I think that for our purpose these two criticisms can be regarded as variants of a single basic one, for the connection between human interests and human vocabulary is a very intimate one. It is an anthropological and linguistic commonplace that the concern of a culture with a given phenomenon is reflected in the vocabulary of that culture, as in the several Eskimo words which denote subtly different kinds of snow. In our own culture new interests lead continually to innovations in vocabulary; and surely it is the decline of interest in certain things that leads to the obsolescence of words used to refer to them.

Both variants of this criticism were formulated long ago by Locke, and developed at considerable length in his *Essay*. Locke paid comparatively little attention to the problem of change, but where he did discuss it his treatment was very similar to Aristotle's. Thus we are assured in the *Essay* that: ". . . an oak growing from a plant to a great tree, and then lopped, is still the same oak; and a colt grown up to a horse, sometimes fat, sometimes lean, is all the while the same horse. . . ."[12] The oak ". . . continues to be the same plant as long as it partakes of the same life . . ."[13] and the identity of animals is explained in similar terms. Personal identity is explained in terms of sameness of consciousness.[14] If we ignore the Cartesian dualism implicit in that last case, and if we are not too critical of the reappearance of the term "same" in the explanation of *sameness,* we can recognize these answers to be the Aristotelian ones, for according to Aristotle the soul is the principle of life,[15] the life of a plant is the nutritive soul,[16] that of an animal its sensitive soul,[17] and that of man his rational soul,[18] these souls constituting the substantial forms or essences of the respective substances.[19] On the other hand, in his brief discussion of identity as applied to non-living things, Locke construes it very strictly to apply only to things which ". . . vary not at all. . . ."[20] But the following passage has a characteristically Aristotelian flavor: "Thus that which was grass to-day, is to-morrow the flesh of a sheep; and within a few days after becomes part of a man: in all which, and the like changes, it is evident their real essence, i.e. that constitution,

[12] Bk. 2, ch. 27, § 3.
[13] *Ibid.*
[14] Bk. 2, ch. 27, § 8, § 9, § 10, § 16, § 17, § 23.
[15] *De Anima* 402a6, 415b8.
[16] 432a29, 434a22–26; cf. also *De Plantis* 815b28–34.
[17] 432a30.
[18] *Politics* 1332b5.
[19] *De Anima* 412a20, 412b13, 415b10.
[20] Bk. 2, ch. 27, § 1.

whereon the properties of these several things depended, is destroyed, and perishes with them."[21]

Despite this partial similarity of their views, the bases for distinguishing between the essential properties and other properties of a thing are very different for Locke than for Aristotle. For Aristotle, the distinction is twofold: first, the essential properties of an object are those which are retained by it during any change through which the object remains identifiably the same object; and second, the essential properties of an object are most important in our scientific knowledge of it. For Locke, on the other hand, the *real* essence of a thing is a set of properties which *determine* all the other properties of that thing.[22] Since all other properties depend on its real essence, *any* change in an object entails a change in its real essence. Hence for Locke the essential properties of an object are *not* retained by it during any change. This view is very different from Aristotle's, on which the accidents of a thing are not bound to its essence but can change independently of it. The epistemological difference is equally striking. Whereas for Aristotle all scientific knowledge is knowledge of the essence, for Locke there is *no* knowledge of the real essences of things.[23]

Locke was more interested in what he called "nominal essences," which are more nearly analogous to the Aristotelian notion of essence. Our idea of a particular substance, according to Locke, is a complex idea composed of a number of simple ideas which are noticed to "go constantly together," plus the notion of a substratum "wherein they do subsist."[24] A general or abstract idea of a sort or species of substance is made out of our complex ideas of various particular substances that resemble each other by leaving out "that which is peculiar to each" and retaining "only what is common to all."[25] Such an abstract idea *de-*

---

[21] Bk. 3, ch. 4, § 19. But cf. Bk. 3, ch. 6, § 4, § 5.
[22] Bk. 3, ch. 3, § 15.
[23] Bk. 3, ch. 3, § 15, § 17, § 18; ch. 6, § 3, § 6, § 9, § 12, § 18, § 49; ch. 9, § 12; ch. 10, § 18.
[24] Bk. 2, ch. 23, § 1.
[25] Bk. 3, ch. 3, § 7.

termines a sort or species,[26] and is called a "nominal essence,"[27] for "every thing contained in that idea is essential to that sort."[28]

The properties contained in the nominal essence of a thing can be distinguished from the other properties of that thing on the same basis as that on which the Aristotelian essence is distinguished from accidents. In the first place, a particular substance of a given species can change with respect to some property whose idea is *not* included in the nominal essence of that species, and will continue to be recognizably the same thing; whereas it must be regarded as a quite different thing if it changes with respect to some property whose idea *is* included in the nominal essence.[29] And in the second place, the nominal essence is more important in knowledge than other properties. To have knowledge of a thing is to know what *sort* of thing it is, and to know the nominal essence is to know the sort. Locke says, moreover, that the leading qualities of a thing, that is, the most observable and hence, for Locke, the most knowable, are ingredient in the nominal essence.[30] Finally, it is argued in the *Essay* that knowledge of nominal essences is required if we are ever to be certain of the truth of any general proposition.[31] Since Locke's nominal essences play so similar a role to that of Aristotle's essences, Locke's arguments intended to prove their subjectivity and relativity to human interests and vocabulary can be interpreted as applying to Aristotle's notion as well as his own.

One fairly minor difference should be noted before going on. Since Locke's nominal essences are abstract *ideas,* they are immediately subjective in a way that Aristotle's essences are not. But that difference is not decisive, for substances may well have objective properties that nominal essences are ideas *of,* or objective *powers* that correspond to them exactly.[32]

[26] Bk. 3, ch. 3, § 12.
[27] Bk. 3, ch. 3, § 15.
[28] Bk. 3, ch. 6, § 2.
[29] Bk. 2, ch. 27, § 28.
[30] Bk. 3, ch. 11, § 20.
[31] Bk. 4, ch. 6, § 4.
[32] Bk. 2, ch. 23, § 7.

Locke urges that essences are subjective in a less trivial
sense. Since they are "inventions"[33] or the "workmanship"[34] of the understanding, different persons in fashion-
ing abstract ideas which they signify by the same term can
and do incorporate different simple ideas into them. Acts
of choice or selection are involved here, and people do
make different choices, as proved by the disputes that so
frequently arise over whether particular bodies are of certain species or not.[35]

That essences are relative to vocabulary is argued by
Locke in terms of an example: "A silent and a striking
watch are but one species to those who have but one name
for them: but he that has the name watch for one, and
clock for the other, and distinct complex ideas, to which
those names belong, to him they are different species."[36]

That the ". . . boundaries of species are as men, and
not as nature, makes them . . . ,"[37] proved by the verbal
disputes already referred to, is explained by the fact that
since we have ". . . need of general names for present
use . . ."[38] we ". . . stay not for a perfect discovery of all
those qualities which would best show us their most material differences and agreements; but we ourselves divide
them, by certain obvious appearances, into species. . . ."[39]
Nominal essences are made for *use,* and different intended
uses or interests will determine different essences. Even
the *noticing* of similarities between distinct particulars is
relative to our interest in them, so our selection of simple
ideas for inclusion in a nominal essence is relative to such
interests. These determining interests are not scientific, for
as Locke observed, ". . . languages, in all countries,
have been established long before sciences."[40] The situation is rather that the terms of ordinary discourse ". . .
have for the most part, in all languages, received their

[33] Bk. 3, ch. 3, § 11.
[34] Bk. 3, ch. 3, § 12, § 13, § 14.
[35] Bk. 3, ch. 3, §14; ch. 6, § 26, § 27; ch. 9, § 16; ch. 10, § 22;
ch. 11, § 6, § 7.
[36] Bk. 3, ch. 6, § 39.
[37] Bk. 3, ch. 6, § 30.
[38] *Ibid.*
[39] *Ibid.*
[40] Bk. 3, ch. 6, § 25.

birth and signification from ignorant and illiterate people. . . ."[41] And for the purposes or interests of those
practical people, the properties selected by them as essential to the objects they deal with are adequate enough. For
"Vulgar notions suit vulgar discourses; and both, though
confused enough, yet serve pretty well the market and the
wake."[42]

Now do these arguments succeed in establishing that
the distinction between essence and accident is subjective
rather than objective, that is, relative to human interests and vocabulary?

I think that the objections are not utterly destructive of
the Aristotelian doctrine, although they do call attention
to needed modifications of it. Locke's case, it seems to me,
depends upon his distinction between real and nominal
essences, and his belief that real essences are unknowable. But his doctrine that real essences cannot be known
flows from two peculiarities of his philosophy, which I see
no reason to accept. One of the bases for his belief that
real essences are unknowable is his view that the only
objects of our knowledge are the ideas that we have in our
minds.[43] Locke's other basis for his belief that real essences
are unknowable is his doctrine that experiment and observation yield only ". . . judgment and opinion, not
knowledge. . . ."[44] Here the term "knowledge" is reserved
for what is *certain*.

I would reject these two doctrines on the following
grounds. The first of them, that knowledge is only of ideas,
is the germ of scepticism. Locke's premises lead necessarily to Hume's conclusions, and the partial scepticism we
find explicitly set forth in Locke is but a fragment of the
complete scepticism that Hume later showed to be implicitly contained there. It seems to me that if a philosophy
denies the very possibility of scientific knowledge, then so
much the worse for that philosophy. As for reserving the
term "knowledge" for what is certain, that usage has but

[41] *Ibid.*
[42] Bk. 3, ch. 11, § 10.
[43] Bk. 2, ch. 1, § 1.
[44] Bk. 4, ch. 12, § 10; cf. also Bk. 4, ch. 3, § 28.

little to commend it. It seems more reasonable to accept the results of experiment and observation, although probable rather than demonstrative, as knowledge nonetheless.

It must be admitted that the doctrine of the unknowability of real essences was not an unreasonable conclusion to draw from the relatively undeveloped state of science in Locke's day. For chemistry, at least, if we can believe what is said of it in the *Essay,* was in a very bad way in the seventeenth century. Locke tells us of the "sad experience" of chemists ". . . when they, sometimes in vain, seek for the same qualities in one parcel of sulphur, antimony or vitriol, which they have found in others. For though they are bodies of the same species, having the same nominal essence, under the same name; yet do they often, upon severe ways of examination, betray qualities so different one from another, as to frustrate the expectations of very wary chemists."[45]

Contemporary science, however, presents a quite different picture. Locke characterized the (allegedly unknowable) real essences of things as the ". . . constitution of their insensible parts; from which flow those sensible qualities, which serve us to distinguish them one from another. . . ."[46] Now modern atomic theory is directly concerned with the insensible parts of things. Through the use of his Periodic Table, interpreted as dealing with atomic number and valency, ". . . Mendeléev was enabled to predict the existence *and properties* . . ." of half a dozen elements whose existence had not been previously known or even suspected.[47] And other scientists have subsequently been able to make similar predictions. Modern science seeks to know the *real* essences of things, and its increasing successes seem to be bringing it progressively nearer to that goal.

It must be granted that Locke's distinction between real and nominal essence is a helpful one, even though it is not absolute. The construction of nominal essences is

[45] Bk. 3, ch. 6, § 8.
[46] Bk. 3, ch. 3, § 17.
[47] J. D. Main Smith, in the *Encyclopaedia Britannica* (14th ed.; 1947), Vol. 17, p. 520 (my italics).

usually relative to practical interests, and the ordinary notion of the essence of a thing is relative to the words used in referring to it. I think that Locke (and Dewey and Lewis) are correct in that contention. Surely different interests lead different people to classify or sort things in different ways, and thus to adopt different nominal essences, the more permanently useful of which receive separate names in ordinary language. Thus it is that: "Merchants and lovers, cooks and taylors, have words wherewithal to dispatch their ordinary affairs. . . ."[48]

The distinction, however, is not absolute. Not every interest is narrowly practical. The interest of the scientist is in knowledge and understanding. The scientist desires to know how things behave, and to account for their behavior by means of explanatory hypotheses or theories which permit him to predict what will occur under specified conditions. He is interested in discovering general laws to which objects conform, and the causal relations which obtain among them. The scientist's sorting or classifying of objects is relative to this interest, which is not well served by classifying things on the basis of properties which are either most obvious or most immediately practical. It is better served by classifying things in terms of properties which are relevant to the framing of a maximum number of causal laws and the formulation of explanatory theories. Thus a foodstuff and a mineral source of aluminum, common salt and cryolite, are both classified by the chemist as sodium compounds, because in the context of modern chemical theory it is this common characteristic which is most significant for predicting and understanding the behavior of these substances. In the sphere of scientific inquiry, the distinction between real and nominal essence tends to disappear. The scientist's classification of things is intended to be in terms of their *real* essences. And here, too, the process is reflected in vocabulary, not necessarily or even usually in that of the man in the street, but rather in the technical jargon of the specialist.

The essences which science seeks to discover, then, are

[48] Bk. 3, ch. 11, § 10.

real essences rather than nominal ones. Since the arguments for subjectivity or relativity to interest or vocabulary were concerned with nominal rather than real essences, they simply do not apply to real essences as either Locke or Aristotle conceived them.

In one passage of his *Essay,* though, Locke does make the further claim that even a real essence relates to a sort and supposes a species.[49] But on Locke's own account of real essence, the real essence of a particular must be that set of its properties on which all of its other properties depend. And that can be investigated independently of any sorting or classifying we may do—although once its real essence is discovered, that will determine how we should classify it scientifically if the occasion for doing so arises.

At this point let me indicate the direction in which I think the Aristotelian doctrine of essence and accident might well be modified. Aristotle definitely held that there could be no scientific knowledge of accidents,[50] but contemporary science would admit no such limitation. It seems to me that both Locke's and Aristotle's views about unknowability should be rejected. Contrary to Locke, I should hold that real essences are in principle knowable, and contrary to Aristotle, I should hold that non-essential or accidental properties can also be objects of scientific knowledge.

It seems to me also that neither Locke nor Aristotle gives a satisfactory account of the relationship between essence and accident. For Locke, all (other) properties of a thing depend on its "real constitution" or real essence[51]; but it is not clear whether the dependence is supposed to be causal or logico-deductive. The former is obviously the more acceptable doctrine. Aristotle, on the other hand, held that some properties of a thing, namely, its accidents, do not in any way depend upon its essence. I think that Locke's view, understood as asserting a causal dependence of accident on essence, is the more plausible one, and that the Aristote-

---

[49] Bk. 3, ch. 6, § 6.
[50] 1064b30–1065a25.
[51] Bk. 3, ch. 3, § 18.

lian doctrine ought to be so modified as to accord with that of Locke in this respect.

Now if both essences and accidents are scientifically knowable, on what basis are they to be distinguished from each other? I suggest that the epistemological or methodological distinction is still valid. For example, common salt has many properties, some more obvious than others, and some more important than others relative to different practical interests. The scientist singles out its being a compound of equal parts of sodium and chlorine as its essential nature. In doing so he surely does not mean to imply that its chemical constitution is more easily observed than its other properties, or more important to either cook, tailor, merchant, or lover. He classifies it as sodium chloride because, within the context of his theory, that property is fundamental. From its chemical formula more of its properties can be inferred than could be from any other. Since the connection is causal rather than logical, the inference from essence to accident must make use of causal law premisses or modes of inference as well as strictly logical ones. Hence to derive conclusions about *all* accidental properties of a substance, we should need to know both its real essence and all relevant causal laws. That is an ideal towards which science strives, rather than its present achievement, of course. To the extent to which one small group of properties of a substance can serve as a basis from which its other properties can be causally derived, to that extent we can be justified in identifying that group of properties as its real essence. This view, it should be noted, is in agreement with Aristotle's doctrine that the definition of a thing should state its essence,[52] and that definition is a scientific process.[53]

There is a certain relativity implied in this account, although it is quite different from those previously discussed. Our *notion* of what constitutes the real essence of a thing is relative to the science of our day. Centuries hence, wiser men will have radically different and more adequate theories, and their notions will be closer approxi-

[52] 91a1, 101b21, 38.
[53] 1039b32.

mations than ours to the real essences of things. But it will still be the real essences of things that are destined to be known by Peirce's ultimate community of knowers.

There is one other and more radical sense of accident that I would agree to be relative. Each separate science is concerned with only some of the properties or aspects of things which it studies. Those left out will be accidental relative to the special science which ignores them. They will not be derivable from what that science considers to be the real essences of those things, although a different special science might be much concerned with them, and even include them in *its* notion of the thing's real essence. But as (and if) the sciences become more unified, no properties of a thing will be wholly accidental in this sense, and all will be causally derivable from the real essence.

In closing, I should like to refer once again to the topic of change. If all of a thing's properties depend on its real essence, then it would seem to follow that every change is an essential one. In my opinion, that unwelcome conclusion can be evaded in two ways. In the first place, with respect to common-sense, practical usage, our ordinary sortings will continue to be based on nominal rather than real essences, so that changes can continue to be classified as accidental or essential in the traditional way. And in the second place, with respect to scientific usage, we can say the following. The real essence of a thing will consist very largely of powers or, in modern terms, dispositional properties. An essential change in a thing will involve the replacement of some of its dispositions or powers by other dispositions or powers. But a change which is non-essential or accidental would involve no such replacement; it would rather consist in differently actualized manifestations of the same dispositional property or power. Unfortunately, lack of space prevents an adequate development of this suggestion.

ESSENCE AND ACCIDENT

Hugh S. Chandler

Quine holds that we cannot draw a distinction between essential and accidental properties of individuals.

> Mathematicians may conceivably be said to be necessarily rational and not necessarily two-legged; and cyclists necessarily two-legged and not necessarily rational. But what of an individual who counts among his eccentricities both mathematics and cycling? Is this concrete individual necessarily rational and contingently two-legged or vice versa? Just insofar as we are talking referentially of the object, with no special bias toward a background grouping of mathematicians as against cyclists or vice versa, there is no semblance of sense in rating some of his attributes as necessary and others as contingent. Some of his attributes count as important and others as unimportant, yes; some as enduring and others as fleeting; but none as necessary or contingent.

> Curiously, a philosophical tradition does exist for just such a distinction between necessary and contingent attributes. It lives on in the terms 'essence' and 'accident', 'internal relation' and 'external relation'. It is a distinction that one attributes to Aristotle (subject to contradiction

From *Analysis*, Vol. XXVI (1966). Reprinted by permission of the author, the editor of *Analysis*, and Basil Blackwell and Mott, Ltd.

by scholars, such being the penalty for attributions to Aristotle). But however venerable the distinction, it is surely indefensible . . .[1]

What, on Quine's view, would show that a "concrete individual", c, had an accidental or essential property? The requirements are complicated. We can specify c in an indefinite number of ways; *e.g.* c is a fox, an animal, a furry creature, a mother, *etc.*[2] Now we can ascribe a property, P, to c *simpliciter,* or we can ascribe P to c *under one of c's specifications.* We can say 'c is female', or we can say 'This fox is female' [where 'this fox' specifies c]. Apparently Quine holds that some property, P, would be an essential property of c if and only if every true proposition of the form 'This S is P' [where 'this S' specifies c] were necessarily true. I say this simply because in the argument given above Quine takes it to be sufficient to show that being two-legged is not an essential property of his eccentric friend to show that 'This mathematician is two-legged' [where 'this mathematician' specifies his friend] is not a necessary truth. Presumably Quine also holds that we could show that P is an accidental property of c only by showing that every true proposition of the form 'This S is P' [where 'this S' specifies c] is contingent. 'P is an accidental property of c' might be taken to mean only that P is not an essential property of c; *i.e.* that there is at least one specification of c, 'this S', such that 'This S is P' is not necessarily true. Quine cannot read 'accidental property' in this way because he would then have to hold that his proof that being two-legged is not an essential

---

[1] Willard van Orman Quine, *Word and Object,* The Technology Press of the Massachusetts Institute of Technology, 1960, pp. 199–200.

[2] My use of the word 'specify' in this paper is not, perhaps, ordinary usage; but I believe that my meaning is clear. Quine occasionally uses this word in describing his view; *e.g.* '. . . the appeal to analyticity can pretend to distinguish essential and accidental traits of an object only relative to how the object is specified not absolutely.' (*From a Logical Point of View,* Harper and Row, New York, 1963, p. 155.) Note that Quine uses the terms 'essential' and 'accidental' in describing the view he rejects.

property of his friend is also a proof that his friend has at least one accidental property.

Suppose our concrete individual, c, is a vixen, a mother, a fox, *etc.* Surely Quine does not hold that there is any proposition of the form 'This S is P' [where 'this S' specifies c] that is necessarily true? On his view 'This vixen is female' entails the existence of this vixen. And, Quine would no doubt hold, the existence of any vixen is contingent. Thus he must hold that every true proposition of this form is only contingently true. It would seem to follow that every property of our vixen is 'accidental'.

Let's say that 'This vixen is female' is 'quasi-analytic', and mean by this that, *given the existence of the subject as specified,* the truth of the attribution follows. I think Quine's real view is this: Some property, P, would be an essential property of c if and only if every true proposition of the form 'This S is P' [where 'this S' specifies c] were quasi-analytic; and P would be an accidental property of c if and only if no such proposition were quasi-analytic. I think he would argue, for example, that being female is not an essential property of such and such a vixen, c, on the grounds that 'This fox is female' [where 'this fox' specifies c] is not quasi-analytic. Or, again, having offspring, on Quine's view, cannot be an accidental property of c because 'This mother has offspring' [where 'this mother' specifies c] is quasi-analytic.

It seems obvious that in Quine's odd sense of 'accidental' no concrete individual can have an accidental property. Let P be any property of concrete individual c. 'This thing having property P' can specify c. But 'This thing having property P has property P' [where 'this thing having property P' specifies c] must be quasi-analytic. Thus P cannot be an accidental property of c.

I do not see why a concrete individual cannot have an 'essential' property in Quine's sense. It would seem, for example, that it would be quasi-analytic of any concrete individual, no matter how specified, that it must have the disjunctive property of *weighing ten pounds or not weighing ten pounds.* But perhaps such disjunctive properties are not to be allowed.

So far, our discussion has suggested certain very general features of the logic of the phrase 'concrete individual'; but now we ought to try to see in greater detail what might be meant by this phrase. It is natural to suppose that when we ask whether concrete individuals have accidental or essential properties we are just asking whether individuals, *persons, cities, pets, etc.* [*i.e.* things given proper names] have accidental or essential properties. If Mr. Smith has an accidental property then at least one concrete individual has an accidental property; if Mr. Smith has an essential property then at least one concrete individual has an essential property.

The phrase 'concrete individual' may also signify something less obvious. Imagine that I have a watch that my father recently had made in Switzerland out of an ancient piece of metal my grandfather found in Persia. In this case, perhaps, one and the same individual thing can be specified as my watch, an example of Swiss artistry, a product of Persian metallurgy, *etc.* If the 'concrete individual' here is envisaged as something having *all* of these properties it is not clear that there could be a proper name that names this individual. Suppose I name *this ancient piece of metal* 'George'. Then George was not made in Switzerland out of an ancient piece of metal. On the other hand suppose I name *this watch* 'William'. William was not one of my grandfather's Persian finds.

Incidentally, the case we have just considered suggests that one of the widely accepted principles of identity is false: namely, 'If this S and this T are numerically one and the same individual, and if this S has property P, then it is logically possible for this T to have property P.' An ancient piece of Persian metal cannot have the property of having been made recently in Switzerland.

There are cases in which a great deal turns on what sort of individual we have in mind. Something that is not a person can become a person, and a person can become something that is not a person. A blastula grows slowly into a person, or a young lady becomes a bit of shrubbery. In these metamorphoses do we have one and the same concrete individual persisting throughout the change? Of course there is an individual in each of these cases that does persist throughout the transformation. One and the same thing is at first not a person and then a person, or at first a person and then a non-person. But in each of these cases there is also an individual that does *not* persist throughout the change. Mr. Smith was a blastula, but when he was a blastula he was not Mr. Smith. Similarly we can say 'That bush is poor Daphne' after she has been transformed; but the bush is not Daphne. It is all that is left of her.

I now wish to offer an alternative to Quine's sense of 'accidental' and 'essential'. If c has property P, and we can conceive c to be without property P while remaining c, then P is an accidental property of c; if we cannot conceive this then P is an essential property of c.

This definition is not meant to be a novelty. I believe it gives a traditional sense of 'essential' and 'accidental'. Saint Anselm, for example, argues that being supreme, and greater [than anything else] are not essential properties of the supreme Nature [*i.e.* God], on the grounds that if nothing other than the supreme Nature existed '. . . it would not be conceived as either *supreme* or *greater,* yet it would not, therefore, be less good, or suffer detriment to its essential greatness in any degree'.[8] The argument turns on a notion of 'essential' like the one I have just sketched.

Among the properties not essential to a thing Anselm distinguishes between true accidents and properties 'improperly' called accidents.

> For, of all the facts, called accidents, some are understood not to be present or absent without some variation in the subject of the accident —all colours, for instance—while others are known not to effect any change in a thing either by occurring or not occurring—certain relations, for instance. (p. 84)

Anselm, I believe, holds that P is a true accident of c if and only if (1) c has property P; (2) we can conceive

[8] Saint Anselm, *Basic Writings,* trans. by S. W. Deane, Open Court, La Salle, Illinois, 1963, p. 62.

c to be without property P while remaining c; and (3) gaining or losing property P would constitute a change in c.

Suppose that our concrete individual is a vixen named 'Pat'. Pat is thus female; but it is an accidental property of Pat's that she is female. She could, so far as logic is concerned, be sent to Denmark and be made a male. Of course in the transaction she would lose the nature of a vixen; but she would remain Pat. This is sufficient to justify saying that being female is one of Pat's accidental properties. We might also note that since the operation would produce a *change* in Pat, Anselm could say that being female is one of Pat's *true* accidents.

What about essential properties of individuals? Mr. Smith was once an ordinary blastula, *i.e.* not one that hummed softly to itself, or brooded about the future. But not being an ordinary blastula is an essential property of Mr. Smith. We cannot conceive Mr. Smith to be an ordinary blastula while remaining Mr. Smith. Similarly Daphne can be changed into a perfectly ordinary laurel bush, *i.e.* a bush only extraordinary in that it is what has become of Daphne. But we cannot conceive Daphne to remain Daphne while thus a bush. One of Daphne's essential properties is not being an ordinary laurel bush.

Quine may be right in holding that concrete individuals cannot have 'accidental' or 'essential' properties, in his odd sense of these terms. He is almost certainly right in holding that individuals cannot have 'accidental' properties in his sense. But we found another, more traditional, meaning of 'accidental' and 'essential', and with this in mind sense can be made of the claim that individuals have such properties.

THE INDIVIDUATION OF THINGS
AND PLACES

David Wiggins

The principal object of this paper is to discuss a circularity
which, it seems, would have to infect any account of the
identity of persisting things. One such account is given and
defended in Section I. Its circularity is exposed in Section
II and discussed in subsequent sections.

I

Definition of identity-statement—Truth-grounds
of such statements

For an utterance to express what I shall refer to in this
paper as an "identity-statement" the first three conditions
which follow must be satisfied. For the resulting statement to be true the fourth condition must be satisfied.
(Utterances of "The evening star is the morning star"
standardly satisfy all four.)

(1) The two noun-phrases A, B, flanking "=," must
each serve to pick out a particular which is strictly *referred*
to by the speaker. And, if he knows what he is saying,

Reprinted with substantial changes and some amendments from
Proceedings of the Aristotelian Society, Supplementary Volume
XXXVIII (1963). A few passages which were excised from the
original for reasons of space have been restored. The strategy of
the paper has made thorough revision difficult but a Postscript has
been added (May 1969). Reprinted by permission of the editor of
the Aristotelian Society, copyright 1963.

each must be directly or indirectly identifiable by him under some substance-concept. The answers to the questions
of which particular he means by A and which he means
by B must be specifiable without prior inquiry into the
statement's truth-value.

Thus an utterance of "Darius was the King of the
Persians" would not standardly express what I mean here
by an identity-statement, not in those cases anyway where
it would be silly to ask, "Which particular individual are
you referring to by 'the King of the Persians'?" The only
answer to this silly question would be, "The one Darius
was," which violates the condition as stated above. There is
and must be a better explanation of the meaning of the
utterance, one not involving the discovery of an answer to
the silly question. Nor would "Point p is the center of
gravity of body b" normally express an identity-statement,
in the usage of the term here proposed. (Suppose the
speaker were told that his statement was false. Before making further tests, he would not be able to identify any point
which he intended by "center of gravity of body b." He
would only be able to say that he meant whatever point the
weighing test would determine, if it were correctly performed. But to know which point this was would involve
knowing a *true* statement of the form "point p is the center
of gravity of body b.")[1]

[1] This condition restricts the notion of identity-statement very se-
verely, and even on the Russellian kind of theory of reference to
which I should now wish to revert there could be no good reason
to deny that the two cited sentences at least *import the identity-
predicate*. It must figure in the uniqueness condition within the
composite Russellian predicate which (on the Russellian analysis)
Darius or point p are said to satisfy. There are also serious difficulties both of principle and of execution in any piecemeal treatment
of definite description which counts some definite descriptions as
truly referential and some as merely predicative. The complications
of making the requisite distinctions (as in e.g., Wiggins, "Identity-
Statements," *Analytical Philosophy*,—an article I should now totally
disown) seem to me both interminable and intolerable.
    There is still, however, a point in isolating that subclass of utter-
ances which make identity-statements to the effect that the reference
of A = the reference of B whose verification or falsification most
typically and directly involves the basic judgments of the congruence
or coincidence of individuals separately intentionally identified by

(2) There must be some substance-concept f (e.g., *planet, horse, tree*) which could in principle be specified in answer to the question "these particulars are the *same what?*"[2]

(3) A predicate f expresses a substance-concept for the purpose of conditions (1) and (2) if it is possible to divide up the contents of the world and isolate the *f's* in it in one and only one way. (Cp. Aristotle 2^b 29–30, Strawson 168–69.) If f satisfies this condition there will be the possibility of a definite and finite answer to the question "How many f's are there in region R at time t?" *Planet* or *man* or *tree* passes this test. Dummy-terms expressing formal concepts like *individual, particular, part* or *thing* do not qualify as substance-concepts by this or any other condition.[2]

(4) If one locates the particulars in question (and in the case of "identity through time," traces them in space and time) under a covering-concept provided under condition (2) one must find that the particulars completely coincide.

referring expression A and referring expression B. These judgments were the concern of this symposium and other occurrences of "=" presuppose them. More is said below about *identify* but it should be said that the notion can be used in a way which is quite independent of theories of strictly semantic reference. The fact that the identificatoriness (identifyingness) or referentiality of a definite description A cannot, on the Russellian theory of reference, be any *semantic* feature of it, or contribute anything extra to the truth-conditions of a sentence *s* of which A is one constituent, does not debar the definite description from making it possible to locate the individual which satisfies A in order to make a judgment about it of coincidence or non-coincidence with the individual answering to another name or definite description B. If this is the best or only route to verifying the statement made by *s* this is not something dictated by the *semantics* of *s*, which only determine *what* has to be so for *s* to be true. But it is still something important if this is the best or only route to that verification.

[2] For the rationale of requirements (2) and (3), and for rather more general conditions both of being a substance-concept and of coincidence see Wiggins, *Identity of Spatio-Temporal Continuity*, Part Three, now.

II

An inevitable limitation (A) *and a circularity* (B) *in the foregoing account—Three answers to* (B)

(A) Even if it is a gesture at something general, this is hardly a general account of identity, even of the sort of identity I want to discuss. The words "the same" do not have any special or peculiar sense in statements about times and places, and one cannot discuss the identity of persisting things in isolation from that of times and places. Yet conditions (3) and (4) are not very readily applicable to their case. Still less is this any *definition* of identity, nor does it really suggest one. Except for the case of material things, "coincidence" is hardly more than a metaphor. Yet there is no more general word which could do duty for it in some attempt at a general definition of identity. (Indeed "coincidence" hardly *analyzes* identity even in our unambitious and specialized account.) Similar difficulties might be encountered in trying to make requirement (3) sufficiently general to cover all possible terms in all possible identity-statements.

(B) Places and times are not labelled. They depend for their identification on identification of the persisting things which *occupy* places *at* times. If being in the same place at the same time and spatiotemporal continuity are necessary conditions of coincidence, then we presuppose in our account of identity the prior identifications of enough persisting things to fix times and places. The limitations of our account of identity are again apparent. What is a new and different point, it seems inadequate even as a special account of the identity of persisting material things. For it is circular. (See in *Works Consulted* Anscombe, pp. 92–94; compare Williams (1), pp. 315–20.)

The first, (A) above, is the less serious problem. One can no more enumerate all the sufficient conditions of "being an individual" than one can definitely and completely capture by the axioms of a set-theory all the conditions of "being a set." One can mention sufficient conditions (cats are particulars, planets are particulars . . . , the union of two sets is a set, the set of the members of any set is a set . . .). One can teach someone to identify particulars of any given kind. But one cannot teach them to identify all particulars of all possible kinds. The limitations and necessary conditions one can lay down in advance on what shall count as an individual or set can only be general and unspecific requirements of coherence and non-contradictoriness (for instance, the requirement of continuity for individuals perhaps, see Williams (2) and Wiggins (2), p. 73, and compare the axiom of regularity for sets.)[3]

There is no clear limit to the interests with which we can explore the world to individuate its contents. Analogously, in the theory of sets it is demonstrably impossible to define exhaustively and definitely, once for all, all the ways in which we can assemble aggregates. (For one explanation see Goodstein, p. 97.) There should be nothing surprising therefore about the impossibility of giving an account which is truly general and more than schematic of what identity is. Places, times, the various species of material things, numbers, etc. are different sorts of individual and must have quite different criteria of identity. We know well enough (in general) what the activity of identifying is—from particular cases. Though we cannot define it, and though there is no very informative list of necessary conditions nor any complete list of sufficient conditions of being an identifiable particular, this does not mean we cannot learn and teach the skill for any particular kind of object. It is absurd, however, to ask for general directions about how to individuate. It is like asking for *one* single method of performing many or *all* classifications.

More serious is (B), sc. that the special account of the identity of persisting material things given in 1 covertly presupposes a prior understanding of the identity-conditions of enough members of the class of persisting material things to fix places and times and the sense of "spatio-

---

[3] Cf. Frege (3), p. 32. ". . . the question arises what it is that we are calling an object. I regard a regular definition as impossible, since we have here something too simple to admit of logical analysis."

temporal continuity." This circle may not matter however if some term or terms in it have specially direct and unproblematic application to reality, or if "spatiotemporal continuity" is a concept which can be (in some suitable sense of "directly") directly acquired. If one or a few persisting things can be identified by a thinker in a direct or privileged manner without support from the spatiotemporal framework then a start can be made from this basis on times, places, and spatiotemporal continuity. Then the original account will work well enough for other persisting things.

Candidates for this privileged role which suggest themselves are (1) oneself or one's own body (cf. Hampshire, pp. 30, 68–69, 87), (2) one's own spatiotemporal location (cf. Strawson, p. 30), (3) an object directly and continuously observed by some thinker (A. M. Quinton in conversation; cf. Nerlich, p. 207; Popper, whose solution must at least involve this; and Williams (1), p. 317).

(1) I only have knowledge of my own identity and can only reidentify myself if I know who I am. To break the circle at this point in the way in which some have envisaged breaking it I should have to be able to say who I was without alluding at all to other persisting things, and then go on *afterwards* to pin down other things by relating them to myself. But if I cannot allude to my commerce with other persisting things, I cannot say where I am, where I have been, or, it seems, anything. Even supposing I could say what I am thinking and have been thinking, others might have had the same thought. So no definite description of me would have been achieved. Self-knowledge without the possibility of reference to any other thing than myself either collapses into the tautology that I = I or, dubiously, into a statement about my inner life which does not determine who I am. (See generally Williams (1), *loc. cit.*) Nor is it any help to plead that I might be able to identify *myself* or *my own body* and reidentify them (whatever that would mean) without *saying* what I was doing. For I should in any case need *another* point of origin, as well as this, in order to *make use* of this alleged grasp of *my own* or *my own body's* identity in the project of pinning

down other persisting things and getting a spatiotemporal frame started for identifications and reidentifications in general. But then we presuppose one of the things which was to be *explained* by this proposal to start with *one's own body* or *oneself,* namely the identification and re-identification of a particular. And now, if we can have that particular as well it is not clear either why there was any special advantage in starting with *oneself* or *one's own body.*

(2) Waive difficulties about "I." Can I get started with the place where I am? Without reference to other objects all that can be said about where I am is "here," and about here only that here = here. It is no doubt true in this very strange sense that I can never get lost. I am always in a place I can refer to as "here." Even if one allowed (as I do not) that this came to something, making a beginning with *here,* or *here* and *myself*—if each is so far contentless neither can be used to give the other content—still does not *by itself* help me in identifying anything I could not identify before. And anything we used to supplement them with might *by itself* be all that was needed. See (3) below.

(3) Should I then start with some persisting thing other than myself? A demonstrative with substance-concept backing could be used to refer to a persisting thing kept under continuous observation (*c*-observation) and successively related to other objects in a thinker's environment. It was in this sort of manner that Leibniz (p. 69) explained "how men come to form to themselves the notion of space":

> They consider that many things exist at once and they observe in them a certain order of co-existence, according to which the relation of one thing to another is more or less simple. This order is their *situation* or distance. When it happens that one of these co-existent things changes its relation to a multitude of others, which do not change their relation among themselves; and that another thing, newly come, acquires the same relation to the others, as the former had; we then say, it is

come into the place of the former; and this
change, we call a motion in that body, wherein is
the immediate cause of the change. . . . And
supposing, or feigning, that, among these co-
existents, there is a sufficient number of them,
which have undergone no change; then we may
say, that those which have such a relation to
those fixed co-existents, as others had to them
before, have now the *same place* which those
others had. . . .

The mutual dependence of places and things now seems
harmless, because both are grounded in the possibility of
demonstrative identification, which is itself grounded in
the possibility of *c*-observation. (For reasons of space I
shall largely neglect the not completely analogous problem
of times.)

A number of remarks need to be made about this passage. (a) I do not take myself to be committed by this
approach to Leibniz's thesis of the identity of relations or
space, or to any attempt to reduce spatial relations to something else. The approach only commits me to the view that
the apprehension of spatial relations is dependent on the
prior individuation of some persisting things. (b) The passage prompts the questions "How does the thinker proceeding in the suggested way eventually get the idea of himself?" and "What gives the thinker the idea of supposing or
feigning what he feigns?" For our purposes it does not
matter. (c) Our problem is—*if* a thinker gets these ideas,
then what term is logically suited to serve as a fastening
point into which he can securely latch his whole system of
identifications? What *grounds* his identifications and reidentifications (including those he has to do to say who
and where he is)? The answer now offered is that they could
theoretically be anchored, in the first instance, on the
identity of some *f* or other, referred to by the thinker as
"this *f*" and continuously observed by him, and then on a
succession or chain of landmarks each fixed by reference
to the last.

III

Development of the more promising answer

It follows from the third suggested answer that the way in which a thinker's own identity and location are involved in identification and reidentification is simply this. (Contrast Hampshire, p. 30; Strawson, pp. 30, 42–43.) It is *he,* located wherever he is located, who continuously observes an object in its relations with others. If he succeeds in doing this he identifies and reidentifies successfully. He is of course a persisting self. But this imports no circularity. (Contrast Williams (1), pp. 318–19.) For he need not, for the purpose in hand, identify or reidentify himself at all. The question which was asked was how I or you or anybody can identify and reidentify things with certainty, things other than ourselves. My (or your) identity is presupposed, in the *question,* "How do I (or you) reidentify successfully?" If it weren't, the question couldn't be asked.

I should here make explicit how "identify" and "reidentify" would be used within this solution and how I try to use them throughout the paper. In the case where the identified object is present to the senses (*direct identification,* or simply *identification*) "identify" comes to something like "pick out" or "fix on." One (only sufficient) condition of this is the ability to touch or handle or point to the object knowing some substance-concept it falls under. When an object *a* is not present to sense (*indirect identification*) identifying involves knowing which particular I am thinking of when I make judgments, ask questions, etc. about *a.* It is sufficient for this to be able to fill out a referring expression "*a*" in a judgment "*φa*" so that "*a*" becomes a definite description uniquely relating the object to the speaker's environment and to things he can identify directly. (This criterion for indirect identification is suggested by Strawson, chap. 1 and *passim,* but is not the same as his.)

Negatively, I do not mean by *"identify" "assign to its proper kind"* nor *"identify to an audience"* (cf. Strawson, chap. 1, on whom see Williams (1), pp. 310–18) nor *"refer."* (Identification of some sort is a precondition of knowingly doing any of these.) Nor is it a necessary condition of identifying that a complete articulation of the identifier's information yield any identity-statement at all. If it were he could never identify for the first time.

I have no clear idea at all of how to define "identify," or formulate its necessary conditions. A rough and unsatisfactory attempt at a more general sufficient condition is:—I identify a if, for any ϕ such that I understand fully what it is for something to be ϕ, I (i) know what it is for "ϕa" to be true and (ii) know without preliminaries what it is effectively to investigate whether "ϕa" be true. Finally, for me to identify a there must be an x such that $x = a$. (Nevertheless one limb of any complete analysis of "identify" will be intensional.)

"Reidentify," given "identity," is easier. I reidentify b at time t_m if at an earlier time t_n I have directly identified b and now at t_m (1) I directly identify b, (2) I realize there was some earlier occasion when I directly identified b. Here a *full* articulation of the thinker's information must (with any necessary supplementation of that information to specify the first occasion and link it with the second) yield an identity-statement. My definition allows a second identification of something c-observed throughout as a (trivial) reidentification, but the interesting case is reidentification over a gap in observation.

IV

Direct identification grounds reidentification

As a demonstration of the partial adequacy of the third solution I shall now try to show that, if c-observation grounds direct identification securely (and I examine whether it does in V), then direct identification of a c-observed configuration of objects securely anchors reidentifications and indirect identifications. For an upholder of the solution can argue (with Strawson, (p. 34), against Pears) that the possibility of certain reidentification is already fully implicit in direct identification.

A thinker reidentifies if he employs the same referring

expression for x, (1) in judgments involving direct identification of x at time t_1 and trivial reidentification of x at t_3, where x has been c-observed throughout, (2) in judgments involving a reidentification of x at t_3 when it has been obscured from view since direct identification at t_1, (3) in judgments involving the indirect identification of x at t_2 while it is hidden from view.

A skeptic might try to drive a wedge between trivial and non-trivial reidentification and object that this notation obscured the vital difference that one had the best conceivable evidence in direct identifications, whereas in reidentifications and indirect identifications there was a small irremovable gap between the purport of the judgment and the best possible evidence for it. (Cf. Pears, pp. 175–76.) There are two notational proposals that a skeptic can make if he forbids us to use "a" for an object a which we should say we had reidentified. (1) He might propose "a'" for use when we should say we had reidentified an object, "a''" for a second "reidentification." . . . (2) He might propose "b" for the first reidentification of a, "c" for the second reidentification of a. . . .

If he opts for (2) then we must ask whether it is possible to use "a" for one object held in mind and c-observed for a period of time (trivial reidentification). If (possibility (2.1)) he decides to give up using "a" to refer even to a at t_1 and a at t_2 when a is c-observed throughout, then we can say that he has given up our conceptual scheme. For us, but not for him, an object is something persisting. His complaint must then either fail to affect our concept or be the recommendation of another concept of object. What sense can be given to mistake or correctness, in judgments about this kind of object? (Cf. Hampshire, pp. 30, 42.) To admit anything about the object at t_{1+n} as evidence about the object at t_1 is to use our conceptual scheme while pretending to reject it.

Suppose then (possibility (2.2)) that he admits the use of "a" when a is c-observed throughout, only using "b" when there has been a gap. The skeptic's possible grounds for preferring his convention for reidentification over a gap are (2.21) belief that $a \neq b$, (2.22) belief that it is a real possibility that a $\neq$ b, (2.23) belief that it is a logical possibility that a $\neq$ b. Hovering between these will not create another possibility.

(2.23) is useless and everybody would agree that mistakes are *logically* possible. What grounds does the skeptic have for (2.21) or (2.22)? Sharing our view that objects *can* persist he must suppose either that objects are annihilated or that they behave oddly when we cease to perceive them. But he has no grounds for suggesting this even as a real but remote possibility, and it would be harder to establish this very complicated belief than our simple belief that in general observation neither affects the behavior of objects nor creates them. The only grounds a skeptic could have for questioning our view that intermittent observation of one and the same object is possible would be grounds for (2.21) or (2.22), which we still await. It would undermine the skeptic's own approach to suggest (what we admit) that *slightly* more mistakes are made in reidentification over unobserved tracts.

Notation (1) above, if the skeptic opts for this, is even more clearly hopeless. How can the skeptic reproduce a feature of our notation (use again the sign "*a*") and at the same time deny it has any genuine basis (by adding a prime to "*a*")? If the addition of primes simply signifies a gap in observation we have ways of indicating this already. Surely, the skeptic is not simply proposing a more concise notation.

It may still be felt that there must in all cases be some small gap for the skeptic to exploit between the meanings of statements involving reidentification and their best possible evidence (cf. Pears, p. 176). "It is a reidentification over an unobserved tract" may be put forward as a ground for doubt because these "are all cases in which the claim to reidentify entails 'If I had continued to observe it from t_1 onwards (when in fact I ceased to observe) then what I observed at t_2 would have coincided with what I in fact observed at t_3 . . . but I did not.' And such a counterfactual conditional cannot be straightforwardly verified." (Compare Pears, *loc. cit.*) To this there are two replies.

To establish such a counterfactual I must produce gen-

eralizations about the behavior of objects of the relevant
kind. To object that these generalizations might be true and
the counterfactual still false and do so without support of a
specific objection to them is simply to renounce counterfactuals. It may be said, "There is a special difficulty about
this case because I was elsewhere, so I couldn't verify it."
Is it then that I *physically* could not have verified it, if I had
chosen? But not all cases will be like this, and anyway
what could ground the suspicion that there was something
special about the behavior of objects in such cases? Is it
then that I *logically* couldn't verify it, since I was looking elsewhere (and nobody can look in two places at the
same time)? But does this come down to any more than
the truism that I am I, *sc.* the person who was looking in
another direction? How could this truth count against a
counterfactual?[4] The objection may be "The generalizations
are all based on observation by you. So you only shift the
blind spot [Pears' phrase], you do not lift it." But I could
allow others' testimony. "But that does not remove it altogether," it may be said. This objection begins to look like
an objection to observation *as such* as a way of finding
out about the possibility of abnormal behavior by objects.
But how else can counterfactuals be ultimately grounded
than in observation? To preserve counterfactuals *and* make
his objection the skeptic must give reason to suggest
that there is a real possibility that unobserved objects
behave oddly. This complicated hypothesis is much harder

---

[4] How, similarly, can it be an objection to our practice of tolerating the possibility of intermittent observation of one and the same
persisting thing that our practice involves tolerating the intermittent
observation of one and the same thing? There must be something
else about this practice, and something relevant if there is even to
be the possibility of trying to subtract this part of our practice from
the rest of our practice. But it is not even clear what it adds to our
conception of a *persisting* thing that it can persist *unobserved,* and
therefore quite unclear what subtraction there ever could be. We
can only make a persisting *unobserved* something relevantly extra,
something over and above persisting, if we can be *told* what extra
is relevantly involved. Otherwise the subtraction endangers the whole
structure on which it is performed, the notion of a persisting material thing. The point of what is going on in the text is to show
the difficulties of saying what this extra is while retaining the concept of persisting material things and refraining from making untenable statements about material things.

to ground than anything his opponents wish to say, and as a thesis about unobserved objects uncomfortably close in form to the kind of statement the skeptic is attacking.

Secondly, is not Pears' view the wrong way round? What surely underpins the counterfactual is a fully backed claim to have reidentified. It is only in the context of the activity of reidentification that such counterfactuals have a sense. This retort can come with the challenge "What amendments to our practices and our standards of certainty in reidentification do you propose?" This brings us back to the possibilities (1), (2.1), (2.21), and (2.23).

There is no gap between meaning and evidence in a standard favorable case which is of any particular utility to a rational skeptic. Solution (3) survives its first test.

V

C-observation and its difficulties

Direct identification grounds reidentification over a gap. Does c-observation *ipso facto* secure direct identification and reidentification, both trivial and non-trivial? If it is to do so in a way which solves our problem, it would seem that a thinker must be able to exercise and apply (with certainty when appropriate) the concept under which a c-observed object *o* is to be identified without recourse to (1) prior knowledge of *place*—for we cannot ground the fixing of places separately from that of things, (2) prior knowledge of those other things than *o* in relation to which it moves or is at rest, (3) prior temporal knowledge. Our exercise of substance-concepts in identification is normally supported and corrected by just this kind of information. Are there favored cases where we can subtract its support and reach what we need to break the circle, *self-supporting* identifications of persisting things?

How does one defend the claim to have observed continuously? Having attended hard and closely is not necessarily enough. Conjurors regularly puzzle people who are doing just that. What if it is suggested that I have confused two similar objects and that there was a gap in what I thought to be c-observation? Normally one could perhaps appeal to the position of each object at every point during the period in question. But for our present purposes and by our present standards this seems unsatisfactory. It presupposes a prior fixing of places, presupposes re-identifications, and leaves unaffected the suggestion that my attention may have wandered momentarily. To rebut this last by giving an account of every stage of some continuous process is to appeal in regressive fashion to something else already verified to behave in a certain reliable way, and so to something already identified (say, the second hand of a clock). Again, to see something, and therefore to identify something, depends on an understanding of the possibility of illusion. Guarding against illusion depends on perception from different points of view (cf. Hampshire, pp. 42–43, 47–50). Does this not reintroduce the identity of places at an earlier stage than we can accommodate it?

There is the suspicion that these standards of certainty are illegitimately exacting and that we are trying to take apart things which are not even divisible in reason. The best way to base the suspicion, which will be confirmed in VII, is to continue the attempt.

An attempt might be made to guard solution (3) against these difficulties by distinguishing two elements in the criterion of individuation associated with a substance-concept, a procedure (hereafter application of *criterion of distinctness*) for telling any ϕ from its environment and a procedure (hereafter application of *criterion of identity*) for reidentifying any ϕ as the same ϕ (terminology of chap. VII, Strawson; cp. Hampshire, pp. 12, 16, 31; Anscombe, pp. 86–87). It could then be argued that considerations of place and spatiotemporal continuity were only relevant to questions for which one needed the *criterion of identity,* and that in the case of c-observation by one observer (his identity not in question, see III) questions about the identity of what he observed could be left to look after themselves, provided only that he applied the *criterion of distinctness* correctly. In this way, it might be said, landmarks and frames of reference could be fixed independently of circular reference to *place,* and identifying could be "extended" by importing a criterion of identity and the notion of identity over a gap.

Identity is not so easily taken to pieces, nor, I suspect, is control on *place* so easily extruded from the exercise of substance-concepts.

It will not secure the required distinction to point out that a man might claim that he could tell cats from other creatures but simply could not reidentify any particular cat. Nor is it enough to suggest that he might certainly, as he promised, fail any test for reidentification of cats. For, perversity apart, he might be overlooking information already implicit in his capacity to recognize the species. I suspect it is a defensible thesis that a decision about what marks are relevant to the reidentification of members of any species (what marks are reliable, persist, etc.) not only depends on the species of things these members belong to, but is also almost wholly determined by the nature of that species and hence by any criterion which was adequate to perform the task of settling questions of *distinctness*. Slighter difficulties than this however are enough to undermine the solution. (1) A man can only classify things if he can rectify a mistake in classification and knows what creates a need for this. This application of subsequent evidence involves reidentification of things. (2) The possibility of illusion would already arise in the application of a criterion of distinctness even if that were something separate from a criterion of identity. So, if guarding against illusion already involves different points of view, both *place* and *reidentification* are already involved in distinctness. Again (3) a test of a man's correctly applying a criterion of distinctness would be his getting right the answer to the question, "How many cats are there?" But this involves not counting the same thing twice, and reidentifying a cat as the same cat if he is mistakenly about to count it again.

At root the difficulty is this. The capacity to distinguish an f from another thing implies *a fortiori* the capacity to distinguish an f from another f. To understand "f′ $\neq$ f′″" is to understand the sense and truth-grounds of its negation, "f′ $=$ f″." The retort may be this: "f′ $\neq$ f′″"

is a statement about present data, "co-existent" particulars, whereas "f′ = f‴" asserts, in an informative case, an identity *holding between an object and itself observed at different times.* These statements answer different kinds of questions. But when one says that "f′ = f‴" one means by "f′" and "f‴" *persisting* things and therefore things which *logically may change.* To understand the truth-grounds of "f′ = f‴" (and hence of "f′ ≠ f‴") already involves an understanding of change and a grasp of the criterion of identity for *f*'s.

What these difficulties and our difficulties at the beginning of the section seem to me to show is that, though *c*-observation yields the greatest certainty there is or could be, it does not yield (1) a logically privileged access to identity or (2) a different kind of certainty or (3) what seemed to be needed to make the third solution work, the autonomous or self-supporting exercise of substance-concepts.

If anyone is more optimistic than I am about the third solution surviving these difficulties then I suspect that his optimism rests on some kind of faith in the power of *edges* to mark things off in a way which is proof against illusion. I believe, however, that it is a mistake to think that my eye cannot (and simply in virtue of the fact that there is no break in my attention cannot) "slip off" or wander from within the edges of what I am observing. Admittedly edges *are* joints in nature which any determinate interest we have will forbid us to hack across in the manner of Plato's bad carver (*Phaedrus* 271D). Admittedly, unlike lines, they are "out there," features of nature. But even if we disallow the possibility of discontinuous changes in persisting things, and even if edges (as they do not) in and of themselves drew distinguishing lines round objects, they would not in and of themselves distinguish objects in *just one way.* The ease with which we identify everyday objects makes us forget how useless it would be to try to apply the criterion "look for any continuous edge" to the individuation of, say, a moving wave or breaker. What must be added is something about the character, shape, and path such a wave has *and has through time*. Nothing less will suffice to teach someone to look for the right edge. To invoke this however is to renounce any claim to find the desiderated access to identity which is absolutely independent of *time* and *place*. *C*-observation must be supported by understanding of change and identity through time and space.

In fact the criterion of "same edge" is given by what it is an edge of, not vice versa. The respect in which the edges of some one thing at one time resemble its edges at a later time need only be that they are edges of the same thing. The point holds everywhere but is clearest if we take an unusual case, for instance Homer's Proteus:—"Then with a shout we leapt upon him and flung our arms round his back. But the old man's skill and cunning had not deserted him. He began by turning into a bearded lion and then into a snake and after that a panther and a giant bear. . . . But we set our teeth and held him like a vice." (*Odyssey* IV 453–63, trans. Rieu.) When particulars like Proteus move, individuation is complicated by the need to check that the magic repertory is rehearsed on a continuous path in space. Ignoring the difficulty that this may reintroduce place-identity, the major point is that I have no idea of what to look for if I am told to look for some one edge of some one kind throughout. At very best I could look for *some* edge in one *place*, which reimports the circularity, and anyway does not guarantee my discerning the *right* edge.[5]

---

[5] Homer has provided himself with *some* defense [which I now (1969) feel raises rather larger issues] against the objection that Proteus exceeds the bounds of the logically possible. For he indicates that Menelaus had taken the trouble, before going to the cave, to find out from the sea god's natural daughter Eidothea just what behavior could, and of course *could not*, be expected from her (not infinitely wayward) father. We need not suppose that Proteus could have changed into simply *anything*. There is moreover an unidiomatic answer to the "same what?" question—Proteus-creature—to fall under which concept a thing must have form *x* or form *y* or form *z* . . . (these must be dots of laziness), and keep to a continuous path in space and time. More difficult, why not decide to say that one creature has *succeeded* another there? This does genuinely seem to be a matter for decision. But surely it is absurd to claim to be able to demand on *a priori* grounds that the annihilation-replacement decision be preferred to the metamorphosis decision. We surely might have scientific or other reasons to postulate metamorphosis.

VI

A Leibnizian attempt on the problem

At this point we may feel that we have to despair of grounding the identification and trivial reidentification of persisting things, as that task has so far been understood, in isolation from the skill one would wish to progress to, the identification of places. But this might seem to involve giving up the evident dependence of *place* on *persisting thing*. So we may feel the attractions of a conceptual guarantee, if such can be had, which will make mistakes about the identity of things impossible, on the condition that no mistakes be made about the monadic properties of things. Without commitment to any Leibnizian reductivism about space one might give up the search for "pre-eminent" individuals which motivated solutions (1), (2), (3) of II above (Miss Anscombe's sense of "pre-eminent," *loc. cit.*, p. 93) and might be tempted to consider a proof the fact that it was a conceptual requirement of substance-concepts being applicable to a world at all that nothing have all its monadic predicates in common with anything else and that the Identity of Indiscernibles hold in its strongest form.[6] For on this supposition one could re-

---

[6] The I. of I. would come to this. There must be some predicate I can appeal to in any case of doubt to vindicate the assertion that individuals *a* and *b* are the same or distinct. (Cf. VIII below.) It is not even necessary to suppose that every particular has a known finite number of characteristics. The logic or dialectic of identity-debate might be that if doubt is cast on F or FG . . . as identifying characteristics, then I can ask for the reason for doubting. This reason would have to take the form of saying "but it's not H or I, so it can't be the one you say it is." If such reasons are not given or doubts terminate then my assertion is acceptable. (Certain very strong and implausible assumptions would also have to be made about the laws governing the changes undergone by each particular individual, and about our knowledge of these.) Given a world as kind as this we get $(x)(y)[(x \neq y) \equiv (\exists F)(Fx - Fy)]$. This implies that $(x)(y)[(x = y) \equiv (F)(Fx \equiv Fy)]$. In these statements the predicate variables exclude from their range one place predicates manufactured with the help of proper names or demonstratives and "same," "different," "distinct," or something similar, all predicates compounded with the help of proper names or terms

identify with *some* kind of certainty however often one got lost or confused. Anything one found could serve as a kind of landmark.

Given such a proof, it might be said that individuation could proceed *as if* the world were one to which substance-concepts had application, but without needing the I. of I. as a premise. (Compare the Uniformity of Nature construed not as a premise in causal reasoning but as the hope that there are some regularities which will not let us down.) Though the status of the I. of I. will be something short of logical truth, there will be no such thing as a counter-example to it describable in substance-terms. The variables for individuals would have no assignable range.

Leibniz wrote in defense of the I. of I. (p. 36) a passage in which, if we pursue this thought, we shall have to find nothing bizarre. "There is no such thing as two individuals indiscernible from each other. An ingenious gentleman of my acquaintance, discoursing with me, in the presence of her Electoral Highness the Princess Sophia, in the garden of Herrenhausen, thought he could find two leaves perfectly alike. The Princess defied him to do it, and he ran all over the garden a long time to look for some; but it was to no purpose. Two drops of water, or milk, viewed with a microscope, will appear distinguishable from each other."

Let us formulate the Principle of Sufficient Reason as follows:—if p is true then (there is a reason R for p, and there is no proposition q such that (both (q is logically incompatible with p) and (R is as good a reason for q as it is for p))). This principle is defensible enough if we read for "reason," "grounds." To suppose that p could be true without grounds is to make incomprehensible the manner in which p was given a sense (cp. Dummett).

---

like "right" and "left" (which depend on the designation of points of origin relative to some thinker).

Leibniz's own recourse to the Identity of Indiscernibles was not very differently motivated. Cp. (2), II–XXVII, "It is always necessary that beside the difference of time and place there be an internal principle of distinction . . . ; thus although time and place [external relations, that is] serve in distinguishing things we do not easily distinguish by themselves . . . the essence of identity and diversity consists . . . not in time and space."

And to suppose p's grounds equally good grounds for q is to make incomprehensible both the distinction in their import and the application of p. From this principle, with certain natural-looking assumptions, I shall show that the I. of I. can be deduced.

Suppose, what might seem plausible enough, that it is a necessary condition of asserting a relation to hold between two individuals a and b that one first identify a and b. Suppose further, what our whole approach commits us to, that locations can only be identified by reference to occupants of space and that spatial facts are similarly dependent on prior identifications of persisting things. Then all identifications will have to be brought off by dint of monadic predicates of persisting things. For nothing else remains.

Now suppose the negation of the I. of I., sc., that two distinct individuals a and c share all their monadic predicates. Imagine that proceeding in the approved way and identifying individuals by their monadic predicates, I get the best possible grounds to assert that a completely encloses a third individual b. These, by hypothesis, will be equally good grounds for asserting that c completely encloses b. But, since nothing can be completely and contiguously enclosed by more than one thing, any grounds I can get for "a encloses b" are equally good grounds for what is incompatible with it, "c encloses b." The Principle of Sufficient Reason shows that to suppose the I. of I. false reduces identity, relation and place to ineradicable confusion. (This argument is the analogue of Leibniz's argument that God could not create a world with two identical individuals since he would have had as good a reason to place them the other way about from the way he actually placed them.)

One apparent fault in this argument is this. Either it is possible to locate individuals (in terms of this theory one would say "provisionally identify" them) by a few of their monadic predicates, and to pin them down with demonstratives, or it is not. If it is not possible, then some ancient puzzles become insoluble. (See Plato, *Meno,* 80d, 71b; *Theaetetus,* 188–89.) One can never find out anything about an individual. For one is unable to identify or locate it before one knows all its properties. If on the other hand we suppose that it is possible to identify without knowing all monadic predicates, then the individuals a and c can be distinguished by research into their relational predicates, and this in spite of the fact that the monadic predicates by which they were initially and provisionally located were identical. A world might be susceptible of individuation even though there were distinct things with similar monadic, dyadic, n-adic predicates (for any finite n). All that would seem to be needed (but by our present premises this much would be needed) is that there be some m-adic predicate ($m > n$ and finite) such that if one has mistakenly assimilated distinct individuals (on some such principle as "provisionally associate apparent identicals") then one can eventually detect the mistake and make sense of the world again by dissociating them.

The I. of I. might, in the light of this apparent oversight in the previous argument, be weakened to allow the predicate variables to range over many-place predicates. This version, like the previous one, would disallow a universe consisting of three monadically identical objects arranged in an equilateral triangle. (There would be nothing, or nothing admissible, in virtue of which they were distinct.) Unlike the previous version, however, the weakened version would admit a world consisting of three monadically identical objects arranged in a 3-4-5 triangle. For the distinctness of the three objects would be grounded by one object's having it true of it that it was opposite the longest side, by another's being closer than any other object to the object opposite the longest side, etc.

Unfortunately this proposal too is incoherent. In the first version of the I. of I. we had to assume that we knew what it would be for something to be characterized by F (and so that we could identify particulars) in order to explain the way in which particulars could be identified. Now, in the second version, we have first to identify the objects at the three corners of a 3-4-5 triangle in order to be able to check on their differentiating relational predicates. If this is possible then identification and, by the argument of IV and V, trivial reidentification, is already being performed. And what is the matter with this sort of identification and reidentification? If it is not possible, then we can never get started in investigating relational properties.

If anyone were to put forward the I. of I. as a *definition* of identity (as Leibniz did not) these difficulties would be even more severe. (Compare II(A).) Either it is or it is not understood what the range is of the principle's variables. If it is not, then the definition gets nowhere. If it is, then identity, in the shape of the pre-existing possibility of identifying members of that range, is already presupposed in the definition. Identity and identification are too primitively and deeply embedded in the very possibility of speech (cp. Hampshire) to receive any more than piecemeal account (in Frege's sense of that word, (2)(ii) sections 56–67). The Leibnizian approach is an attempt to get back to a logically primitive level, the individuation of substances, from a level either equally primitive or logically dependent on it, namely, predication. We must look at the original problem again.

VII

A more realistic and more unsatisfying solution based on solution (3)

It might have been objected at the end of V that we made the difficulty of circularity insoluble by trying throughout to think ourselves into a situation where we attempted to individuate from a posture of total disorientation. Surely, it might be said, it is a precondition of even debating an identity-question that one be able to refer to its terms. "We can surely rely on demonstratives to secure the prerequisite of debate, the frame of reference without which there cannot even be doubt. All fruitful enquiry into identification, reidentification or individuation must take the activity as a going concern."

The objection may look as if it leaves our original problem completely unsolved. The dependence of places on things had led us to search for grounds of certainty independent of *place* in individuating persisting things. The objection wholly ignores this demand for controls on correctness (construed by solution (3) as a search for favored things as anchoring points), and simply states that there will always be something we can as a matter of fact identify and reidentify correctly. This of course we readily admit while still wanting to know about *grounds*. Furthermore, is total disorientation really so difficult to imagine? People are not identified differently from other objects so that we cheat if we exploit the speaker-hearer situation (cp. Williams (1), pp. 317–19). Suppose I argue with a voice which is everywhere equally tonal. I point at a thing x at time t_1 and a thing y at t_2, the voice says "Yes" to agree to both references at the time. I say x is y (thinking myself to have c-observed); it says x is not y. If it induces doubt then may I not find myself as disoriented as you wish? As for demonstratives, one might complain, these work within a frame of reference but since they depend on one they cannot found one.

In fact the objection is not so easily overruled. If the voice gives me a *rational* doubt, then this must either rest on facts about the framework within which the two identifications took place (but then adequate certainty seems to have been attained about some persisting things) or on considerations of the nature of what was identified and reidentified. Let the object be an apple. Then the voice must suggest a specific doubt based on the peculiar pitfalls of recognition (and reidentification, trivial and non-trivial) of apples. But *now* we find a body of individuative beliefs again presupposed, some of them again concerning the framework; whereas we had hoped to get below that level to some fastening point for the whole framework which would give a control on correct exercise of any such skill as the recognition of apples. I can criticize the standards actually employed and suggest more stringent ones. But to do this is to take over and presuppose a part of what I had wanted to ground—the whole skill of identifying and reidentifying apples. On the other hand, I cannot criticize those standards from a level where nothing is presupposed—for how can one appeal to individuative practice in general? (See II(A).) There is no such thing.

We are stuck. To my demand, the answer can only be:

"Your whole project bears too strong a resemblance to another fruitless search, the search for a criterion of truth, to be a sensible one. These skills exist—identifying and reidentifying birds, apples, mountains, waves. . . . Each species carries with it its own criteria of continuity, and its own criteria of certainty and correctness. You must have expected in view of (IIA) that any general or schematic answer about controls would be uninformative till made specific and applied to a delimited class of cases. What you did not expect and ought to have expected is that there is no particular answer for each particular species which does not presuppose something—namely, (1) that this going concern is a going concern, and (2) that all is well with the identification and reidentification of everything, places and persisting things, which form the framework within which the skill is exercised. In the individuation of each kind of particular enough is enough. What is enough in each case you will only know by taking instruction in individuating the thing-kind in question. It is equally fatal to the formulation of your question at the end of section II and to its answer that such instruction can only be given within a framework of other spatially related things. What would it be for it to be given *in vacuo*? To look for any other answer than this is to refuse to take identificatory and reidentificatory skills as you find them. If you refuse to do this you no longer know what you are looking for.

"As for demonstratives, although they cannot *in isolation* found a frame of reference, they can, in the required context of a whole system and in conjunction with substance-concepts (even though these are multiply satisfiable), pin down or fasten the system as firmly as it makes sense to demand."

If this is roughly right, then c-observation retains what importance it does because instruction characteristically begins in the situation where what is to be individuated is present to the senses. This situation provides a paradigm of certainty. This certainty will be ordinary certainty (what other sort would there be?) not the virtually extra-systematic certainty which solution (3) postulated. *C*-observation obviously yields greater certainty than that provided by reidentification over a gap, which indeed it may still in some way underpin, but not a different sort of certainty.

The dependence of places on things led us to an expectation which we find disappointing: that the coherence of a whole system of identifications and reidentifications could be made to rest on *the certainty in isolation* of certain parts of it, favored persisting things. Rather it can only be tested as a whole in use. *C*-observation will not yield the required certainty in isolation. Is our apparent need for this a symptom that the dependence of *place* on persisting things has not been stated in an unqualifiedly correct way?

The suspicion that it has not can be strengthened.

VIII

Problems consequential on this solution

If *c*-observation had yielded what we wanted, then it would have been possible to get started in identification in a systematic way with *c*-observed objects or configurations of objects. Demonstratives plus substance-concept would have worked in isolation. (This is another aspect of the same thing.) Spatial relations could then have been approached in an orderly way. As things are, we have a puzzle. Objects cannot be satisfactorily individuated without a simultaneous temporal and spatial understanding. Temporal and spatial facts about objects are relational facts about them. How then do we ever get started? (The difficulty is analogous to that discussed in VI.) Either we were wrong in abandoning solution (3) (but it did seem unworkable), or the individuation of persisting things, times, and places must be brought into being simultaneously (but this *seems* to conflict with what has up to this point seemed absolutely manifest, the logical dependence of the concept of space on the persisting things which serve to map it).

It is perhaps worth remarking that matters will not be

put to rights in one stroke by saying that what has been overlooked is the possibility of apprehending objects together in configurations. Configurations of definite structure are simply complex substances which satisfy requirement (3) of part I. It is unclear how they would escape the difficulties raised at V in a privileged manner.

Perhaps the answer to the problem lies in some rough and ready thesis about individuation as a self-correcting procedure involving successive approximations and provisional hypotheses, and in a rigorous distinction between questions of certainty and questions about how we do things, get started, etc. I am just as inclined, however, to think that some mistake has been made in reaching this point and that the suggestion in the last paragraph must be interpreted in an *unstraightforward* way so that we can somehow admit spatial apprehension at an earlier stage than was envisaged in solution (3) or the solution of VII.

Another consideration suggests that something has gone wrong. It looks as if some form of the I. of I. will be an unwanted consequence of some of the things we have been led to want to say and of the whole original formulation of the problem.

Suppose first that we dismiss as systematically unanswerable the question "What is identity?", and focus attention on the classificatory activity which gives a sense to any particular substance-concept; this after all is what II, VII, and our whole approach have suggested one should do. Then it becomes peculiarly clear that, if substance-terms are not to "idle" and forfeit the claim to help say anything, then they cannot be used where the activity they presuppose is systematically denied an application. To speak of *systematically* indistinguishable particulars, particulars which sensory exploration *systematically* fails to differentiate, is to employ a concept while depriving of any possible application the activity which gives it a sense, namely, individuation.

Suppose next that we take maximally seriously the original thesis about the dependence of *place* on *persisting thing*. Then "There is a space between *a* and *b*" cannot be the true, or anyway the ultimate, grounds for distinguishing *a* and *b,* since this kind of spatial fact is posterior to identification (and trivial reidentification). The discovery of their distinctness must, it seems, be anterior to the apprehension that there is a space between them.

Suppose, finally, that we have particular distinct individuals *a* and *b.* Then there must be something or other expressible at least in a two-place pseudo-predicate, one relative to any particular observer, which he could find to be true of *a* and not of *b,* and which would serve to justify his distinguishing them. Suppose I am the observer. Then we get the principle

$$(x)(y)((x \neq y) \rightarrow (\exists R)(x \text{ has } R \text{ to me}) \text{ and not}$$
$$(y \text{ has } R \text{ to me})).$$

The principle should not however be relative to me. My identity cannot be fixed independently of anything else. Excluding pseudo-predicates applying to me or, for the same reason, to any other particular observer (for observers are particulars and not specially identified) we reach

$$(x)(y)((x \neq y) \rightarrow (\exists R)(\exists \text{ observer } O)(x \text{ has } R \text{ to } O)$$
$$\text{and not } (y \text{ has } R \text{ to } O)).$$

But there need be no observers, and anything could be an observer, so we must weaken the thesis to read

$$(x)(y)((x \neq y) \rightarrow \text{Possible } (\exists R)(\exists w)$$
$$(xRw \text{ and } yRw)).$$

What could ground or count as satisfaction of the righthand side in the particular case of *a* and *b?* Assertions of possibility need grounds. To invoke the distinctness of *a* and *b* would be blatantly circular. It looks as if we are inevitably thrown back on something true of *a* and not true of *b.* If so, we get something of the form,

$$(\exists R)(\exists w)(aRw.-bRw)$$

or of the form

$$(\exists F)(Fa. -Fb).$$

In either case we get some form of the classical I. of I.

This conclusion may seem fantastic, and it draws us into bizarre and irrelevant inquiries. Why should any observer there may happen to be not take in *a* and *b as distinct,* or as elements in a configuration of a certain structure? If all appeal to the "spread" or "grasp" of his sensory exploration is disallowed then how are shapes distinguished at all? How, for instance, could the apprehension of a thing shaped "8" be explained? If on the other hand such things can be correctly apprehended in isolation, so can a thing shaped "O—O." If this can, why cannot a configuration shaped "O O" be correctly apprehended? If it can be apprehended in isolation, and as a configuration of *two* things, what appeal has the I. of I.?[7]

I have got the subject into something of a mess and bequeath it thus to Mr. Woods. If I had time to rewrite my contribution to this symposium I should try to state the dependence of *place* on *thing* more carefully and pay more attention to the apprehension of the shapes of things, something which is already spatial and needs to be worked in at an earlier stage than in solution (3). I should also look for mistakes in my concept of grounds and in my rejection of the distinction between criteria of identity and criteria of distinctness.

[7] If O O cannot be apprehended as two circles when O and O are exactly similar, then how can O be apprehended as a *circle* if *it* is *perfectly* circular? Ought it not to collapse into ∪ and thus into ⊂ ? The Identity of Indiscernibles has as one of its more extraordinary consequences the impossibility of any symmetrical object.

WORKS CONSULTED OR REFERRED TO:

Anscombe, G. E. M., "The Principle of Individuation," *P.A.S. Supplement*. Vol. 1953.

Aristotle, *Categories*.

Black, M., "The Identity of Indiscernibles," *Mind*. 1952.

Dummett, M. A. E., "Truth," *P.A.S.* 1958–59.

Frege, G., "Function and Concept" in Geach and Black, *Translations*. London: Blackwell. 1952.

——, *Grundgesetze der Arithmetik*. (Excerpts printed in Geach and Black.)

——, "Sense and Reference" in Geach and Black.

Goodstein, R. G., *Mathematical Logic*. Leicester. 1957. (1st Edition.)

Hampshire, S., *Thought and Action*. Chapter one. London: Chatto and Windus. 1959.

Leibniz, G. W., *Correspondence with Clarke*. Edited by H. G. Alexander. Manchester. 1956.

——, *Nouveaux Essais*.

Nerlich, G. C., "Evidence for Identity," *Australasian Journal of Philosophy*. 1957.

Pears, D. F., Critical Study of *Strawson* (Part I). *Philosophical Quarterly*, 1961.

Plato, *Meno. Theaetetus. Phaedrus*.

Popper, K., "The Principle of Individuation," *P.A.S. Supp.* Vol. 1953.

Strawson, P. F., *Individuals*. London: Methuen & Co. 1959.

Wiggins, D., *Identity of Spatio-Temporal Continuity*. London: Blackwell. 1967.

——, "Identity-Statements," *Analytical Philosophy*. Second series. Edited by R. J. Butler. Blackwell Oxford. 1965.

Williams, B. A. O., "Bodily Continuity and Personal Identity," *Analysis*. December, 1960.

——, "Mr. Strawson on Individuals," *Philosophy*. October, 1961.

POSTSCRIPT 1969

In the 1963 Symposium from which the piece is reprinted I never really thought properly into the consequences of the fact (noted in the penultimate sentence) that to apprehend a thing with a shape is *already* to apprehend a spatial thing and apprehend a spatial fact directly. The dependence of spatial facts on facts about individuals must not be stated in such a way as to obscure this obvious point. To be able to distinguish shapes at all *is,* for instance, to be able to apprehend configurations as configurations of a certain shape—which is in itself to be able to apprehend separately identifiable elements within a spatial framework and apprehend them as spatially related to one another in a geometrically definite way within the configuration. The fact that the individuation of places and spatial facts logically depends on that of persisting things in no way prevents the apprehension of some persisting things from itself *being* the apprehension of spatial relations or the apprehension of relative placing of objects in a configuration.

The proposition which generates the puzzling regression (the proposition my symposiast, Michael Woods, so clearly formulated [p. 206 *P.A.S.,* 1963] as his (i)), sc. that every time someone identifies or reidentifies an object he must have already identified a place or another material object, *can* then be disarmed by reference to the possibility of the apprehension and continuous observation of favored individuals. Such favored individuals might be sufficiently complex individuals, e.g., configuration with separately articulable elements which could themselves count as single persisting things. The regress is only generated if the apprehension of space and places in space is something *necessarily separate* from and posterior to continuous observation of persisting things. And now we see it is not. The strength of my fourth solution, which was (as it stood) unsatisfactory, was to make this much evident. Properly understood and amended, this is only a further refinement of the original solution (3). But I am not entirely sure that this is the end of the whole matter.

SELECTED BIBLIOGRAPHY

The majority of the works cited in this bibliography were published after 1945, but an attempt has been made to include some important works published before that date. Although most of the materials cited deal explicitly with the problems of universals and individuation, I have also included some materials which, while not devoted explicitly to a discussion of these topics, touch on issues central to them.

Journals frequently cited are abbreviated as follows:

A   *Analysis*
AJPP   *Australasian Journal of Psychology and Philosophy*
ASP   *Aristotelian Society Proceedings*
ASSV   *Aristotelian Society Supplementary Volume*
JP   *Journal of Philosophy*
M   *Mind*
P   *Philosophy*
PPR   *Philosophy and Phenomenological Research*
PQ   *Philosophical Quarterly*
PR   *Philosophical Review*
PS   *Philosophical Studies* (Minnesota)
RM   *Review of Metaphysics*

Aaron, R. I., *The Theory of Universals.* 2nd ed., rev. London: Oxford University Press, 1967.
———, "Two Senses of 'Universal,'" M, XLVIII (1939), 168–85.
Acton, H. B., "The Theory of Concrete Universals," I, M, XLV, 9(1936), 417–31; II, M, XLVI (1937), 1–13.
Aldrich, V. C., "Colors as Universals," PR, LXI (1952), 377–81.
Allaire, E. B., "Existence, Independence, and Universals," PR, LXIX (1960), 485–96.
Alston, W. P., "Ontological Commitments," PS, IX (1958), 8–17.
———, "Particulars—Bare and Qualified," PPR, XV (1954), 253–58.
Anscombe, G. E. M., "Substance" (in symposium with S. Korner), ASSV, XXXVIII (1964), 69–78.
———, "The Principle of Individuation" (in symposium with J. Lukasiewicz and K. R. Popper), ASSV, XXVII (1953), 83–96.

—— and Geach, P. T., *Three Philosophers.* Oxford: Blackwell, 1963.

Austin, J. L., *Philosophical Papers.* Edited by J. O. Urmson and G. J. Warnock. Oxford: Clarendon, 1961. (Especially I, II, VIII.)

Ayer, A. J., "On What There Is" (in symposium with P. T. Geach and W. V. O. Quine), ASSV, XXV (1951), 125–36.

——, "Universals and Particulars," ASP, XXXIV (1933–34), 51–62.

Basson, A. H., "The Problem of Substance," ASP, XLIX (1948–49), 65–72.

Baylis, C. A., "Logical Subjects and Physical Objects" (in symposium with P. F. Strawson and W. Sellars), PPR, XVII (1957), 478–87.

——, "Meanings and Their Exemplifications," JP, XXVII (1930), 169–74.

Bennett, J., "Substance, Reality and Primary Qualities," *American Philosophical Quarterly,* II (1965), 1–17.

Bergmann, G., "The Identity of Indiscernibles and the Formalist Definition of 'Identity,' " M, LXII (1953), 75–79.

——, "Individuals," PS, IX (1958), 78–85.

——, "Particularity and the New Nominalism," *Methodos,* VI (1954), 131–47.

——, "Strawson's Ontology," JP, LVIII (1961), 601–22.

Bobik, J., "A Note on a Problem About Individuality," AJPP, XXXVI (1958), 210–15.

Bochenski, I. M., "The Problem of Universals," *The Problem of Universals.* Notre Dame, Indiana: University of Notre Dame Press, 1956.

Braithwaite, R. B., "Universals and the 'Method of Analysis' " (in symposium with H. W. Joseph and F. P. Ramsey), ASSV, VI (1926), 27–38.

Brandt, R. B., "The Languages of Realism and Nominalism," PPR, XVII (1957), 516–36.

Brody, B. A., "Natural Kinds and Essences," JP, LXIV (1967), 431–46.

Butchvarov, P. K., "Concrete Entities and Concrete Relations," RM, X (1957), 412–22.

——, *Resemblance and Identity.* Bloomington: Indiana University Press, 1966.

Campbell, K., "Family Resemblance Predicates," *American Philosophical Quarterly,* II (1965), 238–44.

Carmichael, P., "'Derivation' of Universals," PPR, VIII (1948), 700–5.

——, "Professor Ayer on Individuals," A, XIV (1953), 37–42.

Carnap, R., "Empiricism, Semantics, and Ontology," *Revue Internationale de Philosophie*, XI (1950), 20–40.

Chandler, H. S., "Essence and Accident," A, XXVI (1966), 185–88.

Chappell, V. C., "Sameness and Change," PR, LXIX (1960), 351–62.

Church, A., "Propositions and Sentences," *The Problem of Universals*. Notre Dame, Indiana: University of Notre Dame Press, 1956.

Cohen, L. J., *The Diversity of Meaning*. London: Methuen, 1962. (Especially IV, V.)

Cornman, J. W., "Language and Ontology," AJPP, XLI (1963), 291–305.

Dawes-Hicks, G., "Are the Characteristics of Particular Things Universal or Particular?" (in symposium with G. E. Moore and G. F. Stout), ASSV, III (1923), 123–28.

Ducasse, C. J., "Some Critical Comments on a Nominalistic Analysis of Resemblance," PR, XLIX (1940), 641–48.

——, "Some Observations Concerning Particularity," PR, LVIII (1949), 613–14.

Dummett, M., "Nominalism," PR, LXV (1956), 491–505.

Duncan-Jones, A. E., "Universals and Particulars," ASP, XXXIV (1933–34), 63–86.

Emmett, E. R., "Philosophy of Resemblances," P, XXIX (1954), 146–51.

Feibleman, J. K., "On Substance," RM, VIII (1955), 373–78.

Frege, G., *Translations from the Philosophical Writings of Gottlob Frege*. Translated and edited by P. T. Geach and M. Black. Oxford: Blackwell, 1952. (Especially II, III, IV.)

Gasking, D., "Clusters," AJPP, XXXVIII (1960), 1–36.

Geach, P. T., *Mental Acts*. London: Routledge and Kegan Paul, 1957.

——, "On What There Is" (in symposium with A. J. Ayer and W. V. O. Quine), ASSV, XXV (1951), 125–36.

——, *Reference and Generality*. Ithaca, New York: Cornell University Press, 1962.

——, "Subject and Predicate," M, LIX (1950), 461–82.

——, "What Actually Exists" (in symposium with R. H. Stoothoff), ASSV, XLII (1968), 7–16.

Ginascol, F. H., "The Question of Universals and the Problem of Faith and Reason," PQ, IX (1959), 319–29.

Goddard, L., "Predicates, Relations, and Categories," AJPP, XLIV (1966), 139–71.

Goodman, N., *The Structure of Appearance*. Cambridge, Massachusetts: Harvard University Press, 1951.

——, "A World of Individuals," *The Problem of Universals*. Notre Dame, Indiana: University of Notre Dame Press, 1956.

—— and Quine, W. V. O., "Steps towards a Constructive Nominalism," *Journal of Symbolic Logic*, XII (1947), 105–22.

Gregory, J. C., "Leibniz, the Identity of Indiscernibles, and Probability," PPR, XIV (1954), 365–69.

Grossman, R., "Conceptualism," RM, XIV (1960), 243–54.

Hampshire, S., "Identification and Existence," *Contemporary British Philosophy* (3rd ser.), ed. by H. D. Lewis. London: George, Allen, and Unwin, 1956.

——, *Thought and Action*. London: Chatto and Windus, 1959.

Hinton, J. M., "Perception and Identification," PR, LXXVI (1967), 421–35.

Hochberg, H., "Elementarism, Independence, and Ontology," PS, XII (1961), 36–43.

——, "Ontology and Acquaintance," PS, XVII (1966), 49–55.

Jones, J. R., "Are the Qualities of Particular Things Universal or Particular?" PR, LVIII (1949), 152–70.

——, "Characters and Resemblance," PR, LX (1951), 551–62.

——, "What Do We Mean by an 'Instance'?" A, XI (1950), 11–18.

Joseph, H. W., "Universals and the 'Method of Analysis'" (in symposium with F. P. Ramsey and R. B. Braithwaite), ASSV, VI (1926), 1–16.

Joske, W. D., *Material Objects*. London: Macmillan, 1967.

Keene, G. B., "A Note on the Identity of Indiscernibles," M, LXV (1956), 252–54.

Khatchadourian, H., "Common Names and 'Family Resemblances,'" PPR, XVIII (1958), 341–58.

——, "Natural Objects and Common Names," *Methodos*, XIII (1961), 51–63.

Klemke, E. A., "Universals and Particulars in a Phenomenalist Ontology," *Philosophy of Science*, XXVII (1960), 254–61.

Kneale, W., "The Notion of a Substance," ASP, XL (1939–40), 103–34.

Knight, H., "A Note on 'The Problem of Universals,'" A, I (1933), 7–9.

Knight, T. A., "Questions and Universals," PPR, XXVII (1966), 564–76.

Korner, S., "On Determinables and Resemblances" (in symposium with J. R. Searle), ASSV, XXXIII (1959), 125–40.

——, "Substance" (in symposium with G. E. M. Anscombe), ASSV, XXXVIII (1964), 79–90.

Kultgen, J. H., "Universals, Particulars, and Change," RM, IX (1956), 548–68.

Kung, G., *Ontology and the Logistic Thesis of Language*. Translated by E. C. M. Mays. Dordrecht, Holland: D. Reidel, 1967.

Lazerowitz, M., "Substratum," *Philosophical Analysis*. Ed. by M. Black. Englewood Cliffs, New Jersey: Prentice-Hall, 1963.

——, "The Existence of Universals," M, LV (1946), 1–24.

Lloyd, A. C., "On Arguments for Real Universals," A, XI (1951), 102–7.

Lowe, V., "The Concept of the Individual," *Methodos*, V (1953), 155–74.

Lukasiewicz, J., "The Principle of Individuation" (in symposium with G. E. M. Anscombe and K. R. Popper), ASSV, XXVII (1953), 69–82.

MacDonald, M., "The Philosopher's Use of Analogy," ASP, XXXVIII (1937–38), 291–312.

——, "Things and Processes," A, VI (1938), 1–10.

McCloskey, H. J., "The Philosophy of Linguistic Analysis and the Problem of Universals," PPR, XXIV (1964), 329–38.

McMullin, E., *The Concept of Matter*. Notre Dame, Indiana: University of Notre Dame Press, 1963.

McTaggart, J. M. E., *The Nature of Existence*. Cambridge: Cambridge University Press, 1920.

Moore, G. E., "Are the Characteristics of Particular Things Universal or Particular?" (in symposium with G. Dawes-Hicks and G. F. Stout), ASSV, III (1923), 95–113.

——, "Identity," ASP, I (1900–1), 103–27.

——, *Some Main Problems of Philosophy*. London: George, Allen, and Unwin, 1953.

Moravscik, J., "Strawson on Ontological Priority," *Analytical Philosophy*. Ed. by R. J. Butler. Oxford: Blackwell, 1965.

Nerlich, G. C., "On Evidence for Identity," AJPP, XXXVIII (1959), 201–14.

O'Connor, D. J., "Names and Universals," ASP, LIII (1952–53), 173–88.

———, "On Resemblance," ASP, XLVI (1945–46), 47–77.

———, "Stout's Theory of Universals," AJPP, XXVII (1949), 46–69.

Odegard, D., "Indiscernibles," PQ, XIV (1964), 204–13.

Oliver, W. D., "Essence, Accident, and Substance," JP, LI (1954), 719–30.

Pap, A., "Nominalism, Empiricism, and Universals," I, PQ, IX (1959), 330–40; II, PQ, X (1960), 44–60.

Passmore, J., Philosophical Reasoning. New York: Charles Scribner's Sons, 1961.

Pears, D. F., "A Critical Study of P. F. Strawson's Individuals," I and II, PQ, XI (1961), 172–85 and 262–77.

Phillips, E. D., "On Instances," A, I (1934), 60–61.

Pompa, L., "Family Resemblances," PQ, XVII (1967), 63–69.

Popper, K. R., "The Principle of Individuation" (in symposium with J. Lukasiewicz and G. E. M. Anscombe), ASSV, XXVII (1953), 97–120.

Price, H. H., Thinking and Experience. London: Hutchinson's University Library, 1953. (Especially I.)

———, Thinking and Representation. London: G. Camberlege, 1946. (British Academy Lecture.)

Prior, A. N., "Determinables, Determinates, and Determinants," I and II, M, LVIII (1949), 1–20 and 178–94.

Quine, W. V. O., From a Logical Point of View. Cambridge, Massachusetts: Harvard University Press, 1953.

———, "On Universals," Journal of Symbolic Logic, XII (1947), 74–84.

———, "On What There Is" (in symposium with P. T. Geach and A. J. Ayer), ASSV (1951), 149–60.

———, Word and Object. Cambridge, Massachusetts: MIT Press, 1960.

Quinton, A., "Properties and Classes," ASP, LVIII (1957–58), 33–58.

Raju, P. J., "The Nature of the Individual," RM, XVII (1963), 33–58.

Ramsey, F. P., "Universals," The Foundations of Mathematics. New York: Harcourt and Brace, 1931.

———, "Universals and the 'Method of Analysis'" (in symposium with H. W. Joseph and R. E. Braithwaite), ASSV, VI (1926), 17–26.

Randall, J. H., "Substances as Processes," RM, X (1957), 580–601.

Raphael, D. D., "Universals, Resemblance, and Identity," ASP, LV (1954–55), 109–33.

Rose, T. A., "The Nominalist Error," AJPP, XXVII (1949), 91–112.

Russell, B., *The Analysis of Matter*. New York: Harcourt and Brace, 1927.

——, "On Denoting," M, XIV (1905), 479–93.

——, "On the Relations of Universals and Particulars," ASP, XII (1911–12), 1–24.

——, "The Philosophy of Logical Atomism," *Logic and Knowledge*. Ed. by R. C. Marsh. London: George, Allen, and Unwin, 1956.

——, *The Problems of Philosophy*. London: G. Cumberlege, 1912. (Especially IX and X.)

Russell, L. J., "Substance and Progress," ASSV, XII (1933), 1–17.

Ryle, G., "Systematically Misleading Expressions," ASP, XXXII (1931–32), 139–70.

Savery, B., "Identity and Difference," PR, LI (1942), 205–12.

Saw, R. L., "Our Knowledge of Individuals," ASP, LII (1951–52), 167–88.

Searle, J. R., "On Determinables and Resemblance" (in symposium with S. Korner), ASSV (1959), 141–58.

——, "Proper Names," M, LXVII (1958), 166–73.

Sellars, W., "Abstract Entities," RM, XVI (1963), 627–71.

——, "Grammar and Existence: A Preface to Ontology," M, LXIX (1960), 499–533.

——, "Logical Subjects and Physical Objects" (in symposium with P. F. Strawson and C. A. Baylis), PPR, XVII (1957), 458–72.

——, "Meditationes Leibniziennes," *American Philosophical Quarterly,* II (1965), 105–18.

——, "On the Logic of Complex Particulars," M, LVIII (1949), 306–38.

——, "Particulars," PPR, XIII (1952), 184–99.

Shimony, A., "The Nature and Status of Essences," RM, I, 3, 38–79.

Shwayder, D. S., *The Modes of Referring and the Problem of Universals*. Berkeley: University of California Press, 1961.

Sinisi, V. F., "Nominalism and Common Names," PR, LXXI (1962), 230–35.

Smith, N. K., "The Nature of Universals," I, II, and III, M, XXXVI (1927), 137–57, 265–80, and 393–422.

Stebbing, L. S., "Concerning Substance," ASP, XXX (1929–30), 285–308.

Stoothoff, R. H., "What Actually Exists" (in symposium with P. T. Geach), ASSV, XLII (1968), 17–30.

Stout, G. F., "Are the Characteristics of Particular Things Universal or Particular?" (in symposium with G. E. Moore and G. Dawes-Hicks), ASSV, III (1923), 114–22.

——, *The Nature of Universals and Propositions*. London: Oxford University Press, 1921. (British Academy Lecture.)

——, "Things, Predicates, and Relations," AJPP, XVIII (1940), 117–30.

Stove, D. C., "Two Problems About Individuality," AJPP, XXXIII (1955), 183–88.

Strawson, P. F., *The Bounds of Sense*. London: Methuen, 1966.

——, *Individuals*. London: Methuen, 1959.

——, *Introduction to Logical Theory*. London: Methuen, 1952.

——, "Logical Subjects and Physical Objects" (in symposium with W. Sellars and C. A. Baylis), PPR, XVII (1957), 441–57 and 473–77.

——, "A Logician's Landscape," P, XXX (1955), 229–37.

——, "On Referring," M, LIX (1950), 320–44.

——, "Singular Terms and Predication," JP, LVIII (1961), 393–412.

——, "Singular Terms, Ontology, and Identity," M, LXV (1956), 433–54.

Stroll, A., "Identity," *Encyclopedia of Philosophy*, IV, 121–24.

——, "Meaning, Referring, and the Problem of Universals," *Inquiry*, IV (1961), 107–22.

Thompson, M. H., "Abstract Entities," PR, LXIX (1960), 331–54.

——, "Abstract Entities and Universals," M, LXXIV (1965), 365–81.

Thomson, J. J., "Space, Time, and Objects," M, LXXIV (1965), 1–27.

Toms, E., "Non-Existence and Universals," PQ, VI (1956), 136–44.

Urmson, J. O., "Recognition," ASP, LVI (1955–56), 259–81.

Vaught, C. G., "The Identity of Indiscernibles and the Concept of Substance," *Southern Journal of Philosophy*, VI (1968), 152–58.

Wallace, J. R., "Sortal Predicates and Quantification," JP, LXII (1965), 9–13.

Webb, C. W., "The Antinomy of Individuals," JP, LV (1958), 735–39.

Wiggins, D., *Identity and Spatio-Temporal Continuity*. Oxford: Blackwell, 1967.

——, "Identity Statements," *Analytical Philosophy* (2nd ser.). Ed. by R. J. Butler. Oxford: Blackwell, 1965.

Williams, B. A. O., "Mr. Strawson on Individuals," P, XXXVI (1961), 309–32.

Williams, D. C., "Matter and Form," I and II, PR, LXVII (1958), 291–312 and 499–521.

——, "The Elements of Being," I and II, RM, VI (1953), 3–18 and 171–93.

Wilson, N. L., "The Identity of Indiscernibles and the Symmetrical Universe," M, 506–11.

——, "Space, Time, and Individuals," JP, LII (1955), 589–98.

——, "Substances Without Substrata," RM, XII (1959), 521–39.

Wittgenstein, L., *The Blue and the Brown Books*. Oxford: Blackwell, 1958.

——, *Philosophical Investigations*. Translated by G. E. M. Anscombe. New York: Macmillan, 1953.

——, *Tractatus-Logico-Philosophicus*. Translated by D. F. Pears and B. F. McGuiness. London: Routledge and Kegan Paul, 1961.

Wolterstorff, N., "Are Properties Meanings?" JP, LVII (1960), 277–81.

Woods, M. J., "Identity and Individuation," *Analytical Philosophy* (2nd ser.). Ed. by R. J. Butler. Oxford: Blackwell, 1965.

——, "The Individuation of Things and Places" (in symposium with D. Wiggins), ASSV, XXXVIII (1963), 203–16.

Woozley, A. D., "Universals," *Encyclopedia of Philosophy*, VIII, 194–206.

——, "Universals," *Theory of Knowledge*. London: Hutchinson University Library, 1949.

Zabeeh, F., *Universals*. The Hague: Martinus Nijhoff, 1966.

Zink, S., "The Meaning of Proper Names," M, LXXI (1963), 481–99.